COMMANDER IN CHIEF

Abraham Lincoln

AND THE CIVIL WAR

★ ★ ★ ★ ★ ★ ★

COMMANDER IN CHIEF

Abraham Lincoln

AND THE CIVIL WAR

★ ★ ★ ★ ★ ★ ★ ★ ★ ★ ★

ALBERT MARRIN

DUTTON CHILDREN'S BOOKS   NEW YORK

Text copyright © 1997 by Albert Marrin
This trade paperback edition copyright © 2003 by Albert Marrin

PHOTO CREDITS: pages ii, vii, 4, 6, 14, 28, 30, 33, 36, 53, 55, 56, 57, 61, 62, 67, 72, 73, 78, 79, 89, 104, 105, 114, 125, 134, 162, 180, 187, 197, 204, 223, 224, 225, 226 courtesy of the Library of Congress; pages 12 and 22 courtesy of *The Life of Abraham Lincoln*, by Ida Tarbell; pages 17, 81, 99, 107, 141, 175, 189 courtesy of the author; page 20 courtesy of *Recollections of Abraham Lincoln*, by Ward Hill Lamon; pages 34, 179, 193, 214, 216 courtesy of *Frank Leslie's Illustrated Newspaper*; pages 40, 69, 77, 121, 171, 222 courtesy of *Harper's Weekly*; page 43 courtesy of *The Kentucky Statesman*; pages 45, 46, 54, 74, 75, 91, 96, 109, 110, 113, 118, 130, 132, 142, 147, 148, 153, 156, 158, 163, 174, 185, 190, 200 courtesy of the National Archives; page 48 courtesy of *The Liberator*; page 65 courtesy of the Illinois State Historical Society; page 83 courtesy of *Harper's Illustrated History of the Great Rebellion*; pages 100 and 119 courtesy of the National Park Service; page 188 courtesy of the White House; pages 117, 169, 200 courtesy of *Punch*.

CIP Data is available.

Originally published in hardcover 1997 by Dutton Children's Books.
This edition published in 2003 by Dutton Children's Books,
a division of Penguin Putnam Books for Young Readers,
345 Hudson Street, New York, New York 10014
www.penguinputnam.com

Designed by Lilian Rosenstreich
Maps by Richard Amari
Printed in USA
ISBN 0-525-47069-7
1 2 3 4 5 6 7 8 9 10

This book is dedicated to the memory of our dear friends
Mary Ann and Walter Porcher

The President shall be Commander in Chief of the Army and Navy of the United States.

—UNITED STATES CONSTITUTION, ARTICLE II, SECTION 2

CONTENTS

COMMANDER IN CHIEF

Abraham Lincoln

AND THE CIVIL WAR

PROLOGUE:
An Affectionate Farewell

Springfield, Illinois. Monday, February 11, 1861. A cold, windy day, made doubly miserable by the steady downpour.

A crowd of over one thousand people had been gathering at the Great Western Railroad depot since before dawn. The locomotive *L. W. Wiley* waited at the siding, hitched to a two-car train decorated with American flags and wreaths of artificial flowers. An engineering marvel, the *Wiley* could zip along at the amazing speed of thirty miles an hour!

The people stood patiently under a canopy of umbrellas, their coat collars turned up against the wind, seldom speaking above a whisper. It was a serious occasion, a gloomy occasion, with no laughter and few smiles.

At precisely 7:55 A.M., the conductor stepped to the rail of the passenger car. "Board," he cried in a clear voice, cupping his hands to his mouth. "All aboard!" At those words, the door of the waiting room swung open, and a group of fifteen travelers filed onto the platform.

All eyes turned to the group's leader. A tall, thin man, he wore a suit of the blackest black and a "stovepipe" hat of the same color, which

made him look even taller and thinner. Towns-people had known him as a friend and neighbor for many years. Yet things were different now, for Abraham Lincoln was going to Washington, D.C., to take office as the sixteenth President of the United States.

Just one day short of his fifty-second birthday, the President-elect was a striking figure. Having seen him once, you remembered him always. He *was* unforgettable. "Shriveled" and "queer-looking," "ghostly" and "cadaverous," folks called him. Upon being introduced to him, a reporter named Donn Piatt marveled that so strange a being could really be alive. "Mr. Lincoln is the homeliest man I ever saw," Piatt wrote. "His body seemed to me a huge skeleton in clothes. Tall as he was, his hands and feet looked out of proportion, so long and clumsy were they. Every movement was awkward in the extreme."[1]

Lincoln accepted the unflattering descriptions. He had always thought of himself as ugly, joking about it to put others at ease. One of his favorite stories concerned the stranger who put a pistol to Lincoln's head, saying he had sworn to kill the first person he met uglier than he. Lincoln looked at him thoughtfully for a moment, then replied: "If I am uglier than you are, I don't want to live. Go ahead and shoot."[2]

The President-elect stood six feet four inches in his stocking feet, an incredible height at a time when poor diet often stunted growth in childhood. Proud of his height, Lincoln enjoyed measuring himself, back to back, against any tall man he might pick out of a crowd.

Most of his height, however, was in his legs. When sitting, he was no taller than an average man; but when he stood up, he kept going until he towered over everyone. Friends said he could lick salt off the head of anyone in Springfield.

His high forehead was topped by unruly black hair, which, he said, had a way of getting up as far as possible in the world. In addition, he had the start of a beard, grown at the suggestion of an eleven-year-old girl, who thought it might improve his appearance. Lincoln weighed 180 pounds, had a dark complexion, leathery skin, large hands, and feet that friends compared to snowshoes. He had big ears and a big nose with "the tip glowing in red," according to a neighbor. Lincoln's cheekbones were high, his mouth wide, his lips thick, and a mole grew on his right cheek. Apart from his size, his gray eyes were his most outstanding feature. Oh, those eyes! How they seemed to bore into a person, reading their innermost thoughts! Upon meeting a shady character, an aide recalled, Lincoln looked clear through the fellow "to the buttons on the back of his coat."[3]

People reached out to touch the President-elect as he passed through the crowd. Every few feet he paused to shake an outstretched hand, grasping it with both of his. Arriving at the edge of the platform, he kissed his wife and their two younger sons good-bye; they would take a later train and catch up to him farther down the line. Climbing the steps to the passenger car, he paused for a moment, looking down at the upturned faces. He had not intended to speak, but they expected some parting words, and he could not disappoint them.

"My friends," said Lincoln, his voice rising above the pitter-patter of raindrops on umbrellas. "No one, not in my situation, can appreciate my feeling of sadness at this parting. To this place, and the kindness of these people, I owe every thing. Here I have lived a quarter of a century, and have passed from a young to an old man. Here my children have been born, and one is buried. I now leave, not knowing when, or whether ever, I may return, with a task before me greater than that which rested upon Washington. Without the assistance of that Divine Being, who ever attended him, I cannot succeed. With that assistance I

OPPOSITE: *This full-length photograph of "Long Abe" shows Lincoln's powerful physique. It was taken by an unknown photographer in Springfield during the summer of 1860. Until Lincoln received the Republican presidential nomination, few Americans had any idea of his appearance.*

The first photograph of Lincoln with a full beard was taken in Springfield on January 13, 1861, by Christopher S. German, a local photographer.

cannot fail. . . . To His care commending you, as I hope in your prayers you will commend me, I bid you an affectionate farewell."[4]

Scarcely had the words left his lips when the engineer swung into action. The train's bell clanged, its whistle hooted, and jets of steam hissed from the brakes. To the sound of iron wheels grinding against iron rails, the train slowly began to move. And with it began Abraham Lincoln's journey into history.

The President-elect needed all the assistance he could get. He was not merely leaving a familiar way of life, but taking up a challenge that would have tested the wisdom and courage of George Washington, who had led the rebellious colonies to victory in the war for independence.

The nation Washington had fought to create was breaking apart. Already seven Southern states had seceded, left the Union. Three days earlier, on February 8, their representatives had met in Montgomery, Alabama, to form the Confederate States of America. The next day, the Confederate Congress elected Jefferson Davis—a former United States senator and secretary of war—president. On the day Lincoln left for his inauguration, Davis left his plantation near Vicksburg, Mississippi, bound for *his* inauguration in Montgomery. Two months later, war exploded across the land.

The Civil War is at once the great American tragedy and the central event in our history, more important even than winning independence from Great Britain. It defined us as a nation and shaped our character as a people, answering questions that had troubled citizens since the beginning of the Republic.

Are Americans one people united under a single national government? Or are they many peoples loyal to separate countries called states?

Should all the nation's inhabitants be equal under the law? Or should one race rule while another is legally its property with no rights whatever?

Can a minority violently resist a freely elected government? Or must it abide by the will of the majority at any cost?

The Civil War answered these questions, but at a frightful price. In cold cash, the federal government spent $3.4 billion, plus another $8.2 billion for veterans' pensions afterward, making a total of $11.6 billion. In today's money, that sum would be approximately $300 billion. We cannot begin to calculate the toll in human misery. The war claimed the lives of an estimated 620,000 soldiers—360,000 Union and 260,000 Confederate. That is more than the deaths in all other American wars combined, from the Revolution to Vietnam, when the total reached 648,000.

Nearly every American family lost a relative, friend, or neighbor, and for decades veterans without an arm or a leg were a common sight in most communities. The South suffered especially, losing a quarter of its white males. As Mary Chestnut, the wife of a Confederate senator, noted in her diary, Southern women had to change their ideas about male beauty, since whole men scarcely existed anymore.

The President was the key figure in this tragedy. Make no mistake about it: the Civil War was also Mr. Lincoln's War. It was he who refused to yield to Confederate demands, which their leaders interpreted as an attack. It was he who decided to fight the war to the bitter end, with no compromise on the basic issue of secession. It was he who decided to free, or emancipate, the slaves as a war measure, beginning what some historians call "The Second American Revolution," a struggle for human rights that continues to this very day.

In taking the oath of office, Lincoln swore to "preserve, protect, and defend the Constitution of the United States." Those words became his guiding stars, governing his every official action. Under the Constitution, only Congress may raise armies and declare war. The President, however, is commander in chief, directing the armed forces once war has begun.

Nothing had prepared him for this responsibility. Prior to entering the White House, his only military experience had been as a youthful volunteer in a minor Indian uprising. Nor was he emotionally prepared to be a war leader. A man of reason, he believed human beings should settle their differences by discussion, debate, compromise, and the rule of law.

War? Nothing could be more unreasonable. It was all brute force and destruction, killing and tears. Lincoln detested it.

Yet, by some quirk of fate, destiny had chosen him to wage this most terrible war. That fact always amazed him. "Doesn't it seem strange," Lincoln asked a White House visitor, "that I should be here— I, a man who couldn't cut a chicken's head off—with blood running all around me?" Another time, he asked: "What has God put me in this place for?"[5]

A highly emotional man, the ordeal moved him to say, "I shall never be glad any more." On another occasion, he admitted, "I am the loneliest man in America."[6] Lincoln did not pretend to hide his feelings, and sometimes he wept in front of generals and Cabinet members. Nevertheless, as they came to realize, he was no softy. The man never wavered in his determination to fight on to victory.

In every survey made in the past fifty years, scholars have voted Lincoln the best president in American history. Not that they considered him a perfect human being, someone without faults. Far from it! Lincoln made mistakes. He had his share of human failings: self-doubt, hesitation, prejudice. Still, he had that most precious of human qualities—the capacity for growth.

It is that capacity, no less than his achievements, that continues to fascinate us. Lincoln was scarcely more than a small-town politician when the Civil War began. But despite every obstacle, he "overcame," growing as a leader and a human being. If George Washington is the father of our country, then, surely, Abraham Lincoln represents the unity and brotherhood of the American people. As such, he remains an everlasting symbol of how a person—*any* person—can learn from experience and rise above prejudice and limitation.

This book is not a history of the Civil War. Nor is it a biography in the usual sense of a detailed account of a person's life. Besides, Lincoln distrusted biographers, saying they cared more about glorifying or damning their subjects than about telling the truth. Some of his distrust was well placed. Those who knew Lincoln well, or met him only once or twice, sometimes misquoted him, either deliberately or because they "misremembered" his words when they tried to recall them years later. In their recent book, *Recollected Words of Abraham Lincoln,* historians Don E. Fehrenbacher and Virginia Fehrenbacher show that many "Lincoln quotations" and "eyewitness accounts" of his actions are at best errors, at worst frauds.[7] Yet scholars often disagree. Other historians, people with equally high reputations, accept these very same accounts.

My aim has been to bring our greatest President to life by placing him in the context of his own personal background and the larger circumstances of our country's greatest conflict. Only by doing so will he emerge as the "necessary man," the one person without whom it is impossible to imagine those trying times.

1 BEGINNINGS

Well, Scripps, it is a great piece of folly to attempt to make anything out of my early life. It can all be condensed into a single sentence, and that sentence you will find in Gray's Elegy—"The short and simple annals of the poor." That's my life, and that's all you or anyone else can make of it.

ABRAHAM LINCOLN TO JOHN LOCKE SCRIPPS, 1860

It had happened eighty years earlier, but Dennis Hanks remembered it as clearly as if it were yesterday. On that frosty morning of February 12, 1809, ten-year-old Dennis was busy at his chores when Thomas Lincoln bolted out of the forest. Tom was married to Dennis's cousin Nancy. A powerful man with a barrel chest and a ruddy complexion, he had run two miles at top speed. "Nancy's got a baby boy," Tom blurted out, pausing only to catch his breath.[1]

"Denny," as everyone called him, shouted the news to his mother and raced back with Tom to his home. The Lincolns lived on a farm alongside Nolan Creek in Hardin County, Kentucky. Known as the "dark and bloody ground," Kentucky was a place where Indians and whites had fought savagely to control the fertile countryside. Although the Indians were no longer a threat, Kentucky was still the nation's far frontier, with no state in all the West beyond it.

Denny followed Tom into his house, a log cabin built in a clearing. There he found Cousin Nancy, age twenty-five, lying in bed with her daughter Sarah, age two, sitting by her side. A quiet child with large

The house in which Lincoln was born, rebuilt on the original site in Hardin County, Kentucky.

round eyes, Sarah pointed to her baby brother. Denny recalled that he looked "like red cherry-pulp squeezed dry, in wrinkles."[2]

"What you goin' to name him, Nancy?" Denny asked.

"Abraham," she replied, after Grandfather Lincoln, who had crossed the Allegheny Mountains with a distant relative named Daniel Boone, only to die in an Indian ambush.[3]

The family had been pioneers ever since Samuel Lincoln, a weaver's helper, came to Massachusetts from England in 1637. Over the years, Samuel's descendants moved southward through Connecticut, Pennsylvania, and Virginia, then westward into Kentucky.

It had been that way ever since the first Europeans settled in the New World. For ambitious people, the frontier was a land of opportunity where, the saying went, "kin and kin-in-law didn't count a cuss." Striking out for the frontier meant starting afresh. Family background meant nothing in the wilderness. Out there, people judged one another by their character and deeds, not by their ancestry. The road to success was open to all equally. If you worked hard and made the right decisions, you prospered. If not, the failure was yours alone.

Thomas Lincoln earned his livelihood as a carpenter and farmer. Although he did not prosper, he was a decent man who became a respected member of the community. He never learned to read, and his only writing consisted of painstakingly drawing his name one letter at a time. We know little about his wife, the former Nancy Hanks, except that she was gentle and kind. She could neither read nor write, but signed legal documents by making her mark in front of witnesses.

Abraham shot up like a weed, outgrowing his clothes faster than Nancy could make new ones. When he turned seven, Tom decided to move to greener pastures. Late in 1816, the family headed for Indiana, admitted into the Union that same year. The boy was lucky to be going with them. A few days before leaving, he fell into a stream and would have drowned had Denny and a neighbor's son not been walking nearby. They pulled him out, rolled him on the ground, and pounded his back until the water poured from his mouth and he revived.

Although the Lincolns' destination was barely a hundred miles away, it could have been on the far side of the planet. The way to Indiana led through a virgin wilderness. Wherever you turned, a traveler reported, you saw "woods, woods, woods, as far as the world extends."[4] Ancient trees reached heights of seventy feet and more, making people feel tiny and insignificant. The family marveled at a sycamore sixty-five feet in circumference. What made the going so difficult was not the trees themselves but the underbrush. Tom often had to chop a path through the tangle of interlaced branches, bushes, roots, and vines.

As a boy of ten, Dennis Hanks saw baby Abraham only hours after his birth. His recollections of the future President's early years give an intimate account of life in frontier America.

Eventually, they reached Pigeon Creek in the southwestern corner of Indiana. The place took its name from the passenger pigeon, a bird now extinct. In Lincoln's day, it flew in large flocks that darkened the sky, as during an eclipse of the sun. The flapping of wings created gusts of wind that caused trees to sway and sounded like the rushing of a river.

It was December, and Tom had no time to build a cabin before the first big snow. So he made a "half-faced camp," a temporary shelter enclosed by logs on three sides, with a roaring fire at the open end for warmth and protection against dangerous animals. Indiana had plenty of these: wolves, bobcats, grizzly bears. Occasionally buffaloes drank from the Ohio River nearby. Strays from the main herds on

Thomas Lincoln, Abraham's father, was a hardworking farmer who opposed slavery.

the Great Plains further west, these "shaggies," as settlers called them, had wandered far from their home ranges. Shooting a buffalo was a blessing, since its meat could feed a family for a month.

Tom built a cabin in the spring, a simple affair with log walls, earthen floor, and clay chimney. Then he cleared a few acres for farming, backbreaking work that lasted from sunrise to sundown. He began by felling the smaller trees, leaving the larger ones standing. He split the felled trees into firewood and piled the smaller branches around the uncut trees. During the summer, when the wood dried, he set fires to kill the trees, which he then easily chopped down. Young Abraham was a natural with the axe. As Tom did the heavy work, he cleared the underbrush. Years later, he recalled how "A. though very young, was large for his age, and had an axe put into his hands at once; and from that till within his twenty-third year, he was almost constantly handling that most useful instrument—less, of course, in plowing and harvesting seasons."[5]

Although farms lay miles apart, farm families depended on one another in countless ways. No family, no matter how smart or industrious, could survive by its efforts alone. Everyone depended upon everyone else; in fact, helping others was a kind of insurance policy, because you never knew when you might be in the same situation. Nobody dreamed of asking for money. Helping was "right neighborly," something neighbors owed one another.

Helping also gave an excuse for socializing. Families traveled many miles for corn huskings, barn raisings, and hog butcherings. Afterward, everyone had fun at dances, wrestling matches, horse races, and shooting contests. The hosts provided food and lodging. But since log cabins were small, and there might be as many as twenty guests, everyone slept on the cabin floor. Men and women hung their clothes, except for their underwear, on wall pegs. Then, a traveler reported, they lay down on corn-husk mattresses, their feet toward the fire, with "no consciousness of impropriety or indelicacy of feeling."[6]

Frontier women probably worked harder than men, who could at least vary their routine by hunting. Women definitely worked longer hours: cooking, cleaning, caring for the children, grinding grain, baking bread, milking the cows, spinning thread, weaving cloth, making clothes, and turning tallow (animal fat) into soap.

Since few doctors lived on the frontier, wives took charge of their family's health. Remedies were poor at best, dangerous at worst. To soothe teething pains, for example, mothers rubbed infants' gums with a paste of crushed rattlesnake tail and bear grease. They applied "nanny tea," a brew of liquefied sheep dung, to skin rashes.

Map of the United States in Lincoln's boyhood.

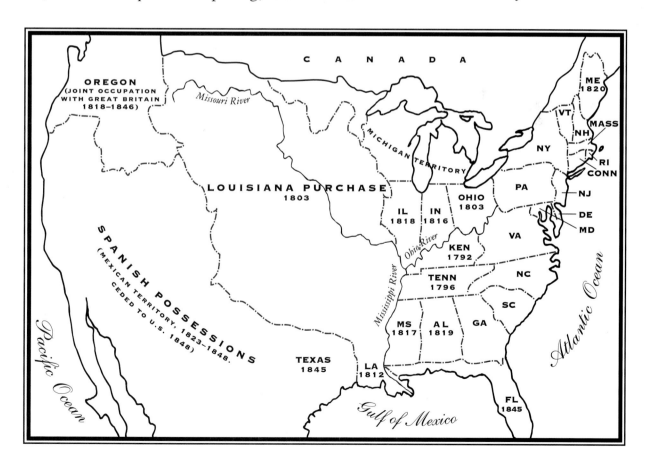

Nobody claimed to have a cure for milk sickness, or "the trembles." In late summer, cattle grazed on white snakeroot, a poisonous plant found along the edges of forests. As the poison took effect, the cows trembled violently, dying within three days. People who drank infected milk died painfully in about a week. Ignorant of its cause, settlers were powerless against the dreaded illness.

In 1818, milk sickness devastated the Pigeon Creek community. Nancy Lincoln, an early victim, died on October 5. She spoke her last words to her son: "I am going away from you, Abraham, and I shall not return. I know that you will be a good boy [and] that you will be kind to Sarah and to your father. I want you to live as I have taught you, and to love your Heavenly Father."[7] For several days, Nancy's body lay in the same room where her family ate and slept. Tom built the coffin. Abraham whittled the wooden pegs to hold its lid in place. When they finished, they held a simple service, since the neighborhood had no minister. Nancy's loved ones buried her on a knoll overlooking the cabin; pioneers usually buried relatives within sight of their home to keep their memory alive. Sarah took over her mother's duties, but the twelve-year-old kept falling behind. Clothes went unwashed. Dirt accumulated. The cabin grew seedy. "Tom, he moped 'round. Wasn't wuth shucks that winter," recalled Denny, who had moved in with the Lincolns.[8]

Sarah Bush Lincoln in old age. A warm, caring person, she encouraged her stepson to study and educate himself.

Come spring, Tom planted corn and returned to Kentucky to find another wife. It so happened that Sarah Bush Johnston, a friend of Nancy's, had recently become a widow. She was, as they said, "available."

Tom came straight to the point. "Well, *Miss* Johnston," he said in a businesslike way, "I have no wife, and you have no husband. I came 'a purpose to marry you. . . . I have no time to lose; and, if you are willin', let it be done straight off."[9]

She was "willin'." So she and her three children—Elizabeth, Matilda, John—piled their things into a rented wagon and left for Indiana with Tom in the driver's seat. The marriage was no love match but a practical arrangement that suited both families. Sarah had a provider.

Tom had a housekeeper and a mother for his children. The children had companions to ease their loneliness.

Abraham always spoke of Sarah as "a good and kind mother." Sarah called him "the best boy I ever saw." He never gave her any trouble or said a cross word in her presence. The idea of causing pain to another living being, let alone a person, gave *him* pain. Horrified after shooting a turkey, for example, he never fired at a live target again. Friends saw him climb trees to put young birds back in their nests, wade an icy stream to rescue a dog, and cry when Tom butchered a favorite hog. Like other frontier children, he played hide-and-seek, prisoner's base, and other games.[10]

By his sixteenth birthday, Abraham's skill with the axe amazed experienced woodsmen. "You'd 'a' thought there was two men in the woods when he got inter it with an ax," Denny recalled.[11] He could take the end of an axe handle between his thumb and forefinger, raise it up to his nose, and hold it at arm's length for several minutes. Abraham was so strong that Tom hired him out to neighbors at twenty-five cents a day to dig wells and split logs into fence rails. Back then, the law said parents owned their children's labor until the age of twenty-one.

The Rail-splitter, *by an anonymous artist, depicts Abraham Lincoln using the axe and wedge to make fence rails from logs.*

Yet Abraham disliked physical labor. In the first place, it seemed to lead to a life of endless toil with little reward. Secondly, he had begun to learn certain things about himself. For as far back as he could remember, he had a thirst for knowledge. Why? When? Where? Who? How? The questions poured out of him. Nothing annoyed him more than hearing adults discuss matters he did not understand and then brush his questions aside.

The youngster vowed to find answers on his own. Since books contained knowledge, he must learn to read. Public schools did not exist on the frontier, only private "blab" schools where pupils studied aloud so the instructor could measure progress by the volume of noise. Abraham had attended a blab school in Kentucky at the age of six. In Indiana, he and Sarah went to blab schools for a few weeks each year after the fall harvest. That was it! He later wrote about attending school "by littles," which totaled about a year. In that year, however, he gained the tools of learning: reading, writing, arithmetic.

His parents encouraged his studies. As a usual thing, his stepmother recalled, Tom never made his son stop reading to do anything if he could avoid it. He did it himself first. If Abraham ran out of paper, he did his arithmetic with charcoal on the wooden fire shovel, "erasing" the exercise with a hunting knife. Denny fashioned the boy's pens from turkey-buzzard quills and made ink out of blackberry roots. Abraham did penmanship exercises, even wrote poetry, in a little notebook. His first poem had these playful lines:

> *Abraham Lincoln*
> *his hand and pen*
> *he will be good but*
> *god knows When*
>
> *Abraham Lincoln is my nam{e}*
> *And with my pen I wrote the same*
> *I wrote in both hast and speed*
> *and left it here for fools to read*[12]

Abraham walked miles to borrow a book from a shopkeeper or a blab-school teacher. If it got damaged, he split rails or dug ditches to repay the owner. A farmer named Josiah Crawford once made him work three days to pay for the damage to a borrowed book.[13] Although he read few books, those he read influenced him deeply. Among them were the Bible, the plays of William Shakespeare, and Daniel Defoe's novel *Robinson Crusoe.* Their beauty awakened his love of words, enabling him as an adult to write some of the finest speeches in the English language.

Murray's *English Reader,* a book forgotten today, served another purpose. Its pages contain moral lessons expressed in short, simple sentences. Abraham learned, for example, that "Revenge dwells in little minds," "To have your enemy in your power and yet do him good is the greatest heroism," and "Gentleness corrects whatever is offensive in our manners."[14] Those lessons became part of his character, the basic rules by which he lived.

Abraham never tired of Parson Mason Weems's *Life of Washington,* a stirring account of the "Father of Our Country" and his role in the Revolution. Washington and the other Founders became the boy's heroes. Their struggle, he believed, had not been about territory, but about human values—the values set forth in the Declaration of Independence. As he said in 1861, "I have never had a feeling politically that did not spring from the sentiments of the Declaration of Independence."[15] Even as a youngster, he believed the mission of the United States was to prove that ordinary people could govern themselves without kings and noblemen. Here was a land where simple folks need not be prisoners of their birth, but could go as far as ambition and talent could take them. It was a land where all should have "an equal chance" and "the right to rise."[16]

A chance to rise came in 1828, when Abe was nineteen. The year began badly. In January, his sister, Sarah, died. Abraham broke down at the news, his whole body heaving with sobs. Soon, however, things changed for the better. In April, he joined Allen Gentry, the son of a local shopkeeper, to take a flatboat loaded with farm produce to New Orleans, Louisiana, a journey of 1,200 miles lasting three months. His pay: eight dollars a month and a return ticket on a steamboat.

The flatboat, described by an English traveler as "an immense coffin" sixty-five feet long by sixteen feet wide, glided down the Ohio

An artist's interpretation of the teenaged Lincoln working as a flatboatman.

River into the Mississippi. As the current carried it southward, Abraham realized that the Mississippi had become the nation's lifeline. The wealth of a continent floated down the "Father of Waters" to the docks of New Orleans, and from there to the world beyond. Whoever controlled the river's mouth controlled nearly a million square miles upstream, more than half the territory of the United States.

The young men could scarcely believe their eyes when they reached New Orleans. Who could have imagined that so many people (over 40,000) could be in the same place, and at once! Everywhere they heard a babble of strange tongues—French, Spanish, Portuguese, Dutch—mixed with Irish brogues. Wandering the narrow cobblestoned streets, they peered through the windows of houses with elegant rooms twice the size of a log cabin. Theaters advertised dancing bears, death-defying acrobats, an Egyptian mummy three thousand years old, and a dwarf said to be the world's tiniest human.

They also saw slaves. New Orleans was a center of the American slave trade. Posters on billboards announced CASH FOR NEGROES, NEGROES FOR SALE, and NE-GROES WANTED. If Abraham read a newspaper during his visit, he would have found advertisements like this: "Virginia and North Carolina slaves for sale. 43 Virginia slaves, women, men, girls, and boys, may be bartered for sugar. . . . North Carolina slaves being 5 large robust men and four women and girls in which a bargain will be offered."[17] Friends later claimed that such "bargains" angered Abraham, and that he vowed to destroy slavery if he ever had the chance. Perhaps he did. Unfortunately, we cannot know what he said at the time. He never wrote about his reaction, nor did his companion.

Meanwhile, Tom had grown restless again. Early in 1830, he sold his farm, put his family in two ox-drawn wagons, and set out on a two-hundred-mile trek to Illinois. After floating their wagons across un-bridged streams, the Lincolns reached the north bank of the Sangamon River in the central part of the state. Abraham and his stepbrother helped Tom build a log cabin, then hired out to a shopkeeper named Denton Offutt for another trip to New Orleans the following year.

Abraham returned a changed man. Now twenty-one, he had finally become his own person. No longer could his father sell his work or claim his earnings. Being on his own, however, raised certain questions. Where should he live? What should he do with his life? How should he earn a living?

Like many people his age, Abraham did not know what he wanted to do. All he knew was what he did *not* want. He did not want his life to be a steady grind of physical labor until he grew old and his bones ached whenever the weather turned cold. In short, he did not want to be like Tom.

Father and son had never been close. Tom had a short temper and would strike out for little or no reason. Abraham's stepmother recalled how he once questioned his father's version of a story, saying "Paw, that was not jest the way it was." For doubting his word, Tom slapped his face.[18] We cannot be sure how such incidents affected the boy, since he never discussed them for the record. What is certain is that, once Abraham left the log cabin, he never looked back. In the years that followed, he seldom saw his parents. After he married, he never invited them to

Where Lincoln lived, 1809–1861.

his home or brought his family to meet them. Informed in 1851 that Tom lay dying, he refused the old man's request for a good-bye visit. Nor did he attend the funeral.

In July 1831, Abraham became a clerk in Offutt's store in New Salem. A typical Illinois prairie community, New Salem had a population of twenty-five families. Besides Offutt's place, it boasted a church, blab school, gristmill, tavern, and blacksmith's shop. Although winters were harsh, with

Unable to attend school regularly, Lincoln studied on his own by the light of the fireplace.

snowdrifts reaching the tops of doors, spring was always a delight. By summer, the prairie grass stood six feet high, swaying in the breeze like ocean waves. Sometimes prairie fires lit up the horizon, burning, it seemed, to the ends of the earth. Vast herds of deer and flocks of wild turkeys still roamed the country-side. The Sangamon River swarmed with bass, catfish, and suckers. These fish were so common they gave Illinois the nickname "Sucker State." When Lincoln ran for President, supporters dubbed him the "Illinois Sucker" and the "Tall Sucker."

Abraham slept on a cot in Offutt's back room. During his time off, he joked and swapped stories with the customers, who gathered around the potbellied stove. Abraham also liked children, and they liked him. He was so much fun to be with that he seemed more like an older play-mate than an adult. Years later, one remembered him as "a great marble player" who "kept the small boys running in all directions to gather the marbles he shot."[19] Little girls adored his stories and gentle ways. He called each girl "Little Sister."

Lincoln continued his self-education, borrowing books from school-master Mentor Graham and joining the New Salem Debating Society. At first, his appearance startled society members. The gangly youth wore coarse linen pants that were held up by one suspender and ended five inches above his ankles. His shirt was of faded calico and he wore brogans, work shoes with wooden soles. Debaters soon found that looks were deceiving, for he had a keen mind and expressed his ideas clearly. "He was already a fine speaker. All he lacked was culture," a society member recalled.[20]

Abraham made a lifelong friend by fighting him. Jack Armstrong led the Clary's Grove Boys, a gang of roughnecks much feared in the neighborhood. The gang's idea of "fun" was to beat up strangers, put burrs under saddles, and roll drunks down a hillside in a barrel. One day, Mr. Offutt boasted that his clerk could "lick" anyone in a fair fight. Armstrong challenged the newcomer to a wrestling match. Abraham had no choice. In that rugged frontier society, a man proved himself by taking on all comers. Refusing a challenge marked you as a coward, and therefore unworthy of trust.

They stripped to the waist and went at it with all their might. There was plenty of grunting and groaning as each tried to lift the other and smash him to the ground. Just as Lincoln was winning, Armstrong's gang joined the fight. Lincoln released his opponent and, putting his back against a wall, offered to fight them all—one at a time.

The gang leader admired courage. Armstrong stood up, brushed the dust from his clothes, and put out his hand in friendship. Lincoln became one of the boys. Although he never interfered in their pranks, his presence had a calming effect. If, for example, a fistfight was getting out of control, he would say "Let's stop it," and they did.[21]

In March 1832, Lincoln decided to run for the Illinois state legislature. Offutt's store had recently failed, and his clerk needed a job. Nowadays, his candidacy would be considered arrogant. He had little education and no experience in public life, important qualifications in twentieth-century politics. Back then, however, these meant little. In a frontier state like Illinois, most lawmakers were no better prepared than Lincoln. Running for office was a sensible move, since politics offered a quick way to advance in the world. The trick was to get elected and then learn on the job.

Lincoln decided to campaign as a Whig. One of America's two major political parties, the Whigs favored a strong central government to build up the economy. Their opponents, the Democrats, favored states' rights—that is, a minimum of interference from Washington. Lincoln's platform dealt with the everyday concerns of his district. He called for public schools, lower interest rates, and clearing the Sangamon River so steamboats could reach New Salem. Every man, he added, had his own special ambition. His was to serve the people and earn their respect. If elected, he would be grateful. If defeated, he was so used to disappointment that it would not matter.

The campaign had hardly begun when Chief Black Hawk led his warriors across the Mississippi into northern Illinois. Thirty years earlier, federal agents had persuaded his tribe, the Sauk and Fox, to leave

Illinois in return for a promise of money and gifts. The government, however, failed to keep its part of the bargain. Now, when Black Hawk tried to reclaim the tribal lands, panic swept the frontier. Army troops rushed to the scene, backed by hastily formed militia companies. New Salem sent a company led by Abraham Lincoln, whom the Clary's Grove Boys had elected captain. It was not much of a war, as the Indians were easily defeated and sent to reservations. Lincoln saw no action. The only casualties he encountered were five farmers with bloody circles on top of their heads where their scalps had been. The captain joked that his worst enemy was the mosquitoes, "with whom I had a good many bloody struggles."[22] He was being modest. One day, a friendly Indian came into camp with a pass. But pass or no pass, some volunteers wanted to lynch the man. Stepping in front of him, Lincoln said they'd have to do it over his dead body. He meant it, and the thugs backed off.

Lincoln returned to New Salem late in July, two weeks before Election Day. He "stumped" the district from end to end, trying to make up for lost time. Frontier voters usually gathered to hear speeches in forest clearings, where the trees had been cut but the stumps left in the ground. A candidate, to be seen and heard, mounted a stump and spoke at the top of his voice.

Lincoln gave scores of stump speeches. He also met voters personally by knocking at cabin doors, tossing horseshoes outside country stores, and wrestling local champions. One day he found thirty men harvesting wheat in a field. When he started to speak, however, they said they would not support anyone "unless he could take a hand." The candidate smiled. "Well, boys," he replied, "if that is all, I am sure of your votes," and pitched in with both hands.[23]

It was not good enough. On election night, Lincoln placed eighth in a field of thirteen. The good news was that he had won 277 of the 300 votes cast in the New Salem area. The lesson was clear: given enough time to campaign, he could win. Wait till next time!

Meanwhile, he opened a grocery store with William F. Berry, a preacher's son. Country groceries carried more than food and household goods; they sold cloth, harness, tools, guns, ammunition, and whiskey. Lincoln hated alcoholic drinks, saying they made him feel "flabby and undone." Berry, however, loved the whiskey barrel. He guzzled away the profits until, as his partner put it, the store "winked out." Berry died soon afterward, leaving bills totaling eleven hundred dollars. Lincoln called it "the National Debt," but repaid every penny during the next ten years. Had he been another type of person, he might have tried to duck the obligation. Yet paying was a matter of honor—of his self-respect as a human being. Folks called him "Honest Abe," a nickname he earned in countless small ways. Once he walked six miles to refund the six cents he had overcharged a customer.

Friends came to the rescue by helping him become the village post-master. It wasn't much of a job, paying only fifty dollars a year. Yet it gave him lots of spare time to earn extra money. He split rails, worked at the local mill, and, aided by Mentor Graham's books, learned survey-ing. Equipped with his chain and compass, he laid out new town sites, farms, and roads. Surveying had a double value to the aspiring politi-cian. Not only did it help pay his bills, but by getting him out into the country it allowed him to meet more people—that is, more voters. "Next time" was never far from his thoughts.

In 1834, when he was twenty-five, Lincoln ran for the state legisla-ture and won. That victory changed his life in an unexpected way. Dur-ing the campaign, he became friendly with John T. Stuart, a candidate from another district. A prosperous Springfield lawyer, Stuart gave him some good advice. He pointed out that, since representatives earned three dollars a day only during the legislative session, Lincoln must still earn a living. Stuart urged him to study law. Practicing law would give him a decent income and expand his political contacts. Lack of formal education need not be an obstacle. America had few law schools at this time, and most lawyers had never gone to college. You simply "read law" by yourself or in a lawyer's office until you could pass the examination. Given orally by a board of practicing attorneys, the examination usually focused on state laws, legal procedures, and the rules of evidence.

Stuart lent the young man law books, and Lincoln did the rest. At New Salem, folks started to wonder about their friend. The more Lin-coln read, the "lazier" he became; that is, the less work he did with his hands. Passersby saw him sitting on a woodpile with his nose buried in a thick book. Often he stayed up all night, reading by candlelight.

Joshua F. Speed was Lincoln's only close friend. They first met when Lincoln arrived in Springfield in April 1837. Speed offered Lincoln his room, and for four years they shared the same bed.

What was he up to? What did it all mean?

"What are you reading?" a farmer asked.

"I'm not reading," said Lincoln. "I am studying law."

"Law," the farmer exclaimed. "Good God A'mighty!" Then he walked off, shaking his head.[24]

Lincoln cleared the first hurdle in March 1836, when the Sangamon County Court declared him a person of good moral character. In September, he received his license after passing the bar examination.

Stuart invited Lincoln to become his junior partner; with the state capital about to be moved from Vandalia to Springfield, he needed help with the expected increase in business. So on April 15, 1837, the new lawyer stuffed his belongings into two saddlebags, said good-bye to his friends, and left New Salem forever. He was twenty-eight years old. Although he could not know it, he had already lived exactly half his life and would die twenty-eight years later to the day.

Lincoln found Springfield a bustling town of 2,500 residents. Wagons arrived daily with manufactured goods from the East, which merchants sold to local farmers for cash or traded for grain, meat, and hides. Carriages sped along the unpaved streets, carrying men in stylish suits and women in dresses of imported silk. In the dry season, the wind blew clouds of dust mixed with particles of dried horse manure into people's faces and onto their food. In the wet season, the streets became muddy streams. The only way to cross dry was over narrow wooden planks or on someone's back. Local farm boys charged five cents to lug a "dude" across on their backs.

On his first day in town, Lincoln ordered a bedstead from a carpenter and visited Joshua F. Speed's store to buy bedding for it. Speed asked seventeen dollars. Lincoln had only seven dollars. Yet his voice was so sad, his expression so downcast, that Speed offered to let him share his bed above the store. Lincoln took his saddlebags upstairs and came down with a broad grin on his face. "Well, Speed," he said, "I'm moved."[25]

While working at his law practice, Lincoln also earned high marks as a politician. During his freshman term in the legislature, he had mastered the fine points of bargaining and deal making. He became so skilled that he could sense an opponent's next move before he knew it himself. Reelected three more times—1836, 1838, 1840—he drafted laws, became a leader in the Illinois House of Representatives, and served on his party's state committee.

Still, there was more to life than work. Springfield had an active social life. People often held "at-homes" to dance, sing around the piano, or read poetry aloud. In December 1839, Lincoln visited the home of Ninian W. Edwards, the son of a former Illinois governor, and his wife, Elizabeth. There he met Mary Todd, Elizabeth's younger sister. His life would never be the same.

Born in 1818 into a wealthy Lexington, Kentucky, family, Mary was attractive, charming, and high-spirited. Short and plump, she had a round face, bluish-gray eyes, a fair complexion, and dark brown hair. Educated at an exclusive girls' school, she spoke French like a native and could hold her own in any conversation. Springfield's bachelors vied for a chance to dance with her, talk with her, and escort her about town. Among her beaux was Stephen A. Douglas, an ambitious Democratic politician already being mentioned as a future presidential candidate. Mary refused his marriage proposal, saying "I can't consent to be your wife. I shall become Mrs. President . . . but it will not be as Mrs. Douglas."[26]

Abraham and Mary fell in love. Others might think them an odd couple, but they believed God had made them for each other. She had everything this rough man from the backwoods could want: good looks, intelligence, and charm, blended with a loving nature. He was shy and, she admitted, "not pretty." No matter. He adored her and seemed destined for greatness even then. Something told her that he was the man to bring her into the White House as "Mrs. President." They became engaged in December 1840.[27]

The Edwardses tried to end the romance. They may have been snobs, but they had Mary's best interests at heart. In pre–Civil War America, a woman lost her legal rights upon marrying. Divorce laws did not exist, meaning that the choice of a wrong mate was literally "until death do us part." A husband could be a drunk, a brute, and a cheat, and still the wife must "love, honor, and obey." Lincoln might

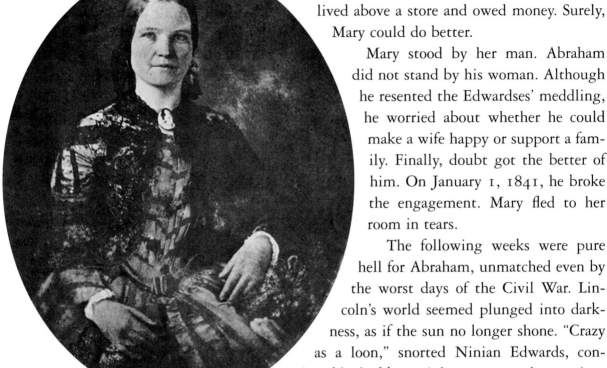

Mary Todd Lincoln at the age of twenty-eight. Perhaps her earliest portrait, this picture was taken by N. H. Shepherd in Springfield in 1846, four years after her marriage to the frontier lawyer. Mrs. Lincoln was an excellent seamstress who often made her own dresses.

have a brilliant future, but no one could be sure of that in 1840. The only certainties were that he lived above a store and owed money. Surely, Mary could do better.

Mary stood by her man. Abraham did not stand by his woman. Although he resented the Edwardses' meddling, he worried about whether he could make a wife happy or support a family. Finally, doubt got the better of him. On January 1, 1841, he broke the engagement. Mary fled to her room in tears.

The following weeks were pure hell for Abraham, unmatched even by the worst days of the Civil War. Lincoln's world seemed plunged into darkness, as if the sun no longer shone. "Crazy as a loon," snorted Ninian Edwards, convinced he had been right to oppose the marriage from the beginning. Joshua Speed hid his friend's razor for fear he might slit his throat. "I am now the most miserable man living," Lincoln wrote his law partner. "If what I feel were equally distributed to the whole human family, there would not be one cheerful face on the earth. . . . To remain as I am is impossible; I must die or be better, it appears to me."[28]

Months passed before his spirits revived. He still loved Mary, but dared not tell her. How could he, given the way he had acted? Finally, after more than a year, a mutual friend arranged for them to meet "accidentally" in her house. "Be friends again," she said earnestly.[29] They took her advice.

On November 4, 1842, they told the Edwardses they intended to marry. The older couple understood; continuing to argue against the marriage would only make matters worse. The wedding took place that night in their parlor before a small gathering. Abraham gave his bride a gold ring with the inscription *Love Is Eternal*.

The newlyweds moved into a furnished room at the Globe Tavern.

Crowded and noisy, charging four dollars a week for food and lodging, it was the best the groom could afford. Yet Mary had fond memories of the Globe. There, in August 1843, she gave birth to their first child, Robert Todd, named after her father. Aided by fifteen hundred dollars from the proud grandfather, the family moved into a frame house at the corner of Eighth and Jackson Streets. Mary gave birth to three more sons in its second-floor bedroom: Edward (1846), William (1850), and Thomas (1853).

The boys were very different from one another. Robert did not make friends easily, perhaps because of his crossed eyes, a birth defect that troubled him all his life. Schoolmates called him Cockeye. Edward died at the age of three, so no one can know how he would have developed. William, better known as Willie, was gentle and inquisitive. He had a passion for railroads and spent hours memorizing timetables. By his tenth birthday, he could take an imaginary train from New York City to Chicago, Illinois, naming every station and giving the exact time of arrival. Thomas, the Lincolns' youngest, was a squirming infant with a big head. So his father nicknamed him Tad—short for Tadpole. Although cheerful and affectionate, Tad also had a violent temper. A speech defect made him difficult to understand, and he was a slow learner; he could not read until the age of twelve.

Abraham used to say that "Love is the chain whereby to bind a child to its parents."[30] He and Mary seldom disciplined their sons, preferring to explain why something was wrong and then allow the child to tell his side of the story. Good deeds earned hugs, kisses, and praise. Even bribery was better than physical punishment, Abraham thought. He gave money in return for promises of good behavior, and if a boy broke his word, put on a sad face. That usually brought a tearful apology and, for the moment, an improvement. The boys could not bear to disappoint "maw" and "paw."

Lax discipline led to wild outbursts, as

Robert Todd Lincoln. The Lincolns' eldest son was a serious youngster who found it difficult to make friends. He eventually graduated from Harvard University, joined General Grant's staff in the closing days of the Civil War, and served as secretary of war from 1881 to 1885.

Mary Todd Lincoln poses with her youngest sons, Willie (left) and Tad (right), shortly before they left for Washington in February 1861.

when Willie and Tad rampaged through a crowded railroad car while their parents looked on with pleasure. William H. Herndon, Lincoln's last law partner, could hardly control his temper once "these little devils" got going.[31] Abraham liked to take the boys to the office on Sunday mornings. The moment they arrived, they began to "scatter the books, smash up pens, spill the ink, and p[is]s all over the floor. I have felt many and many a time that I wanted to wring their little necks, and yet out of respect for Lincoln I kept my mouth shut. Lincoln did not note what his children were doing or had done. . . . He worshipped his children and what they worshipped; he loved what they loved and hated what they hated, which was everything that did not bend to their freaks, whims, follies, and the like." Herndon believed that "had they s[hi]t in Lincoln's hat and rubbed it on his boots, he would have laughed and thought it smart."[32]

Mary must have felt she had another "devil" in the house, only older and taller than the rest. Although Abraham had left the woods long ago, in many ways he remained a child of the frontier. His homespun manners annoyed her no end. Often he answered the door in his stocking feet or came to meals in his shirtsleeves, unheard of in "proper" households, where men wore jackets in the hottest weather. He would lie on the hallway floor, his back propped against an overturned chair, reading newspapers aloud; that way, he explained, he could absorb an article with his eyes *and* ears. If guests arrived while Mary was dressing, he called out, "She will be down as soon as she has all her trotting harness on."[33]

Abraham's jokes embarrassed his wife. She never knew whether he might say the wrong thing at the wrong time. For example, upon arriving for an at-home at a fellow lawyer's house, he announced, "Oh boys, how clean these girls look!" Another time, he saw a well-dressed woman slip in a muddy street. "Reminds me of a duck," he piped up. "Feathers on her head and down on her behind."[34]

Mary was a high-strung woman. At the slightest provocation, she smashed dishes, screamed, and dropped to the floor in tears. If her husband displeased her, she threw books at him, hit him with a broom, or hurled potatoes at his head. A townsman once saw her chasing Lincoln while waving a butcher knife over her head. He could easily have outrun her, and that would have been the end of the incident. But at the sight of neighbors coming from the opposite direction, he suddenly whirled around. Abraham "caught his wife by the shoulder with one hand and . . . quickly hustled her to the back door of their house and forced, pushed her in, at the same time, as it were, spanking her heavy end, saying to her at the same moment: 'There, [damn] it, now stay in the house and don't disgrace us before the eyes of the world.' "[35] He usually tried to calm her with a joke. Failing that, he went off with the children until she came to her senses.

Mary's outbursts owed as much to fear as to anger. A highly sensitive woman, she panicked at anything out of the ordinary. Thunder terrified her. Whenever storm clouds gathered, Abraham hurried home from the office to keep her company. The sight of a bearded umbrella mender at the front door scared her into wailing "Murder! Murder! Murder!" Threats to her children made her lose control. When, for example, Robert tasted some lime, used to disinfect the outdoor toilet, she stood at her front door flailing her arms and shrieking "Bobbie will die! Bobbie will die!" A neighbor washed his blistered mouth. Another time, Robert wandered away from the house. Discovering his absence, Mary ran up and down the street shouting "Bobbie's lost! Bobbie's lost!"[36]

Despite their bad moments, the Lincolns lived by the motto inscribed on Mary's wedding ring. Their love endured. Abraham called her by pet names like "Puss," "Mother," and "my child wife." Mary said he was everything to her: "Lover—husband—father, *all*." On one of his birthdays, she gave him a gift and a speech that ended: "I am so glad you have a birthday. I feel so grateful to your mother." Mary could not imagine a life without her man.[37]

Lincoln ended his partnership with John T. Stuart in 1841 and joined forces with Stephen T. Logan. Three years later, he opened his own office with Billy Herndon as junior partner. Herndon was more than a business associate. Next to Mary, he knew more about Lincoln than any person alive. He was with "the old man" constantly, studying him and sharing his thoughts on every issue. An able writer, his *Life of Lincoln* and *The Hidden Lincoln* are among the most interesting firsthand accounts we have of the future president.

William H. Herndon, from a line drawing made about the year 1880. Not only was "Billy" Lincoln's law partner, he wrote one of the earliest biographies of the sixteenth President. It first appeared in 1889 and is still an important source for Lincoln's life.

Their law office was a second-floor room in a shabby building in downtown Springfield. Reached by climbing a rickety staircase, it had a few battered pieces of furniture and desks that had seen better days. Nobody ever washed the windows or, for that matter, swept the floors. The dirt was so thick that a discarded packet of seeds once sprouted in a dark corner. Lincoln often forgot where he put important documents. Stacks of papers lay on every flat surface, starting frantic searches whenever they were needed. Lincoln joked about his forgetfulness. It reminded him of "the story of an old Englishman who was so absent-minded that when he went to bed he put his clothes carefully into the bed and threw himself over the back of the chair."[38]

A messy office, however, did not mean a messy mind. When arguing before a jury, Lincoln set out the facts with a mixture of logic, humor, and emotion. His teary eyes and quivering voice could win over the most hard-boiled juror. His stinging remarks made witnesses squirm in their seats. An attorney once described how he "pealed" a witness "from head to foot." During another cross-examination, he asked a famous surgeon, an expert witness in a murder case, about his fee for testifying. The amount shocked the jurors. Lincoln rose to his full height, stretched out his right arm and forefinger, and cried: "Gentlemen of the jury, big fee, big swear."[39]

Lincoln became one of his state's top lawyers. Fellow attorneys sought his advice in difficult cases. He handled every type of case from murder, assault, and rape to land titles, disputed wills, and bad debts.

The legal profession had a bad reputation in Lincoln's day. Americans often saw lawyers as greedy men who provoked quarrels and bent the truth for private gain. Comedians made audiences laugh at stories about the fictional law firm of "Catch 'em and Cheat 'em." For Lincoln, however, a lawyer must not be a moneymaking machine. He must be a compromiser, a peacemaker, a lover of justice and mercy. Above all, he must be honest. "There is a vague popular belief that lawyers are necessarily dishonest," Lincoln told some would-be attorneys. "Let no young man, choosing the law for a calling, for a moment yield to this popular belief. Resolve to be honest at all events; and if, in your judgment, you can not be an honest lawyer, resolve to be honest without being a lawyer. Choose some other occupation, rather . . . than consent to be a knave."[40]

He refused to accept clients he believed to be wrong or guilty. During one trial, for example, he discovered that his client had lied to him. Lincoln stormed out of the courtroom. The judge, puzzled at this be-

"X" marks the spot in this photograph of the building housing the Lincoln-Herndon law office in downtown Springfield.

The Lincoln-Herndon law office was a single room, simply furnished and rarely cleaned. When Lincoln and his wife, Mary, quarreled, he might spend the night in the bed shown at the right of the picture.

havior, ordered him to return. Lincoln refused, saying his hands were dirty and needed a good scrubbing. Honesty proved to be the best policy, since his reputation as a man of principle swayed juries as much as his courtroom tactics.

Nothing made Lincoln angrier than for a man to hit a woman. One day the wife of a shoemaker came to his office in tears. What should she do? Her husband liked to get drunk and end his sprees by beating her black and blue. Lincoln said not to worry. He and two friends took the husband aside and warned him to keep his hands to himself—or else. Before long, however, he was at it again. Lincoln and his friends took the fellow into a vacant lot, tied him to a post, and tore the shirt off his back. Then they gave his wife a whip and told her to go to it with all her might. When she finished, they cut him down and sent him away with another warning. If he ever struck her again, they would fix him so that the cut of the whip would feel like a feather brushing against his skin.[41]

Lincoln tried several cases before the Illinois Supreme Court. Most people in the state, however, lived on farms far from any court or lawyer's office. Therefore, if the people could not come to the law, the law must come to the people. The Springfield courts shut down for half the year: three months in the spring and three in the fall. A circuit judge, so-called because he traveled a circular route, rode from one village to another, holding court in each. And since lawyers needed clients, they, too, "rode circuit"—followed the judges on their rounds.

Lincoln practiced in the Eighth Judicial Circuit, an area covering 12,000 square miles of prairie and woodland. Riding circuit took its toll on both him and his family. While away from home, he stayed at country inns, sharing beds not only with other lodgers but with swarms of hungry fleas. Waking before dawn, he gobbled breakfast and rode all day to be at court on time. Without Mary's firm hand, his clothes became wrinkled and dirty. He once refused a dinner invitation, pleading "I am ragged; I am ragged; I am ragged. I cannot meet the ladies with my elbows out." Mary lived in such terror during his absences that he paid a neighbor boy five cents a night to sleep in the house.[42]

If practicing law brought hardships, it also brought rewards. Lincoln's income reached $5,000 a year in the 1850s, or triple the salary of the governor of Illinois. In 1861, he had $15,000 in cash and investments. Not that he charged high fees; he never asked more than he thought a client could afford to pay. In certain cases, he made Herndon return half the fee because, he felt, their services had not been worth so much. That did not sit well with fellow lawyers, who grumbled about his "impoverishing" the profession. In a mock trial, they convicted him of an "awful crime against his brethren of the bar." Nevertheless, he refused to raise his fees.[43]

In 1846, Lincoln won election to the U.S. House of Representatives. By the time he took his seat, the country was at war with Mexico. In the 1820s, Mexico had invited Americans to settle in Texas, a vast land of scattered ranches and nomadic Indians. In 1836, the settlers rebelled and formed their own nation, the Lone Star Republic. After nine years of independence, Texas joined the Union as the twenty-eighth state. Mexico, however, refused to recognize the Rio Grande River as the new border.

Hot words, then hot lead, began to fly. Claiming that Mexico had shed American blood on American soil, Congress used a raid on an American outpost as an excuse for declaring war. After a string of stun-

N. H. Shepherd's companion to the portrait he took of Mary Todd Lincoln in Springfield in 1846. (See page 28.) Lincoln cherished the set. Before leaving for Washington as President-elect, he dusted the pair carefully. "They are very precious to me," he told Maria Vance, a black housekeeper, "taken when we were young and so desperately in love. They will grace the walls of the White House."

ning defeats, ending with the capture of Mexico City, in 1848 Mexico recognized Texas as part of the United States. In addition, it surrendered over half a million square miles of territory. Included in that territory were all of the future states of California, Nevada, and Utah, most of Arizona and New Mexico, and parts of Colorado and Wyoming.

Americans disagreed over their first foreign war. It was a bully's war, many insisted, a war of aggression unworthy of a free nation. Opponents held antiwar rallies in towns across the land. Protesters, including Lincoln, raised their voices in the halls of Congress itself. Although he supported the army and voted for supplies, he accused President James K. Polk, a Democrat, of provoking the conflict. "The blood of this war, like the blood of Abel, is crying to Heaven against him," he told the House of Representatives.[44] He dared the President to name the exact spot on American soil where Mexicans had shed American blood.

Lincoln's attitude angered Illinois voters. In electing him, they had assumed he was a patriot, only to find him "siding" with the enemy. Newspapers called him another Benedict Arnold, after the Revolutionary War traitor. Democrats branded him "Spotty Lincoln" and hoped he would soon die of "spotted fever." A political rival challenged him to a duel. Lincoln had no intention of shedding another man's blood, much less his own, over some silly words. So he accepted the challenge, provided he selected the weapons—"cow-dung at five paces." Everyone laughed, forcing the man to drop his challenge.[45]

Lincoln did not run for a second term, because party leaders decided to run another Whig in his place. Disappointed, he threw his support behind the presidential campaign of General Zachary Taylor, a Mexican War hero. He hoped that Taylor, if elected, would name him Commissioner of the General Land Office, an important post that might further his political career. It was not to be. Taylor offered him a job in the Oregon Territory. He refused because the job seemed a dead end. Besides, Mary protested strongly; she had no intention of leaving Springfield for the wilds of the Pacific Coast.

Lincoln might have quit politics altogether had it not been for the "Peculiar Institution"—slavery in the Southern states. Until the Mexican War, most Americans had agreed to disagree about slavery—that is, not to make it a political issue. The Mexican peace treaty destroyed that arrangement, triggering a debate about whether the new territories should join the Union as free or slave states. The debate grew louder, and nastier, with each passing year. Like a magnet, it drew Lincoln back into politics and set the stage for the Civil War.

2 THE PECULIAR INSTITUTION

We hold these Truths to be self-evident, that all Men are created equal, that they are endowed by their Creator with certain unalienable Rights, that among these are Life, Liberty, and the Pursuit of Happiness. . . .

DECLARATION OF INDEPENDENCE, JULY 4, 1776

He who would be no slave, must consent to have no slave. Those who deny freedom to others, deserve it not for themselves; and, under a just God, can not long retain it.

ABRAHAM LINCOLN, APRIL 6, 1859

In August 1619, almost a year to the day before the Pilgrims sailed aboard the *Mayflower*, a Dutch warship sold twenty Africans at Jamestown, Virginia. Slavery took root quickly, growing as the English colonies grew. Every colony had slaves, though the vast majority lived in the South, roughly the area enclosed by the Mississippi, Ohio, and Potomac Rivers. Owners argued that slavery was a necessity. With land so plentiful in the New World, few immigrants wanted to work for others. Given the constant labor shortage, forced labor seemed the only way to grow the South's chief cash crops: tobacco, sugar, rice.

By the time of the Revolution, attitudes had begun to change. As Americans fought for their own freedom, they also questioned the morality of slavery. They echoed the words of Abigail Adams, the wife of a future president, who demanded justice for "those who have as good a right to freedom as we have."[1] Enlightened Southerners agreed. George Washington and Thomas Jefferson, slave owners themselves, hoped Americans would find a way to abolish this ancient evil.

History seemed to be on their side. Between 1776 and 1804, the

Northern states abolished slavery by law or by freeing the children of slaves born after a given date. Although the United States Constitution recognized the legality of slavery—by the so-called three-fifths clause—it checked its growth by ending America's role in the Atlantic slave trade; the crew of any vessel found with slaves aboard could be hung as pirates. A law passed in 1787 forbade slavery in the Northwest Territory, a vast area between the Ohio and Mississippi Rivers. Meanwhile, some Southerners were either freeing slaves outright or allowing them to buy their freedom with money earned from after-hours jobs. The number of free blacks rose from 59,000 in 1790 to 319,000 in 1832.[2]

Slavery might have died out had technology not come to its rescue. In 1793, Eli Whitney invented the cotton engine, or "gin" for short. Until then, few farmers raised cotton as their chief crop. It was not worth the bother, since a "fast" worker needed half a day to separate a pound of cotton fiber from its seeds by hand. Whitney's gin, however, used mechanical claws to separate a thousand pounds a day. The age of King Cotton had dawned. By 1850, seven-eighths of the world's supply came from Southern fields, accounting for over half the exports of the United States.

Intended as a laborsaving device, Whitney's invention brought untold misery. Rising demand for cotton increased the demand for

Enslaved people pick cotton under the supervision of white overseers. Notice the whip the overseer on the right holds under his arm.

labor to plant and pick it. Slave prices skyrocketed from $300 for a field hand in 1790 to $1,800 in 1860. In that year, 3,953,760 slaves worth $2 billion lived in the South. These were owned by 384,884 masters, or only one-fourth of the white population.

Not all slave owners profited equally. The vast majority owned small farms and five slaves or fewer. During planting and harvesting, they worked in the fields alongside their slaves. Fewer than three thousand persons owned more than a hundred slaves each, and only eleven owned five hundred or more. Since the Southern economy rested on cotton and slaves, these "lords of the cotton kingdom" controlled the press, decided who taught in the colleges, sat in the state legislatures, and went to Congress.

With the birth of King Cotton, racism combined with economics as a justification for slavery. Called "man's most dangerous myth," racism is the belief that certain peoples are biologically, morally, and intellectually inferior to others. Racists denied the existence of a single human family, descended from Adam and Eve, with branches throughout the world. They held that different races were separate species, like gorillas and monkeys, with blacks at the bottom of the scale. Although blacks had human form, racists denied their humanity. Black people, they argued, were "natural-born slaves" created by God to serve their "natural-born masters," the whites. Thus God had given them strong backs, hard skulls, small brains, "heat-resisting" skins, and eyes designed to see in bright sunlight.

It followed that if blacks were inferior, slavery was not "a necessary evil" but "a positive good." Jefferson Davis described slavery in glowing terms: "The forefathers of [the slaves] were gathered from the torrid plains and malarial swamps of . . . Africa. Generally they were . . . untaught in all the useful arts and occupations, reared in heathen darkness; and, sold by heathen masters, they were transferred to shores enlightened by the rays of Christianity. There, put to servitude, they were trained in the gentle arts of peace and order and civilization. They increased from a few unprofitable savages to millions of efficient Christian laborers. Their servile instincts rendered them contented with their lot. . . . Never was there happier dependence of labor and capital on each other."[3]

The facts told a different story. Every slave was like every other in this respect: they were another person's property. They had no more say about their existence than a horse or a house or a hole in the ground. Slaves were sold, traded, awarded as prizes, raffled off, mortgaged, left in wills, wagered in card games, and taken in payment of debts. The wealthy gave them as gifts. "With us," a Virginian boasted, "nothing is so unusual as to advance children by gifts of slaves. They stand with us instead of money."[4] Doting parents knew that if ever their children needed ready cash, they need only "cash in" a slave.

The master was a prince, his plantation a domain where law and custom gave him total power over his human property. Nevertheless, most tried to soften their actions for two reasons. First, since they depended upon slaves to make their fortunes, deliberately mistreating them hurt profits. Second, slavery was an intricate web of human relationships in which a lot depended on individual character.

Masters related to slaves in ways cruel and kind, harsh and gentle, angry and friendly—yes, even loving. Although it was not supposed to happen, more than one slaveholder had an experience like Rachel O'Connor's. Writing from Louisiana in 1830, Rachel told of nursing a sick black child on her husband's plantation. "The poor little fellow is laying at my feet sound asleep. I wish I did not love him as I do, but it is so, and I cannot help it."[5]

Slaves followed many occupations. Town slaves worked as coachmen, barbers, butlers, tailors, shoemakers, blacksmiths, carpenters, painters, plasterers, masons, cooks, maids, and seamstresses. In the country, slaves worked as lumberjacks, dug coal, herded cattle, broke wild horses, built ships, and did everything on riverboats except take command. The majority, however, spent their lives on a plantation, never venturing more than ten miles from it, unless to go to the auction block.

A plantation consisted of various buildings. The owner's home, or Big House, was a two-story structure with at least ten rooms. Slaves lived in "the quarters," a row of one-room cabins that broiled in summer and froze in winter. A cabin often housed two or three families. "In a single room were huddled, like cattle, ten or a dozen persons, men, women, and children," recalled Josiah Henson, a former slave. "There were neither bedsteads, nor furniture of any description. Our beds were collections of straw and old rags, thrown down in the corners and boxed in with boards, a single blanket the only covering. . . . The wind whistled and the rain and snow blew in through the cracks, and the damp earth soaked in the moisture until the floor was miry as a pigsty."[6] Beyond the quarters lay the barns, stables, storage sheds, blacksmith shop, and bake ovens. The fields lay beyond the buildings, and the woods behind these.

There were three classes of slaves. Servants in the Big House were the slave nobility. They dressed well, had fine manners, and scorned the less fortunate, including whites, whom they called "dirt eaters" and "poor white trash." The cook prepared the meals, the butler served them in style, and the housekeepers kept things tidy. "Mammy," the common term for a slave nursemaid, cared for the children and was often closer to them than their own mother. If Mammy or another slave woman gave birth about the same time as the mistress, she nursed the white infant along with her own. Body servants saw to the master's or mistress's personal needs; always available, they slept on a straw mattress at the foot of the bed or outside the bedroom door. Slave children polished shoes, warmed cold beds by lying in them, and did other easy tasks; one boy scratched his master's head so he could fall asleep. Craftsmen worked at the same tasks as their town cousins. Everyone else went to the cotton fields.

The field hands' day began early. Before sunrise, the overseer, a white man hired to manage slaves, rang a bell or blew a horn. The slaves quickly dressed and ate breakfast. They wore the roughest homespun, or "Negro cloth," and usually went barefoot even if they had shoes; shoes were scarce and best saved for wintertime. Meals consisted of salt pork, corn bread, milk, and seasonal vegetables such as sweet potatoes and

Advertisements offering to buy and sell slaves were a regular feature of Southern newspapers.

peas. Masters knew that well-fed hands worked better than hungry ones, so most gave ample rations. Slaves understood the reason for such "kindness." One recalled that his owner "fed us reg'lar on good, 'stantial food, just like you'd tend to you hoss, if you had a real good one."[7]

Only the very sick and the very young escaped work. Elderly women did laundry, cooked, and cared for the babies. Elderly men tended the farm animals, gardened, and cleaned out the barns. Children between six and ten joined the "trash gang" to pull weeds. At the age of ten, they went to the cotton fields for a few hours each day; by eighteen, they worked full-time. Except for a fifteen-minute lunch break, field hands kept at it until sundown. Every year scores of slaves died because their "heat-resisting" skins failed to prevent sunstroke.

Each Southern state had its Black Codes, laws aimed at shaping the "perfect" slave, a person who accepted his or her lowly position as just and natural. In the words of a South Carolina law: "The slave should know that his master is to govern absolutely, and he is to obey implicitly. That he is never for a moment to exercise either his will or judgment in opposition to a positive order."[8]

Black Codes regulated every aspect of slave life. Slaves could not smoke tobacco, ride in carriages, or carry walking sticks. Slaves could not attend church services or make "joyful demonstrations" unless supervised by a white person. Slaves could not use guns, hold meetings, or beat drums and blow horns for fear these might signal a revolt. Slaves could not trade, buy, sell, own property, or learn to count money. Slaves could not leave the plantation without a signed pass. To make sure they obeyed, each district enrolled patrollers, bands of mounted volunteers, to scour the countryside after nightfall. Known as "paddy-rollers" and "the devil's own horsemen," they shot first and asked questions later.

Napoleon used to say he could do everything with bayonets except sit on them. By that he meant that the best way to control people is not through force but through their own minds, so that they obeyed willingly. Similarly, the Peculiar Institution was a form of brainwashing aimed at robbing its victims of their self-respect. Blacks were not referred to as people but as "coons," "darkies," and "niggers," from the Spanish *negro*—"black." Grown men had to answer to "boy" and women

OPPOSITE: *Marks of servitude. The caption on this photo reads: " 'Overseer Artayou Carrier whipped me. I was two months in bed sore from the whipping. My master come after I was whipped; he discharged the overseer.' The very words of poor Peter, taken as he sat for this picture. Baton Rouge, La., April 2, 1863."*

to "girl." Blacks, however, had to treat whites with elaborate courtesy. Adult whites must be addressed as "master" and "mistress," white children as "little master" and "little mistress."

Every Southern state forbade blacks to read and write, or to be taught these skills by whites. The written word has power, and reading could easily "corrupt" the slaves' minds with notions of freedom and equality. Overseers, therefore, watched for anyone with a "stolen education"—anyone who had somehow learned to read. "For God's sake," said Elijah Green, recalling life on a South Carolina plantation, "don't let a slave be catch with pencil and paper. That was a major crime. You might as well had killed your master and missus." Literate slaves faced severe punishment, like the poor fellow who had his thumbs cut off. Strict owners forbade their slaves even to *touch* a Bible.[9]

Every state had its sadists, those who enjoyed hurting others. Newspapers mentioned slaves being shot, stabbed, burned, beaten, hacked to pieces, branded, covered with boiling tar, and forced to eat manure. An ex-slave recalled how "old Missis . . . she'd take a needle and stick it through one of their nigger women's lower lip and pin it to the bosom of her dress, and the woman would go roun' all day with her haid drew down thataway, and slobberin'."[10] The "best" owners, however, frowned upon violence. Yet

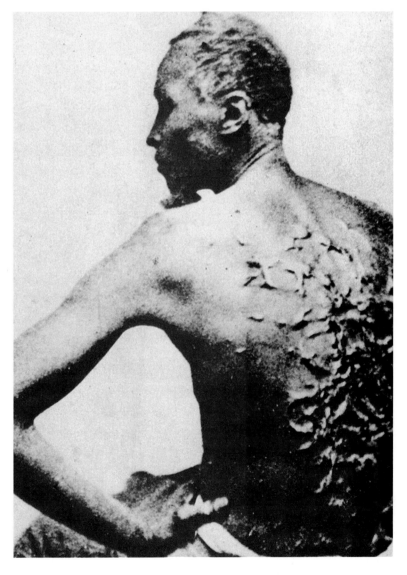

even they used it occasionally, so that few slaves went through life without physical abuse.

Whipping was the punishment of choice. Offenders were stripped naked and given anywhere from a dozen to a thousand strokes with a leather whip applied to every part of the body. The whip cut deep, causing wounds that healed as ugly scars.

Yet the ugliest scars remained hidden from view. As late as the 1930s, ex-slaves could describe whippings in minute detail. Husbands and fathers, wives and mothers, recalled standing by, powerless, as loved ones had the flesh torn off their backs. A ninety-year-old man recalled how, as a youth, he saw his naked mother with blood running from her shoulders down to her heels. "They didn't care nothing 'bout it," he said angrily. "Let everybody look on at it." The overseer kept on with the whip until his arm ached.[11]

Slave families had little in common with those of free people. Young women of "breeding age" could choose their mates or, as often happened, had mates chosen for them. Hilliard Yellerday, a former slave, recalled: "When a girl became a woman, she was required to go to a man and become a mother. There was generally a form of marriage. The master read a paper to them telling them they were man an' wife. Some were married by the master laying down a broom and the two slaves, man and woman, would jump over it. The master would then tell them they were man and wife, and they could go to bed together. . . . A slave girl was expected to have children as soon as she became a woman. Some of them had children at the age of twelve and thirteen years old."[12]

Since slave marriages had no legal standing, they were no more binding than "marriages" of farm animals. Even so, the family played a central role in black life. In the family, youngsters found love, sympathy, and the practical wisdom gained by

Posters like this one in the collection of the National Archives were common throughout the South in the decade before the Civil War. Notice that the slave trader had an office in Lexington, Kentucky, Mary Todd Lincoln's hometown.

$1200 TO 1250 DOLLARS ! FOR NEGROES ! !

THE undersigned wishes to purchase a large lot of NEGROES for the New Orleans market. I will pay $1200 to $1250 for No. 1 young men, and $850 to $1000 for No. 1 young women. In fact I will pay more for likely

NEGROES,

Than any other trader in Kentucky. My office is adjoining the Broadway Hotel, on Broadway, Lexington, Ky., where I or my Agent can always be found.

WM. F. TALBOTT.
LEXINGTON, JULY 2, 1853.

generations of bondage. Parents taught children whom to trust, how to cooperate with one another, and ways to fool the master.

Proud masters showed off their latest "crop" of slave children. Long after the Civil War, Willie Williams, raised on a Louisiana plantation, told an interviewer how "de marster lots ob times looks dem [children] over an' points one out an' says, 'Dat one will be wo'th a thousan' dollahs,' an' he points to anudder an' says, 'Dat one will be a whopper.' You see, 'twas jus' lak raisin' de mules."[13] The interviewer took down Mr. Williams's statement to show the everyday dialect used by black people at the time. Black dialect often expressed ideas and feelings more vigorously—indeed, more passionately—than standard speech. For this reason, abolitionists often used it to hammer home their arguments against slavery, thereby giving them greater force and poignancy. Frederick Douglass, for example, did this in a slave song he quotes in *My Bondage and My Freedom*:

> *We raise de wheat,*
> *Dey gib us de corn;*
> *We bake de bread,*
> *Dey gib us de crust;*
> *We sift de meal,*
> *Dey gib us de husk;*
> *We peel de meat,*
> *Dey gib us de skin;*
> *And dat's de way*
> *Dey take us in;*
> *We skim de pot,*
> *Dey gib us de liquor,*
> *And say dat's good enough*
> *for nigger.*[14]

There was always a market for what slave traders called human "stock." Every day except Sunday, armed guards herded slaves into every large Southern town. Women marched in a line, or coffle, each joined by a rope around her neck. Men wore handcuffs and iron collars linked by a long chain. Locked in the trader's own jail, a series of brick-floored cells

An appeal to human-ity. This illustration is from an 1832 issue of William Lloyd Garrison's anti-slavery journal, The Liberator. *Drawings like this aimed at highlighting the common humanity of all peoples, regard-less of race and sex.*

with barred windows and iron-grated doors, they were sold either to private customers or at public auctions.

The rule was: "Buyer beware." A wise pur-chaser examined the "merchandise" with extreme care. "Every first Tuesday slaves were . . . sold on the {auction} block," a former slave recalled. "They would stand the slaves up on the block and talk about what a fine-looking specimen of black manhood or womanhood they was, tell how healthy they was, look in their mouths and exam-ine their teeth just like they was a horse, and talk about the kind of work they would be fit for and could do."[15] Cus-tomers handled the bodies of women and teenage girls, inspecting them up and down to decide how many children they might bear. All were checked for whip marks, since recent scars indicated a slave was being sold as a troublemaker.

Masters broke up almost a third (32.4 percent) of all slave mar-riages.[16] Families crumbled as husbands, wives, and children went to the auction block separately. Eyewitnesses reported scenes of frantic mothers clinging to the auctioneer's legs, begging him to sell her and her little ones together. Others stood by speechless and with glazed eyes, numbed by the terrible scene. Once separated, family members were taken to dif-ferent parts of the country, the majority never to meet again. Even if they lived on plantations in the same county, chances were they never knew it, much less visited one another, thanks to the paddyrollers.

A female slave had no right to resist the master's sexual advances, nor could her family stand in his way. The law allowed him to mistreat "his" women, even rape them, without punishment. As a result, thou-sands of mulattoes, children of mixed race, came into the world each year. Although the exact number is unknown, some mulattoes were freed by fathers' troubled by guilty consciences. Educated in the North, they often adopted white prejudices, taking pride in their "superior" blood and light skins. Abraham Lincoln discovered this when he moved into the White House in 1861. Among the servants was William John-son, a free black who had come with him from Springfield. Johnson was too dark for the mulatto servants. They made him so miserable that the President had to find him a job elsewhere.[17]

Blacks defied the Peculiar Institution in different ways. A major part of their struggle was to preserve their dignity despite daily humiliation. Take the word *nigger*. Julius Lester, the editor of an outstanding collection of slave recollections, reminds us that the same word can have different meanings. It is not words that wound, but who uses them and how. In white mouths, "nigger" was a coarse insult, a verbal slap in the face. Slaves, however, adopted this hateful word, thus drawing its sting and turning it into its opposite. Calling themselves "nigger" was an act of free will, and thus a form of resistance. It established their identity, showing they could rise above bondage. This tactic is described in the opening lines of a song: "Got one mind for the boss to see; / Got another mind for what I know is me."[18]

Christianity served a similar purpose. White ministers taught that slavery was the blacks' own fault. As punishment for their sins, God was supposed to have created them black, the color of evil, and put them in bondage. Slaves, however, learned different lessons from Christianity. Avoiding the patrollers, they held "hush-harbor" meetings at night in forests and swamps. There, black preachers, people with stolen educations reading from stolen Bibles, explained that God loved them, too. Their religious songs, or spirituals, asked God to deliver His black children from bondage as He had once delivered the children of Israel.

> *Didn't my Lord deliver Daniel,*
> *Deliver Daniel, deliver Daniel?*
> *Didn't my Lord deliver Daniel,*
> *Then why not every man?*
>
> *He delivered Daniel from the lion's den,*
> *Jonah from the belly of the whale,*
> *The Hebrew children from the fiery furnace,*
> *Then why not every man?*[19]

Slaves resisted passively; that is, they worked as little as possible while trying to look busy. Field hands "misunderstood" orders or sang slow "drawling" songs, adjusting their movements to keep time with the tunes. Before the weigh-in at the close of each workday, they put stones into their cotton sacks to make it seem as if they had picked their quota. Some went in for sabotage, breaking tools and "accidentally" cutting down cotton plants while hoeing around them.

Desperate people did desperate things. Court records tell of a field hand who cut off his right hand and another who cut off the fingers of one hand to avoid the auction block. Occasionally, slaves committed suicide or killed their children. Lou Smith, a former slave, recalled a woman who had seen each of her children sold soon after birth. "When her fourth baby was born and was about two months old, she just studied all the time about how she would have to give it up, and one day she said, 'I just decided I'm not going to let ol' master sell this baby; he just ain't going to do it.' She got up and give it something out of a bottle and pretty soon it was dead."[20]

Still others turned their anger against their tormentors. Arson became a major problem, as scores of barns, ginhouses, and cotton sheds went up in smoke each year. Court records also tell of servants poisoning their masters or mistresses with ground glass mixed in gravy. In certain areas, slaveholders guarded against poisoning by forcing a servant to eat a little food from each dish.

Southerners most feared a full-scale rebellion. Historians have counted some 250 American slave revolts. In colonial days, serious outbreaks occurred in New York City, New Orleans, and Alexandria, Virginia. These revolts seldom lasted more than a week, and captured rebels received no mercy. To set an example, executioners strangled captives, locked them in starvation cells, burnt them at the stake, and broke them at the wheel; that is, they tied them to wagon wheels, broke every bone in their bodies with iron bars, and left them to a lingering death.

The worst slave revolt occurred in Southampton County, Virginia. Its leader was Nat Turner, a slave preacher who had visions of battles between black and white spirits. Convinced that God had chosen him to crush "the Serpent" of slavery, on the night of Sunday, August 21, 1831, Turner led seventy slaves and free blacks on a rampage. They did not try to separate brutal masters from innocent women and children. At one farm, rebels clubbed a family of five as they slept; at another, they killed the mistress and her ten children. Fifty-seven whites died before a posse captured the rebels. Not only were they executed, but scores of innocent blacks, including slaves who had protected their masters, died at the hands of vengeful mobs. Turner went to the gallows convinced that he had done God's work. The judge ordered his body handed over to a surgeon for dissection, then skinned and boiled to make grease.[21]

Turner's revolt startled Southerners. Wherever whites turned, they imagined blacks wanted their blood. Masters slept with pistols under their pillows, waking at the slightest sound with pounding hearts. Events in Southampton County, a planter wrote a friend, "have alarmed my wife so as really to endanger her health, and I have not slept without anxiety in three months. Our nights are sometimes spent listening to noises. A hog call has sometimes been the subject of nervous terror, and a cat, in the dining room, will banish sleep for the night. There had been and there still is a *panic* in this country."[22]

The panic was unjustified. News of the brutal retribution for Turner's rampage had spread through the quarters by the slave "grapevine"—word of mouth. It discouraged further rebellions; in fact, no slave revolt ever had a prayer of succeeding. Unarmed and outnumbered, blacks were powerless to break their chains by themselves. Such was the harsh truth, but the truth nevertheless. Only help from outside the slave system offered any hope of freedom.

On New Year's Day, 1831, as Nat Turner made his plans, a frail man with thick spectacles and a shiny bald head began printing a weekly newspaper in Boston, Massachusetts. The son of a drunken father who had abandoned his family, William Lloyd Garrison, age twenty-six, had always identified with the oppressed. His newspaper, *The Liberator,* served the radical abolitionists, a group of Northern men and women determined to end, or abolish, slavery. Although a minority within the abolitionist movement, the radicals had influence far beyond their numbers.

Garrison and his followers attacked slavery from every angle. They described racism as the greatest lie ever invented by wicked men. The Bible tells of God's creation of mankind (not manlike creatures) in His own image. It followed, therefore, that blacks were not a separate species but members of the human family. Articles in *The Liberator* argued there was only one race, "the universal human race in which all men are brothers, and God is father over all!"[23]

Since blacks were God's children, enslaving them was a sin. Abolitionists wanted all slaves freed immediately and given full American citizenship. There must be no calculation of profit and loss. If cotton could not be grown without slave labor, then it should not be grown. If halting cotton production wrecked the Southern economy, so be it. If slave owners lost their investment, too bad for them.

Garrison and his allies bombarded the nation with propaganda. Volunteers stood on street corners, handing out pamphlets and drawings depicting the evils of slavery. Abolitionist groups held rallies featuring runaway slaves as speakers. Their star speaker was Frederick Douglass, a tall mulatto with a rich baritone voice. Douglass's life reads like an adventure novel. Born a slave in Maryland in 1817, he stole an education by tricking white children into sharing their lessons with him. After ferocious beatings, he stole himself by fleeing to the North, where he joined forces with Garrison. Douglass soon became *the* black abolitionist of his time, with his own newspaper, the *North Star,* and magazine, *Douglass' Monthly.*

Douglass's very existence challenged the idea of black inferiority. The man radiated strength, determination, and intelligence. His theme, hammered home in countless speeches, came down to a single word: equality. If blacks seemed inferior, blame the Peculiar Institution, not its victims! "Take any race you please, French, English, Irish, or Scotch," he said; "subject them to slavery for ages—regard and treat them everywhere, every way, as property. . . . Let them be loaded with chains, scarred with the whip, branded with hot irons, sold in the market . . . and I venture to say that the same doubt would spring up concerning either of them, which now confronts the negro. . . . [No wonder] the colored people in America appear stupid, helpless, and degraded. The wonder is that they evince so much spirit and manhood as they do."[24]

Cotton lords blamed abolitionists for their troubles. After Nat Turner's revolt, Southern states banned free speech, making it a crime to say, write, or read anything critical of the Peculiar Institution. Police

OPPOSITE: *William Lloyd Garrison, founder of* The Liberator, *was a leader of the radical abolitionists. During the Civil War, he demanded that Lincoln abolish slavery immediately, regardless of the political and military consequences. After the war, he campaigned against liquor and in favor of justice for the Indians and women's right to vote.*

turned their backs as mobs broke into post offices in search of abolitionist literature. Any white person who protested paid dearly. A mob in Petersburg, Virginia, whipped a man for saying blacks had "a right to their freedom." A Georgian caught with a copy of *The Liberator* was tarred and feathered and dunked in a river until he nearly drowned.[25] It could have been worse. Several state legislatures voted the death penalty for abolitionists. The Georgia legislature offered $5,000 to anyone who kidnapped Garrison and brought him to Georgia for trial.

Millions of Northerners, too, would have liked to see Garrison swinging from a gallows. Although slavery was banned in the North, racism has never respected state boundaries. Signs of bigotry were common. For example, white minstrels wore "black face," depicting black people as clowns with thick red lips and wild eyes. Children learned about black "inferiority" in school. Parents warned naughty youngsters that "the old nigger," a bloodthirsty night demon, "will carry you off."[26]

Just as slave states had Black Codes, free states had Black Laws. Northern blacks faced discrimination at every turn. Laws either forbade blacks to ride in railway trains, streetcars, and steamboats or made them sit in special sections. Blacks could not sleep in most hotels, see a show in most theaters, eat in most restaurants, and live in most parts of town. No black could serve on a jury or testify against a white in court. Black criminals served their time in segregated prisons, and black bodies rested in segregated cemeteries. Black children attended segregated schools. Blacks paid taxes like everyone else; yet they could only vote in Massachusetts, New Hampshire, Vermont, and Maine.

Frederick Douglass, a former slave, was the most influential black abolitionist of his generation. At the start of the Civil War, he said a crusade against slavery was more important than a struggle to preserve the Union. This photo was taken about the year 1850.

Most Northerners despised abolitionists. Businessmen saw them as enemies out to ruin their best customers, the slave owners. Workers accused them of plotting to unleash masses of low-wage blacks in the factory towns. Fear sparked mob violence on a wide scale. White gangs swept through black neighborhoods in New York, Boston, Philadelphia, Cleveland, and Cincinnati, beating people and burning their property. Howling mobs stoned abolitionist speakers and pelted them with filth. In 1835, Garrison narrowly escaped with his life after rioters tied a rope around his waist and dragged him through the streets of Boston until he was rescued by the mayor. A magistrate charged *him* with disturbing the peace!

Although the issue of slavery brought out the worst in people, it could not create a national crisis if it remained outside politics. King Cotton, however, made that impossible.

Cotton is now grown with chemical fertilizers. In the nineteenth century, however, these were unavailable. As a result, the soil wore out quickly, which meant slavery had to expand into new areas or die. Slave owners saw their future in the Western territories. So did Northern farmers, merchants, and workers. Calling themselves Free-Soilers, they wanted to keep both slavery and "inferior" blacks out of the West. By the 1840s, Indiana, Iowa, and Oregon had barred all blacks from their territory. Illinois forbade any more blacks to enter the state without a certificate of good behavior, and the new constitution of 1848 did away with even that concession.

Congress tried to satisfy both sides. The Missouri Compromise of 1820 admitted Missouri as a slave state and Maine as a free state; moreover, it banned slavery "forever" north of Missouri's southern boundary, an immense plain stretching from the Mississippi River to the Rocky Mountains. After the Mexican War, the Compromise of 1850 admitted California as a free state in return for a strong Fugitive Slave Law, a measure long-favored by slaveholders. Yet this law had an unintended effect. By making it easier to pursue runaways in the free states, it stimulated the Underground Railroad, further poisoning relations between North and South.

The Underground Railroad was a secret network of volunteers who guided runaway slaves to safety. Like any railroad, it had "trains," "stations," and "conductors." A train might be a

Harriet Tubman, "the Moses of her people," was the most famous conductor on the Underground Railroad. Brave and resourceful, she threatened to shoot any fugitive who tried to turn back. No one knows exactly how many slaves the conductors rescued; they kept no records, for obvious reasons.

horse, rowboat, or false-bottom wagon. A station was any place that offered a meal and a day's rest: a farmhouse barn, basement, storeroom, church. Conductors were adventurous whites or blacks returning to the South to bring out relatives. No one knows exactly how many slaves the conductors rescued; they kept no records, for obvious reasons. The best estimate is over 100,000 in the fifty years before the Civil War.[27]

Professional slave catchers invaded the North. It was all perfectly legal. The Fugitive Slave Law allowed blacks, fugitive or free, to be arrested and sent south purely on a slave catcher's say-so. It also stripped runaways of basic civil rights like a jury trial and testifying in their own defense. Anyone who refused to aid in the capture of a fugitive, or interfered with an arrest, faced a heavy fine and a jail term. "Niggers are property, sir," a slave catcher declared, "the same as horses and cattle; and nobody has any more right to help a negro that has run away than he has to steal a horse."[28]

Although many Northerners may have disliked blacks, they also despised these arrogant bullies. Jeering crowds lined sidewalks as slave catchers marched entire families, roped and handcuffed, toward trains bound for Dixie. State legislatures passed "personal liberty laws" forbidding local authorities to help slave catchers. Ordinary citizens went further, rescuing captives at gunpoint. Frederick Douglass said the best way to make the Fugitive Slave Law a dead letter was "to make a dozen or more dead kidnappers."[29]

Stephen A. Douglas added fuel to the fire. He had gone far since the days when he courted Mary Todd in Springfield. Nicknamed "the Little Giant" because of his small size—barely five feet four inches tall—and huge ambition, he became Illinois's leading Democrat. Within a decade, Douglas held office as a state judge, a member of the House of Representatives, and a United States senator. As chairman of the Senate Committee on Territories, in 1854 he sponsored the Kansas-Nebraska Act. Without real-

After the passage of a strong Fugitive Slave Law in 1850, professional slave catchers invaded the North to recapture their clients' "property." Local whites protested, as we see in this poster from Boston.

CAUTION!!
COLORED PEOPLE
OF BOSTON, ONE & ALL,
You are hereby respectfully CAUTIONED and advised, to avoid conversing with the
Watchmen and Police Officers of Boston,
For since the recent ORDER OF THE MAYOR & ALDERMEN, they are empowered to act as
KIDNAPPERS
AND
Slave Catchers,
And they have already been actually employed in KIDNAPPING, CATCHING, AND KEEPING SLAVES. Therefore, if you value your LIBERTY, and the *Welfare of the Fugitives* among you, *Shun* them in every possible manner, as so many *HOUNDS* on the track of the most unfortunate of your race.
Keep a Sharp Look Out for KIDNAPPERS, and have TOP EYE open.
APRIL 24, 1851.

THEODORE PARKER'S PLACARD
Placard written by Theodore Parker and printed and posted by the Vigilance Committee of Boston after the rendition of Thomas Sims to slavery in April, 1851.

izing it, he had set the stage for a major political crisis.

The Missouri Compromise had forbidden slavery in the Kansas and Nebraska territories. Senator Douglas, however, favored "popular sovereignty," allowing settlers in a territory to decide if it should become a free or slave state. Popular sovereignty turned the Kansas-Nebraska Act into a formula for murder. As settlers moved into Kansas from the North and South, rival gangs created "Bleeding Kansas." Gang members shot it out in broad daylight, staged midnight ambushes, and burned opponents' farms. Federal troops restored order, but only after two hundred Americans had lost their lives to other Americans.

Meanwhile, the Supreme Court entered the picture. In 1857, the justices handed down a decision in the Dred Scott case. Scott was a slave who had lived with his master in free territory. Upon returning to Missouri, he sued for his freedom, claiming that his time on free soil made him a free man. The justices disagreed. The majority ruled that blacks had never been citizens of the United States and therefore had no rights under its laws. Worse, since slaves were private property, their masters could take them anywhere. Thus, with one blow the justices overturned the Missouri Compromise, opened the West to slavery, and legalized it in *free* America. What made so many Northerners angry was that masters could now drag their human property across the continent. This in turn, they feared, would allow slave owners to undercut the wages of free workers and make them work longer hours.

Dred Scott. In 1846, Dred Scott sued to obtain his freedom because he had lived with his master in free territory. Eleven years later, the Supreme Court rejected his plea, ruling that he was not a citizen and, as a black man, "had no rights which a white man was bound to respect."

The Kansas-Nebraska Act and the Dred Scott decision were political bombshells. As the dust settled in Kansas, unhappy Democrats and Whigs left their parties to form the Republican party. Like the Free-Soilers, Republicans opposed slavery not out of pity for oppressed blacks but out of concern for the interests of white people. Calling themselves "the white man's party," they did not want to interfere with slavery where it already existed, only to keep it out of the West. Nobody defended these aims more forcefully than Abraham Lincoln.

★   ★   ★

Slavery had been a part of Lincoln's boyhood. Kentucky was a slave state, and nearly as many slaves (1,007) as adult white men (1,627) lived in his home county. Among them were slaves belonging to relatives. The boy's uncles, Isaac and Mordecai Lincoln, owned dozens of slaves. A relative of his mother owned three black people.

Abraham saw slaves herded along the wilderness road that ran past the family cabin, bound for plantations in Tennessee and Georgia. Once a dealer asked his father's permission to bed a coffle down for the night on a haystack near the cabin. The youngster never forgot how "all of the slaves, men, women, and children, were chained together" in their sleep, and how "some of the women held babies in their arms."[30] Tom struggled to compete with slave labor, as did most of the neighbors. Slavery stirred such bitterness in Hardin County that the churches split over the issue. One of Tom's reasons for leaving Kentucky was to get away from the Peculiar Institution.

Except for his two trips to New Orleans, Lincoln saw few (if any) black people after moving to Indiana. The Peculiar Institution was not something he examined closely as a teenager. As an adult, he learned more about slavery from his wife than from any other person. Born into a slaveholding family, Mary had a wealth of firsthand information on the subject, much of it favorable. Slaves were not beaten in the Todd household, or called "nigger"; her parents would have punished their children for using this coarse word. The Todds regarded their house servants as family members, particularly Mammy Sally, a kindly woman whom the "chil'en" loved.

Mary knew the other side of slavery, too. An auction house stood a few blocks from the Todd home. On quiet summer days, screams from the whipping post came through the parlor's open windows. Newspapers read at the breakfast table had offers to buy "slaves unfit for labor by Rheumatism &c"; these poor souls ended up being worked to death on Louisiana sugar plantations. Mammy Sally marked the fence to signal runaways that they could get food at the back door late at night. The young Todds, Mary included, discovered her secret but kept it to themselves. Mary even took the slave prayer "Hide me, O my Savior" as her own.[31]

Her husband never hid his opinions about slavery. Lincoln hated it. He hated its cruelty. He hated its abuse of women and its breakup of families. He hated it as "a monstrous injustice" that permitted foreigners to taunt America as a nation of hypocrites. He hated it because it was an injustice that had been suffered not only by blacks but by the downtrodden in all ages. "It is the eternal struggle between these two principles—right and wrong—throughout the world," he declared. "They are the two principles that have stood face to face from the beginning of time. The one is the common right of humanity and the other the divine right of kings. It is the same principle in whatever shape it develops itself. It is the same spirit that says, 'You work and toil and earn bread, and I'll eat it.' No matter in what shape it comes, whether from the mouth of a king . . . or from one race of men as an apology for enslaving another race, it is the same tyrannical principle."[32] These beliefs led him to denounce slavery in the Illinois legislature in 1837 and in the House of Representatives a decade later.

Yet he was no abolitionist. Much as he hated slavery, he accepted it as the law of the land. And Abraham Lincoln was above all a man of the law. He held the law sacred, as if the Almighty had written it in golden letters a yard high. This explains why he resented people like William Lloyd Garrison and Frederick Douglass. Although they were sincere, they put their love of justice above the law. Resisting sin meant more to them than all the laws in all the law books in all the countries on earth. They valued doing "the right thing" more than life itself.

Lincoln saw abolitionists as fanatics who inflamed people's emotions. He accused them of wishing to tear up the Constitution, in his view the finest instrument of self-government ever devised by the human mind. Abolitionists, he said, would wreck the Union in a heartbeat, "even burn the last copy of the Bible, rather than slavery should continue a single hour."[33]

For one who hated slavery as he did, Lincoln's respect for the law put him in an uncomfortable position. On the one hand, he denounced the Fugitive Slave Law as "ungodly" and "very obnoxious."[34] On the other hand, he recognized that slaves were property in the United States. Even before the Fugitive Slave Law, as a member of Congress he voted to return runaways seized in the District of Columbia. Moreover, he called for a gradual end to slavery in the nation's capital provided owners received a fair price and its "free white citizens" approved.

Lincoln shared the views of the white majority in the free states. Hatred of slavery did not prevent him (or them) from holding racist ideas. The future President thought black people "inferior," claimed they belonged to "the inferior races," and urged the Illinois legislature to expel them from the state to avoid intermarriage. When free blacks circulated a petition asking the legislature to allow blacks to testify against whites in court, Lincoln refused to sign. Words like *nigger* and *slave niggers* were part of his vocabulary. He told black dialect jokes and recited this verse about Sally Brown, a pretty mulatto:

> *Sally is a bright Mullatter,*
> *Oh, Sally Brown*
> *Pretty gal, but can't get at her,*
> *Oh, Sally Brown.*[35]

In all his years as a lawyer, Lincoln had only two slave-related cases. In the first, he won freedom for a young woman brought to Illinois by her master. In the second, he represented a Kentucky slaveholder who sued to recover a family that claimed freedom because they, too, had been brought to Illinois. This case he lost.

The man known to history as the Great Emancipator did not start out that way. Like so many Americans, he merely wanted to contain slavery in Dixie, where, in time, he expected it to die a "natural death." Since cotton growing exhausted the soil, preventing the Peculiar Institution from expanding meant that it must eventually die out. After 1849, when the Whigs did not renominate him for the House, he worked at rebuilding his law practice, since, he believed, his political career was over. He had nearly given up on politics when the Kansas-Nebraska Act aroused him as nothing had ever done before. Instead of dying naturally, slavery seemed about to spread through the nation like a "cancer." Rather than see that happen, in 1856 he joined the Republicans and returned to politics.

Lincoln had failed to win election to the Senate as a Whig in 1855. In 1858, as a Republican, he criticized Senator Douglas so forcefully

that his party nominated him to oppose him in the upcoming election. He
launched his campaign with "A House
Divided," the first of his great speeches.
Standing before delegates to the Republican convention in Springfield, Lincoln
warned that the quarrel over slavery was
spinning out of control. Comparing the
nation to a house, he said:

" 'A house divided against itself cannot
stand.'

"I believe this government cannot endure, permanently half *slave* and half *free*.

"I do not expect the Union to be *dissolved*—I do not expect the house to *fall*—
but I *do* expect it will cease to be divided.

"It will become *all* one thing, or *all* the
other."

Either the foes of slavery would halt its
spread, or its allies would keep going "till it
shall become alike lawful in *all* the States,
old as well as *new*—*North* as well as *South*."[36]

Douglas struck back. The Little Giant
crisscrossed Illinois by train, ridiculing Lin-
coln and his "black Republicans" at every whistle-stop. Lincoln followed,
using his own brand of ridicule. Not only did he attack the senator's
ideas, he mocked him with humorous stories. They hurt. "Every one of
his stories seems like a whack on my back," Douglas groaned.[37]

They finally agreed to hold seven debates between August 21 and
October 15, 1858. These Lincoln-Douglas debates are part of the American heritage, shining examples of democracy in action. Unlike the
bland "debates" viewed by twentieth-century television audiences, these
were sharp exchanges by masters of speechmaking. They used logic,
rhetoric, vivid images, and humor to sway their audiences. For example,
when Douglas called him two-faced, Lincoln shot back: "I leave it to
my audience. If I had another face, do you think I'd wear this one?"[38]

*Stephen A. Douglas in
1858. "The Little
Giant" and "Long
Abe" Lincoln had been
rivals for years. Both
men courted Mary
Todd, ran for the
Senate, and were
contenders for the
presidency. Lincoln
won two of the three
contests.*

Victor Perara's drawing of the Galesburg debate, October 7, 1858. The Lincoln-Douglas debates drew vast crowds throughout the state of Illinois. Although Lincoln lost the senatorial race, the debates gave him a national reputation, making him a leading contender for the 1860 Republican presidential nomination.

The debaters respected their listeners. They never talked down to them or gave rehearsed answers to prepared questions. Trusting in the people's judgment and patience, they probed every aspect of the issues. In all, the seven debates lasted twenty-one hours.

Serious discussion, however, did not stand in the way of a good time. Politics was a form of entertainment. People came long distances on horseback and in wagons, camping for the night near a town where a debate was to be held. Marching bands and booming cannons greeted the candidates at the railroad station. Townspeople stretched banners across streets, and Old Glory fluttered from every window.

In one town, cheering supporters hoisted "Long Abe, the Tall Sucker" on their shoulders and carried him past signs reading THE GIRLS LINK-ON TO LINCOLN. The Little Giant's followers hailed him as the friend of ordinary people. Everyone enjoyed the barbecues, ice-cream parties, and banquets set on tables three hundred feet long. Although people were usually on their best behavior, things could get out of hand. Douglas supporters once bombarded Lincoln with rotten eggs. A reporter noted that Lincoln's friends retaliated by smearing the senator's carriage with "loathsome dirt."[39]

What a contrast the candidates made! The Little Giant was a stocky fellow with a large head, a barrel chest, and "a fierce, bull-dog look."[40] Douglas drank whiskey, smoked cigars, and spoke in a booming voice that seemed to come from inside a big bass drum. He spoke with his whole body, shaking his head, flailing his arms, and stamping his feet to make a point.

"Long Abe" had a high-pitched voice that carried a long distance, an advantage in an age without microphones. The moment he opened his mouth, his accent marked him as a Kentuckian. Lincoln pronounced *such* as "sich," and *Mr. Chairman* as "Mr. Cheerman." He said "thar" for *there,* "git" for *get,* and "kin" for *can.* He "keered" about ordinary folks, because he was "one uv 'em," and never tired of "heering" about "them and theirs." To emphasize a point, he bent his bony knees, crouched low, and sprang up on tiptoe to his full height. Mary thought her old beau a dwarf in comparison. "Mr. Douglas," she told neighbors, "is a very little, *little* giant by the side of my tall Kentuckian, and intellectually my husband towers above Douglas just as he does physically."[41]

Neither man said anything new. Each hammered away at familiar points, hoping to drive them home by repetition. Douglas appealed to the racism he knew ran deep in Illinois. Accusing the Republicans of being secret abolitionists, he said they wanted blacks to invade Illinois to take white jobs and white mates. Worse, they wanted blacks to vote, a violation of the Declaration of Independence. According to the senator, America's charter of liberty was made by white men for white men. The Founding Fathers never intended it to apply to blacks, "an inferior race [that] must always occupy an inferior position."[42] Popular sovereignty was the only way to deal with slavery, he insisted. Allowing the people to decide for themselves was the democratic way, the American way! If the people disapproved of slavery, their elected representatives could ban it despite any Supreme Court ruling. All they had to do was—nothing. Without state laws, courts, and police to back it up, slavery was merely a word.

Lincoln denied for the umpteenth time that he was an abolitionist. Like Douglas, he believed in white supremacy. In two separate debates, he denied that blacks should enjoy the privileges of American citizenship. These denials were not slips of the tongue, but statements of principle. In words that are crystal-clear, he told an audience at Charleston, Illinois:

> I will say . . . that I am not, nor ever have been in favor of bringing about in any way the social and political equality of the white and black races—that I am not nor ever

have been in favor of making voters or jurors of negroes, nor of qualifying them to hold office, nor to intermarry with white people; and I will say in addition to this that there is a physical difference between the white and black races which I believe will for ever forbid the two races living together on terms of social and political equality. And inasmuch as they cannot so live, while they do remain together there must be the position of superior and inferior, and I as much as any other man am in favor of having the superior position assigned to the white race. . . . I will add to this that I have never seen, to my knowledge, a man, woman or child who was in favor of producing a perfect equality, social and political, between negroes and white men."[43]

The debaters stood worlds apart on two other issues. First, Lincoln argued that popular sovereignty as used by his opponent was a hoax. No believer in democracy could quarrel with the rule that the people's will should prevail. But *which* people? Wasn't the opinion of citizens nationwide as important as local opinion? Of course it was. He accused Douglas of taking a vital national issue—the spread of a moral cancer—and turning it into a local matter like the price of cranberries. How ridiculous! The territories belonged to the entire American people, Lincoln insisted. They had explored them, fought for them, and paid for them with their hard-earned dollars. It was up to all the people, and not just a tiny minority, to decide how best to use the new lands.

Lincoln took his second point from the Declaration of Independence. It had always been, for him, a statement of principles as true as the Ten Commandments and the Sermon on the Mount. God had created *all* men equal: that was the basic fact. Still, God had not made all men equal in all respects. People differed in appearance and intelligence, abilities, and character. Yet these differences were minor compared to the "inalienable" rights they had as human beings—rights that could never be justly taken away.

"There is no reason in the world," Lincoln declared at Ottawa, Illinois, "why the negro is not entitled to all the natural rights enumerated

in the Declaration of Independence, the right to life, liberty and the pursuit of happiness. . . . In the right to eat the bread . . . which his own hand earns, *he is my equal and the equal of Judge Douglas, and the equal of every living man*."[44] Slavery was definitely wrong, and should at least be limited to the states in which it already existed. Preserving the West for whites would indirectly benefit blacks, Lincoln insisted. By speeding the end of slavery, it would enable them to enjoy their human rights, if not the rights of American citizens.

In those days, senators were elected by state legislatures, not by popular vote. When the polls closed on November 7, Illinois voters had chosen fifty-four Democratic and forty-six Republican legislators. The Little Giant won reelection. The defeat hurt, but Lincoln took it in stride. Asked about his reaction, he said he felt like the boy who had stubbed his toe. "I am too big to cry and too badly hurt to laugh."[45]

Lincoln was no quitter. Defeated in his Senate bid, he turned his eyes toward the White House.

3 AND THE WAR CAME

Both parties deprecated war; but one of them would <u>make</u> war rather than let the nation survive; and the other would <u>accept</u> war rather than let it perish. And the war came.

ABRAHAM LINCOLN, MARCH 4, 1865

On the night of Sunday, October 16, 1859, eighteen men left their hideout at a Maryland farm and crossed the Potomac River into Virginia. Moving swiftly, they headed for the village of Harpers Ferry at the junction of the Potomac and Shenandoah Rivers. The village had no importance in itself. Its attraction lay in a cluster of buildings nestled along the riverbank. Ever since George Washington chose the site, it had housed a federal arsenal, a facility for the manufacture and storage of guns for the U.S. Army.

Upon reaching their destination, the leader called a halt. John Brown—"Captain" Brown to his followers—stood five feet ten inches tall. He had gray hair and hard blue eyes that, an acquaintance said, made him look as if "he could lick a yard full of wildcats before breakfast and without taking off his coat."[1] Brown had followed many careers during his fifty-nine years, failing in all of them. That was to be expected, since business always took a back seat to abolitionism. A deeply religious man, he had convinced himself that he was God's sword, chosen by the Lord to end slavery by force. A veteran of "Bleeding Kansas," he had led a raiding party to Pottawatomie Creek, where they hacked five pro-slavery men to pieces in front of their horrified families.

On this night, John Brown became the most dangerous man in America. He had come to Harpers Ferry to seize the arsenal. Having done so, he planned to carry its guns into the Virginia mountains and send word that the slaves should flee to his stronghold. There he planned to form a black nation, complete with an army loyal to himself. When the time came, he would lead the army southward, destroying the Peculiar Institution and bathing the United States, this "slave-cursed Republic," in blood.[2]

At their captain's signal, his men took the arsenal in a surprise attack. But from then on, everything went downhill. A free black was the first victim, shot to death as he ran for cover. Clanging church bells roused the countryside, summoning scores of armed militiamen. The siege lasted thirty-six hours, until a company of marines under Colonel Robert E. Lee stormed the arsenal's main building. Brown's crusade claimed seventeen lives, ten of them his own men, including two of his sons. No slave rebelled or came to his aid.

A Virginia court sentenced Brown and six accomplices to death for murder and treason. Fearing a rescue attempt, on December 2 the authorities surrounded the gallows with hundreds of armed men. Among them were cadets from the Virginia Military Institute led by Professor Thomas J. Jackson, an ex-army officer and hero of the Mexican War. Nearby, in the rear rank of the Richmond Grays, volunteers from the Virginia state capital, stood a young actor named John Wilkes Booth.

Brown turned out to be more important in death than he had ever been in life. He had planned it that way. Months before the raid, he discussed his idea with Frederick Douglass, an old friend. Douglass could

Opponents called John Brown "the most dangerous man in America," because he wanted to abolish slavery by armed force. In October 1859, Brown and a small band of followers seized the government arsenal at Harpers Ferry, Virginia. Overpowered and convicted of treason, he was hanged on December 2. This photo was taken shortly before the raid.

scarcely believe his ears. An attack on a federal arsenal was an attack on the United States and must end in disaster, he warned. Brown smiled. Even if the raid failed, he explained, it would be successful in a larger sense. Brown felt certain it would provoke a North-South crisis, perhaps even a civil war, which would complete his work. Later, a visitor to his jail cell whispered about a rescue effort by some ardent sympathizers. The condemned man rejected the offer, saying "I cannot now better serve the cause I love than to die for it."[3]

Fellow abolitionists agreed. They wanted him to hang, and considered his death a blessing. It would give them a martyr, one who gladly sacrificed his life for a sacred cause. Brown's martyrdom would arouse the North, spreading the abolitionist message faster than armies of speakers and hundreds of printing presses.

On the fatal day, abolitionists held prayer meetings throughout the North. Church bells tolled, flags flew at half-mast, and people wore black armbands. The poet Ralph Waldo Emerson called Brown "the new saint" who had made the gallows "glorious like the Cross." Joshua Giddings, a prominent lawyer, praised Brown and prayed for the fires of rebellion to "light up the towns and cities of the South, and blot out the last vestiges of slavery." William Lloyd Garrison wished "success to every slave insurrection at the South and in every slave country." No abolitionist mentioned Brown's bloody deeds in Kansas, or calculated how many innocent lives, black and white, would be lost in a slave rebellion.[4]

Southerners saw Brown's raid as a return to the days of Nat Turner, only worse. Letters found at the Maryland hideout implicated six prominent abolitionists. The "Secret Six" had given Brown money to buy weapons for his men. As if that were not bad enough, the outpouring of sympathy for the "martyr" convinced many that the North shared his aims. That was untrue, as any reading of Northern newspapers would have shown. Most editors condemned Brown as a lunatic and a terrorist. Yet people do not think clearly when they expect to be murdered at any moment.[5]

Panic swept the South. Constance Carey, a Virginia teenager, captured the mood in the weeks after Brown's raid. She described "the fear . . . dark, brooding, oppressive, and altogether hateful" that filled everyone's heart. "I can remember taking it to bed with me at night, and awakening suddenly, oftentimes to confront it through a vigil of nervous terror. . . . The notes of the whip-poor-wills in the sweet-gum swamp near the stable, the mutterings of a distant thunderstorm, even the rustle of the night wind in the oaks that shaded my window, filled me with nameless dread."[6]

Ordinary people closed ranks behind the slave owners. Convinced that fellow Americans wished to "Brown us all"—turn them over to bloodthirsty slaves—they tightened security. Evening curfew bells sounded in Southern towns at 9:00 P.M., ordering blacks indoors. The patrollers turned out in force. Militia units were reorganized and equipped with muskets purchased in Europe. This was a dangerous sign, for until then the Southern militias had been a joke. Yet there was nothing funny about these units. In time, they became one the world's greatest war machines: the Confederate army.

All this took place as the nation prepared for a presidential election. Everyone expected a fierce contest in 1860, with the issues set out in the Lincoln-Douglas debates taking center stage. Stephen Douglas seemed sure to win the Democratic nomination. Republican insiders

Victory in the Wigwam. Harper's Weekly printed this drawing of the scene in the great hall before Lincoln won the Republican nomination on May 18, 1860. His victory triggered a near-riot, in which his supporters stamped their feet and shouted themselves hoarse.

leaned toward Abraham Lincoln. His loss in Illinois had only been a momentary setback. Newspaper coverage of the debates had turned his name into a household word nationwide. Speaking invitations came from political clubs and citizens' groups in every free state. Voters increasingly saw him as a contender for the highest office in the land.

On May 10, 1860, Illinois Republicans dubbed Lincoln "The Rail Candidate" at their state convention, a clever move that focused attention on his humble origins rather than his prominence as a lawyer. The following week, the party's national convention met in Chicago's Wigwam, a hall built to hold ten thousand people. Three leading Republicans sought the nomination, but Lincoln's managers undermined their support through secret deals that gave him the nomination on the third ballot. The convention went wild. Delegates hugged, cheered, and shouted themselves hoarse. "Imagine all the hogs ever slaughtered in Cincinnati giving their death squeals together, and a score of big steam whistles going together!" said a reporter. "Lincoln's boys gave a concentrated shriek and stamping that made every plank and pillar in the building quiver."[7]

Back in Springfield, the candidate sat in the telegraph office with a few close advisers. Late that afternoon, May 18, the telegraph key began to clatter. Good news! Lincoln read the message, leaped out of his chair, and bolted out the door. "Excuse me," he called over his shoulder, "but there's a little woman down at our house who will be interested in this."[8]

The whole of Springfield invited itself into the Lincoln house. Crowds packed the rooms to overflowing. When they could not push through the door, people climbed through the first-floor windows, stepping on the furniture and on one another. Night turned to day as hundreds paraded around the house with blazing torches held high. Rockets sped skyward, their fiery trails crisscrossing in the darkness. Barrels of burning tar lined the street, between bonfires built by the town's boys. "We will give you a larger house on the fourth of next March," well-wishers shouted.[9]

That seemed just what the opposition intended to do. The Democratic party split into two factions. The Northern faction nominated Stephen Douglas, while the Southern faction chose John C. Breckinridge of Kentucky as its candidate. Old-line Whigs formed the Constitutional Union party and nominated John Bell of Tennessee. Although Lincoln's name did not appear on the ballot in any Southern state, his opposition could not join forces. To win the election, he had to carry only the free states.

Lincoln followed custom by having supporters campaign on his behalf; Americans thought it "undignified" for a presidential candidate to campaign for himself. He remained in Springfield, making no speeches and giving no interviews to the press. The Little Giant, however, threw custom to the wind and campaigned vigorously. Again he accused Lincoln of being an abolitionist, adding that he had favored John Brown. Douglas's supporters went further, playing upon racial prejudice and fear. They branded Lincoln a "nigger worshipper" and accused his running mate, Senator Hannibal Hamlin of Maine, of being a mulatto.[10]

Republicans did not mince words, either. Noting that Lincoln had denounced Brown as a killer who deserved hanging, they asked voters to support "the true white man's party." Springfield's Republicans displayed banners with red letters two feet high. NO MORE SLAVE STATES, one banner read. NO NEGRO EQUALITY IN THE NORTH, said another.[11] Everywhere Republican organizers whipped up enthusiasm with rallies and torchlight parades. Rail-Splitter Battalions dragged floats featuring woodsmen splitting rails through city streets. Choruses sang "Old Abe Lincoln Came Out of the Wilderness," and crowds chanted:

> *Ain't I glad I joined the Republicans,*
> *Joined the Republicans, joined the Republicans,*
> *Ain't I glad I joined the Republicans,*
> *Down in Illinois?*[12]

Willie and Tad did their part, too. They stood in front of their house, urging passersby to "vote for Old Abe, the poor man's friend." Robert was in Massachusetts, preparing to enter Harvard University. Asked to read the Declaration of Independence at a Fourth of July rally, he said he needed his father's permission. A rally organizer wrote to Springfield and received this reply: "Tell Bob to read that immortal document every chance he has, and the bigger the crowd, the louder he must holler."[13]

The possibility of a Lincoln victory terrified Southerners. True, they knew of his pledge not to disturb slavery where it already existed, only

The Republican standard-bearer, August 8, 1860. After a huge rally in Springfield, Lincoln supporters—many of them friends and neighbors—gathered in front of the candidate's home. In this photograph by William Shaw, Lincoln is the tall figure dressed in the white suit.

to bar it from the territories. Yet they also knew, as he did, that the nation could not remain half slave and half free. Slavery's "natural death" might take longer than abolitionists wished, but the result was inevitable. The end of slavery and the Republican control of the government meant that blacks would eventually become citizens and voters. Once that happened, Southerners believed their "enemies" would have them in their power.

The United States seemed a contradiction in terms. No longer united by shared beliefs and interests, it had become two feuding sections. Southerners asked whether it might be wiser to end the farce by seceding and forming their own country. Everywhere the "fire-eaters," radicals who demanded immediate secession, gained influence. Their motto: "Defend yourselves! The enemy is at your door!"[14]

Final returns on Election Day, November 6, 1860, showed that Lincoln had carried the free states with 1,865,593 votes to 2,823,795 votes for all other candidates combined. In other words, the man from Illinois received less than 40 percent of the vote, which made him the most unpopular man ever to be elected President of the United States. He did not care. Victory was victory, and it tasted sweet.

Lincoln left his campaign headquarters at 2:00 A.M. on November 7. Expecting it to be a long night, he had told Mary not to wait up. He climbed the stairs to their bedroom, opened the door, and gazed down at his sleeping wife. "Mary," he whispered, gently nudging her awake. "Mary, Mary! *We are elected!*" As his words registered, she burst into tears. "There, there, little woman. I thought you wanted me to be President," said Lincoln, taking her in his arms. "I do," she replied, "and I am very happy—that is why I am crying."[15]

News of Lincoln's victory set off a week-long celebration. Merrymakers surged through the streets of Springfield, shouting, singing, and tossing firecrackers by the fistful. Each night, tipsy Republicans rolled out a cannon and blasted the city awake.

The President-elect received well-wishers at the Illinois statehouse. People from all walks of life crowded around their man, pressing him flat up against a wall. Once he charged into the crowd, stopped beside a tall Missourian, and said, "Let us measure." Lincoln overtopped him, but barely.

Mary did not like such informality, particularly when she heard well-wishers ask, "Is that the old woman?" Nor was she thrilled when her husband presented her to a crowd saying, "Ladies and gentlemen, here is the long and short of the Presidency."[16]

Lincoln's victory caused panic in Dixie. Slave prices tumbled as jittery owners, fearing the worst, sold out for whatever they could get. Each day brought a fresh crop of rumors. Northern fanatics were releasing slaves at gunpoint! Free blacks were burning cities! Slaves were poisoning wells! Blame the abolitionists! Blame the "black Republicans"! Blame Lincoln! Normally cautious people shrieked at the sound of his name, and mobs hung him in effigy. Secession talk turned to action.

On December 20, roughly six weeks after Lincoln's election, South Carolina seceded from the Union. From

On December 20, 1860, a special issue of the Charleston Mercury announced the dissolution of the Union.

CHARLESTON

MERCURY

EXTRA:

Passed unanimously at 1.15 o'clock, P. M., December 20th, 1860.

AN ORDINANCE

To dissolve the Union between the State of South Carolina and other States united with her under the compact entitled "The Constitution of the United States of America."

We, the People of the State of South Carolina, in Convention assembled, do declare and ordain, and it is hereby declared and ordained,

That the Ordinance adopted by us in Convention, on the twenty-third day of May, in the year of our Lord one thousand seven hundred and eighty-eight, whereby the Constitution of the United States of America was ratified, and also, all Acts and parts of Acts of the General Assembly of this State, ratifying amendments of the said Constitution, are hereby repealed; and that the union now subsisting between South Carolina and other States, under the name of "The United States of America," is hereby dissolved.

THE

UNION

IS

DISSOLVED!

A former U.S. senator, Jefferson Davis was a Mississippi plantation owner who became president of the Confederate States of America. General Winfield Scott called him "a cheap Judas" who "would have betrayed Christ and the Apostles and the whole Christian church" for thirty pieces of silver.

then until February 1, 1861, an epidemic of "secessionitis" swept the Lower South as Mississippi, Georgia, Florida, Alabama, Louisiana, and Texas joined in the move. Southerners celebrated as if an awful burden had been lifted from their shoulders. "Such a row I never witnessed before," a Texan wrote from New Orleans. "One would have thought that the *Messiah* had come surely."[17] As each state seceded, the citizens of Columbia, South Carolina, the state capital, rang it out with a bell they named "Secessia."

On February 4, delegates met in Montgomery, Alabama. After a few days' discussion, they formed the Confederate States of America and chose Jefferson Davis president. His vice president was Alexander H. Stephens of Georgia, a thin, pale man suffering from tuberculosis.

Stephens left no doubt about where the Confederacy stood on the slave question. "Our new government," he declared, "is founded . . . upon the great truth that the Negro is not equal to the white man; that slavery—subordination to the superior race—is his natural and moral condition. This, our new Government, is the first in the history of the world based upon this great physical, philosophical, and moral truth."[18]

Traitors in Washington, D.C., aided the Confederacy in countless ways. Cabinet members—Southerners for the most part—acted as spies. The secretary of war transferred guns from federal arsenals to Confederate units. The secretary of the navy scattered the fleet thousands of miles from its home ports. Outgoing President James Buchanan, a Democrat, denounced secession as illegal but claimed he could not prevent it. When Confederate forces seized federal property—forts, arsenals, warehouses, shipyards, post offices, custom-houses—he did nothing. The President was no traitor, just a weak man who had given up. Lincoln would have to clean up the mess.

Buchanan's weakness convinced Confederates they had nothing to fear. Secession, they told one another, could never lead to violence. Senator James Chesnut of South Carolina was so sure of this that he offered to drink every drop of blood spilled in a civil war. A fellow South Carolina politician went further; he vowed to eat the bodies of all those killed because of secession.[19] Even if war did come, they promised that the "Yankees"—Northerners—would be pushovers. Everyone knew that one Southerner equaled ten Yankees on the battlefield. Trained to ride horses and shoot guns from childhood, Southerners were born soldiers. Yankees were soft-handed, pasty-faced shopkeepers and oppressed factory workers. "Rebels"—Confederates—boasted, "We could whip the Yankees with children's pop-guns!"[20]

A hero of the War of 1812 and the Mexican War, General Winfield Scott was the army's general in chief at the start of the Civil War. Although born in Virginia, he remained loyal to the Union during the secession crisis.

Lincoln, too, refused to face reality. Before the election, he had called talk of secession an "empty threat," a "bluff," and a "humbug." Southerners, he insisted, were too sensible to tear the nation apart. To be sure, he welcomed their military preparations, because these would make it easier to crush future Brown-style rebellions. Even when secession became reality, he ignored the storm signals from Dixie. There was no crisis, he said repeatedly. Everything would be just fine.

By early February, however, he realized his mistake. Southern newspapers were urging Confederate leaders to prevent Lincoln, the "Illinois ape," from being inaugurated. Each day brought rumors of treason. Lincoln heard of a plot to fill Washington with armed Confederates in civilian clothes, seize the city, and take over government buildings. The plot, whether real or imaginary, made perfect sense. Capturing the capital would paralyze the Union government, making it all but impossible to reunite the country by force.

Lincoln sent an aide to test the army's loyalty. The aide went to Major General Winfield Scott, the nation's most respected soldier. At age seventy-five, Scott stood six feet four inches and weighed three hundred pounds. Rolls of fat hung from his face and neck, and he could not walk without assistance. He had commanded American forces during the Mexican War, rising to the rank of general in chief of the army. A Virginian who despised slavery and loved the Union, he promised to support the President-elect no matter what happened. "If necessary," he growled, "I'll plant cannon at both ends of Pennsylvania Avenue, and if any should raise a finger I'll blow them to hell!"[21]

On February 11, 1861, the presidential party arrived at the Great Western depot in Springfield. The party consisted of the President-elect, his son Robert, a secretary, and Ward Hill Lamon. Since presidents did not have official bodyguards, Lamon had volunteered his services. A lawyer by profession, this man-mountain of muscle stood nearly as tall as Lincoln himself. "The chief" cautioned that, if ever Lamon struck a person, he must not use his fists, but a crowbar or some other object that was not sure to kill! Illinois Republicans promised to murder Lamon if he failed to protect Lincoln's "sacred life."[22]

Inaugural journeys were traditionally happy events. Not this time, however. Alarmed by the news from Dixie, crowds gathered along the route to catch a glimpse of the President-elect. Some cheered as his train sped by, but most stood silently, following it with their eyes. Approaching a city, it passed between solid walls of humanity. Cries of "Save the Union, Abe!" rose above the clacking of iron wheels.[23]

The train followed a roundabout route to allow the largest number of people to see their new leader. The schedule called for a fifteen-day journey with overnight stops at ten cities in Indiana, Ohio, New York, and Pennsylvania. On February 16, as the train approached Albany, New York, word came that Jefferson Davis had taken his oath as president of the Confederacy. To celebrate the event, an actress named Maggie Smith danced on the Stars and Stripes as thousands cheered. Elsewhere, Southerners burnt the American flag.

More troubling news awaited Lincoln at Philadelphia. On February 21, he learned of a plot to attack him as he came through Baltimore, Maryland, next morning. Detectives had overheard members of two criminal gangs, the Blood Tubs and the Plug Uglies, talk of assassinating the President-elect. Advisers urged Lincoln to go straight through to Washington, but he refused. "What would the nation think of its President stealing into the Capital like a thief in the night?" he asked.[24] They held their ground, insisting that no President had the right to risk his life needlessly. He reluctantly agreed.

Lincoln boarded the midnight train from Philadelphia with Ward Hill Lamon and a detective. Entering a sleeping berth reserved for a "sick" passenger, he settled in for the ride. Lamon took no chances. Armed with two revolvers, a dagger, a slingshot, brass knuckles, and his two fists, he stood guard throughout the night. They reached the nation's capital before daybreak on February 23. Without revealing the identity of the tall man in the stovepipe hat, they took a cab to Willard's Hotel at Pennsylvania Avenue and Fourteenth Street.

Lincoln's reluctance proved justified. When his "sneaky" arrival became known, Democratic newspapers blasted him as a coward and a fool. Cartoons showed "old lady" Lincoln wearing a bonnet and shawl, and "spineless" Lincoln staring popeyed at a bristling white cat. Humiliated, he vowed never to give even the appearance of being afraid. Ignoring pleas for caution about his personal safety, he recklessly exposed himself to danger to prove his courage.

Washington bore little resemblance to the city we know today. In many ways, the nation's capital was still a frontier town. The United States Capitol crowned the highest hill, its unfinished dome encircled by cranes and scaffolds.

This cartoon, titled "The Flight of Abraham," appeared in Harper's Weekly *on March 9, 1861. It depicts the President-elect "stealing" into Washington for his inauguration, fearful of threats against his life. Charges of cowardice hurt him deeply, and may account, in part, for his later carelessness about his personal safety.*

The incomplete dome of the U.S. Capitol as it appeared on Inauguration Day, March 4, 1861. Despite the war, Lincoln insisted that work on the dome continue as a symbol of the nation's determination to survive. It was finished in time for his second inauguration.

Cowsheds stood near the Capitol, and congressmen shot birds and squirrels on its grounds. The Capitol's windows overlooked the infamous Georgia Pen, which Congressman Lincoln had described as "a sort of negro-livery stable, where droves of negroes were collected, temporarily kept, and finally taken to Southern markets, precisely like droves of horses."[25] In the distance rose the marble shaft of the Washington Monument, only a third of the way on its five-hundred-foot climb upward. Storage sheds and blocks of marble clustered around the monument's base.

A city of 60,000 inhabitants, including 8,000 slaves, Washington had no police force or sanitation service. It sorely needed both. Shabby rooming houses and gambling dens lined the main streets. Every street had at least one tavern, each producing its share of brawls, robberies, and murders. "Washington is probably the dirtiest and most ill-kept borough in the United States," a reporter wrote. "The streets are seas or canals of liquid mud . . . conglomerations of garbage, refuse, and trash [that give off] seventy separate and distinct stinks."[26] Chickens dodged speeding carriages in the unpaved streets. Pigs rooted in piles of filth along Pennsylvania Avenue, the city's main thoroughfare. Known simply as "the Avenue," it had a brick sidewalk on the west side. An open sewer flowed from Capitol Hill along its eastern side, past the White House.

Until his inauguration, Lincoln and his family lived in a five-room suite in Willard's Hotel. Advertised as the best hotel in town, it had ev-

This portrait of the President-elect was probably made on March 24, 1861, by Alexander Gardner, a leading photographer of the day. Lincoln's right hand was badly swollen, due to lots of handshaking, and he kept it closed during the sitting.

ery modern convenience, from an elevator to running water in each room. Lincoln, however, scarcely noticed these marvels.

Since there was no civil service to fill government jobs, the President appointed every officeholder. Job seekers hounded Lincoln with requests. They made Lincoln miserable. "I hardly have a chance to eat or sleep," he groaned. "I am fair game for everybody of that hungry lot." Another time he compared himself to a mother pig trying to feed her large litter: "There are too many pigs for the tits."[27]

The First Lady had hungry friends and relatives, too. Mary begged. Mary pleaded. Mary turned on the charm. If her husband resisted, she ranted, raved, and tore her hair. A Republican official once saw her sprawled on the floor during a temper tantrum. She would not stop screaming, Lincoln explained, his eyes filled with sadness, unless he promised to help one of her friends.

Another visitor overheard this while passing their room:

"No, Mr. Lincoln, you *shan't* have them! . . . You *can't* have them until you promise me."

"Ma—come now! be reasonable. Look at the clock. I'm already late; let me have them—*please*!"

"Never, Mr. Lincoln!—not till you promise me first."

Finally, Lincoln pleaded, "Ma! How do you reckon I can go to a Cabinet meeting—without my pants!"[28]

OPPOSITE: *The First Lady in the gown she wore to the Inaugural Ball in 1861. The President's wife loved expensive clothes and ran up high bills during shopping sprees in New York City. Mrs. Lincoln loved flowers, and critics made fun of her wearing "flower pots" on her head.*

Noon. Monday, March 4, 1861. Inauguration Day. A bright, sunny day with a brisk wind blowing across the Potomac. At the stroke of noon, the state carriage stopped in front of Willard's Hotel. A tall man in a black suit stood at the main entrance with a stovepipe hat in one hand and a gold-headed cane in the other. President Buchanan nodded his head in greeting and motioned for President-elect Lincoln to sit beside him. Moments later, as a military band struck up "Hail to the Chief," the carriage moved down Pennsylvania Avenue toward Capitol Hill.

General Scott, true to his word, had done everything to protect the President-elect. Cavalrymen surrounded the open carriage with drawn swords. Infantrymen lined the Avenue with bayonets on their rifles. Sharpshooters crouched on rooftops and behind chimneys, scanning windows across the way and the crowds below. Gunners stood by cannons positioned to rake the crowds from all angles. Any attempt to disrupt the inauguration would have resulted in a bloodbath.

If looks could kill, Lincoln would never have reached the platform built along the Capitol's east front. Thousands of spectators watched silently, glaring at the tall figure in the carriage. As he passed, he looked into their eyes and felt their hatred. Catcalls and insults filled the air. "There goes the Illinois ape, the cursed abolitionist," well-dressed women called to one another. "He will never come back alive."[29]

Lincoln took his place on the platform, along with three hundred other dignitaries. Rising to speak, he looked around for a place to put his hat. Stephen Douglas put out his hand. "If I can't be President," said the Little Giant, "I can at least hold the President's hat."[30]

The inaugural address lasted thirty minutes and covered nine printed pages. Lincoln reassured Southerners that he had no intention of attacking slavery where it already existed. If secession led to bloodshed, they, and they alone, would bear the guilt before God and history. He had planned to close with this remark, but things looked so grim that he felt he must address the South personally. The words came straight from his heart. "I am loth to close. We are not enemies, but friends. We must not be enemies. Though passion may have strained, it must not break our bonds of affection. The mystic chords of memory, stretching from every battle-field, and patriot grave, to every living heart and hearthstone, all over this broad land, will yet swell the chorus of the Union, when again touched, as surely they will be, by the better angels of our nature."[31]

Chief Justice Roger B. Taney then administered the oath that made Abraham Lincoln the sixteenth President of the United States. Next morning, he awoke to the first crisis of his presidency.

It involved a tiny piece of federal property. Although South Carolina had seceded, U.S. Army troops still held Fort Sumter on a sandy island in Charleston harbor. Before dawn on March 5, the War Department received an urgent message from Major Robert Anderson, the fort's commander. Anderson reported that Confederate officials were demanding his surrender. To make matters worse, he had less than a month's supply of food on hand. Unless help came in time, the Confederates would either shell or starve his men into submission.

Lincoln called in his advisers, who disagreed about everything except the time of day. Army leaders insisted Fort Sumter could not be held. Navy leaders claimed the opposite; the fort could be resupplied and reinforced by sea. Secretary of State William H. Seward had yet another idea; he wanted to provoke a war with France or Spain to reunite the country against a common foe. The President, caught in the middle, decided to figure things out for himself.

He had to consider three factors. First, abandoning the fort would humiliate him personally and brand his administration as incompetent. Second, a retreat was no guarantee of peace. Sensing weakness, the Confederates would probably make other demands that must eventually lead to war. Finally, if war was inevitable, there must be no question about who fired the first shot. Showing the Confederates as aggressors would unify the North, *the* main condition for waging a successful war. Lincoln did not want a war and would not provoke one. Yet if war must come, he wanted to be in the strongest moral position.

On March 29, Lincoln ordered the army and navy to prepare a relief expedition to leave New York Harbor within a week. The President did not conceal the expedition's sailing date or mission; indeed, the Confederates received that information in an official letter. The expedition had only one purpose: to resupply Fort Sumter. It would use force only if the Confederates blocked delivery of supplies.

Like Lincoln, Jefferson Davis dared not show weakness. So when the

On April 12, 1861, at 4:30 A.M., Confederate artillery commanded by P.G.T. Beauregard opened fire on Fort Sumter, thus beginning the greatest conflict in American history.

Union vessels anchored outside Charleston harbor, he ordered P.G.T. Beauregard, the local commander, to force a showdown. General Beauregard had been Major Anderson's star pupil during his years as a professor at West Point. Friends for twenty-five years, they dreaded having to meet in battle. Nevertheless, as professional soldiers, they could not choose their wars. On April 11, Beauregard demanded the fort's immediate surrender. Anderson refused.

At 4:30 A.M., April 12, the Confederate shore batteries opened fire. Startled awake, the people of Charleston leaped from their beds and ran to their windows. What a sight! All along the rim of the harbor, tongues of flame lashed out across the water. The racket became deafening. Shock waves struck buildings, rattling windowpanes and making people's ears ring. Nobody complained. Excited civilians cheered the gunners, urging them to keep up the good work.

Charleston's slaves showed no emotion, which puzzled Mary Chesnut, the senator's wife. "Not by one word or look can we detect any change in the demeanor of these Negro servants," she wrote in her diary. "Lawrence sits at our door, sleepy and respectful, and profoundly indifferent. So are they all. . . . You could not tell that they even heard the awful roar going on in the bay, though it has been dinning in their ears, night and day. People talk before them as if they were chairs and tables. They make no sign. Are they solidly stupid? Or wiser than we are; silent and strong, biding their time?"[32] Only time could answer her questions.

Fort Sumter's time was running out. Shells plowed into its walls, sending chunks of masonry flying at bullet speed. Explosions ignited the barracks. Flames licked at the iron doors of the magazine, or ammunition storage house, threatening to blow the place sky-high. One by one the guns fell silent, destroyed by enemy action or abandoned to the inferno. Resistance was hopeless. After thirty-four hours of shelling, Major Anderson raised a bedsheet on the flagstaff as a sign of surrender. Despite the fury of the bombardment, the only fatality was a Union private accidentally killed after the surrender. It had been a nearly bloodless beginning to the bloodiest war in American history.

On April 14, General Beauregard allowed the garrison to march out under the Stars and Stripes, a traditional sign of respect among soldiers. Boarding a transport, they sailed for New York City, where crowds welcomed them as heroes. Their tattered flag became a national treasure, like the Liberty Bell.

On April 15, as Fort Sumter's defenders were putting to sea, their commander in chief made his first warlike moves. Lincoln declared a naval blockade of Confederate ports and called for 75,000 volunteers to put down the rebellion.

The effect was like a stone striking a hornet's nest. During the next five weeks, the states of the Upper South—Virginia, Arkansas, North Carolina, Tennessee—left the Union. Unwilling to secede because Lincoln had been elected, they joined the Confederacy when he asked for troops to "coerce" their "sister" states. Although the border slave states—Kentucky, Missouri, Maryland, and Delaware—identified with the Confederacy, they decided against joining, at least for the present. Lincoln, as we shall see, would do anything to keep them in the Union.

The war that began at Fort Sumter had various names: Civil War, War for Southern Independence, War for the Union, War Between the

States. (Since Lincoln did not recognize Confederate independence, war could *not* be declared. The Civil War—legally—was a rebellion.) Yet no name is more revealing than the Brothers' War. This name expresses a vital truth: neutrality is impossible in a civil war. Like it or not, the individual must choose sides, and by doing so shatter the closest relationships. North and South, the war became a struggle of father against son, brother against brother, relative against relative, friend against friend. The conflict reached into the First Family itself. Four of Mary Lincoln's brothers and three brothers-in-law served in the Confederate armies.

Professional soldiers belonged to another kind of family. In April 1861, the U.S. Army numbered 16,367 men, most of them stationed at lonely frontier outposts. Soldiers shared the same experiences, particularly the career officers who had been cadets together at West Point and comrades during the Mexican War. Ties of friendship also became ties of blood, as many a junior officer married his colonel's daughter. Their children were called "army brats."

Secession forced soldiers to follow their consciences into opposing camps. Of the army's 1,080 officers, 767 remained loyal to the Union, while 313 sided with the Confederacy. Nevertheless, some of the Confederacy's leading generals rejected its basic principles. Thomas J. Jackson, Jubal Early, George Pickett, Joseph E. Johnston, A. P. Hill, Braxton Bragg—to name a few—disapproved of slavery and secession. Robert E. Lee, soon to give Lincoln more sleepless nights than anyone else on the planet, echoed him in describing slavery as "a moral and political evil." And, like Lincoln, he loved the Union. "I can anticipate no greater calamity for the country than a dissolution of the Union," said Lee. "Secession is nothing but revolution."[33]

Nevertheless, Lee and the others loved their home states more than the United States. They saw themselves as sons of their states first, as Americans second. Not even Lincoln's offer of the field command of the U.S. Army could tempt Lee after his "mother state," Virginia, seceded.

Lincoln's call for volunteers ignited a firestorm among Southerners. The vast majority, who owned no slaves, would never have fought to protect the Peculiar Institution; that would have been "a rich man's war and a poor man's fight." Nor did they expect to conquer the North. Already an industrial giant with 85 percent of the nation's factories, 66 percent of its railroad mileage, and 98 percent of its shipping, the North had the makings of a world-class military power. Added to this, its population numbered 23,000,000, compared to the 5,220,000 whites who lived in the Confederacy. The South's strategy, therefore, had to be defensive. It must hold the enemy in check, exhausting him and discouraging him until he recognized Confederate independence.

Ordinary people fought for the Confederacy because they felt trapped. Lincoln could not restore the Union by sitting still. He had to take the initiative and wage a war of conquest. Union forces must invade the Confederacy, smash its armies, and overthrow its government. In the process, they would turn the South into a battlefield, making refugees of civilians and destroying the work of generations. Small wonder, then, that Southerners of every class flocked to the Confederate banner.

"Johnny Reb," the Confederate soldier, used the Yankee leader's name as a curse word. Abraham Lincoln came to embody the "evil" enemy. Rebels called the North "Lincolndom"; Republicans were "Lincolnites" and "Baboonites." They called Union troops "Lincolnpoops," "bluebellies," and "doodles," as in "damnyankee doodles." Volunteers sang:

> *Whoop, the doodles have broken loose,*
> *Roaring around like the very deuce!*
> *Lice of Egypt, a hungry pack;*
> *After 'em boys, and drive 'em back.*
>
> *Bull-dog, terrier, cur and lice,*
> *Back to the beggarly land of ice,*
> *Worry 'em, bite 'em, scratch and tear,*
> *Everybody and everywhere.*[34]

Johnny Reb could hardly wait to take a shot at a bluebelly.

Nor could "Billy Yank," the Union soldier, wait to get a crack at *him*. News of Fort Sumter sent a tidal wave of patriotism rolling across the free states. Traitors had insulted the Stars and Stripes! American soldiers had been forced to abandon American property! These insults must be avenged.

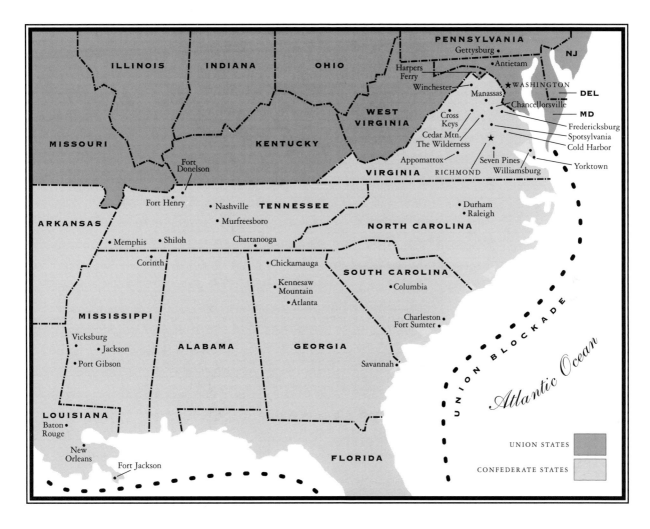

The war spirit showed itself in banner headlines, rousing speeches, and mass meetings. Men flocked to recruiting stations, led by brass bands and flag-waving women wearing "Union bonnets," hats with fluttering ribbons of red, white, and blue. Questioned about the West's reaction, an Ohio man bawled, "The West is one great Eagle-scream!" A fellow in Washington asked a Massachusetts soldier: "How many more men of your state are coming?" The soldier shouted: "All of us."[35] He was not exaggerating; in several towns, every man of military age enlisted.

Washington was linked to the North by a single railroad line across Maryland. On April 19, as the Sixth Massachusetts Regiment changed trains in Baltimore on its way to Washington, mobs gave it the recep-

Major battles of the Civil War.

tion they had failed to give Lincoln. Four soldiers and nine rioters died in the resulting riot. The regiment reached the capital that evening, followed by a line of stretchers bearing its wounded. Two days later, Baltimore's leading citizens called at the White House to demand that no more federal troops "pollute" Maryland's "sacred soil." The President cut them short. "Our men are not moles," he snapped, "and can't dig under the earth; they are not birds, and can't fly through the air. There is no way but to march across, and that they must do."[36]

Washington expected the rebel army any day. The Avenue stood deserted as citizens fled northward. Shops closed, owners nailing their doors and windows shut. Entrances to government buildings had barricades of sandbags and guards with fixed bayonets. A ten-foot pile of cement-filled barrels and timber bared every door of the Capitol, while sharpshooters watched from the windows. Engineers mined the Potomac bridges, ready to blow them up the instant Confederate troops started to cross.

Lincoln waited anxiously for reinforcements. None arrived. "Why don't they come? Why don't they come?" he muttered as he paced back and forth, his hands clasped tightly behind his back.[37] Looking out a window with a spyglass, he did see evidence of troops—Confederates. At Alexandria, Virginia, rebel flags flew over buildings, their Stars and Bars challenging the Stars and Stripes from across the Potomac.

On April 25, early risers heard a loud whistle. People living near the railroad station saw a train pull in, grind to a halt, and unload the Seventh New York Regiment. Washingtonians cheered. Lincoln breathed a sigh of relief. Another ten thousand troops arrived during the next two days, with thousands more on the way.

The capital became an armed camp. Squadrons of cavalry clattered through the streets at all hours. Sweating gunners hauled their weapons into position along the Potomac shore and the ring of forts springing up on the city's outskirts. The city teemed with soldiers, astonishing a presidential aide with "the everywhereness of uniforms and muskets."[38]

Lacking barracks, the first arrivals bedded down wherever they could find a spot. White tents blossomed on Capitol Hill; soldiers even slept on the floor of the House of Representatives and fried their bacon on the furnaces in the basement. The Patent Office and the Smithsonian

Institution, the nation's greatest museum, had rows of triple-decked bunks between their exhibition cabinets. Troops lived for a time in the East Room of the White House, sleeping on the plush carpet. Eventually, permanent camps dotted the landscape in a wide arc. Reporters measured them by the square mile.

The first Union offensive took the Confederates by surprise. On May 24, troops crossed the Potomac bridges to occupy Alexandria and Robert E. Lee's estate on Arlington Heights, where Arlington National Cemetery is today.

Although nearly cost-free, these operations hit the First Family hard. Colonel Elmer E. Ellsworth was among the dead. Ellsworth, age twenty-four, had read law in Lincoln's office, and he and Mary loved him like a son. Together they went to view his body at the Navy Yard morgue. Lincoln needed every ounce of energy to keep his self-control. It was not enough. Asked about the young man, his voice cracked and he said, "Excuse me, but I cannot talk," then burst into tears.[39] This early tragedy personalized the war for him. It taught the President, as nothing else could, that military decisions were not exercises in pure logic. Decisions taken in the White House always translated into flesh and blood, heartbreak and misery.

The May offensive on Alexandria was the opening round of an ambitious effort. Richmond, the Virginia state capital, had also become the capital of the Confederacy. The rebel congress was due to hold its first meeting there within a month. The North demanded immediate action. "On to Richmond! Forward to Richmond!" became the war cry. Although Lincoln thought the army needed more training, he gave the order to advance.

Brigadier General Irvin McDowell invaded Virginia with 30,000 men. Little

The death of Colonel Elmer E. Ellsworth early in the war deeply distressed the Lincoln family. On May 25, 1861, the President wrote the young officer's parents that "our affliction here is scarcely less than your own," and called him "my young friend and your brave and early fallen child."

better than raw recruits, the majority of them had a hard time keeping up with their units. Weighed down by ten-pound muskets and fifty-pound packs, hundreds fell by the wayside or broke ranks to pick blackberries and drink from their canteens.

The civilians who followed them had it easier. Certain of an easy victory, hundreds had come from Washington to experience the "thrill" of battle from a safe distance. Stylish men rode sleek horses or sat beside elegant ladies in elegant carriages. To quench *their* thirst, they sipped champagne from long-necked bottles packed in tubs of ice. Many had tickets for a victory ball in Richmond.

General McDowell headed for Manassas Junction, a railroad center thirty miles southwest of Washington. On July 21, his scouts found the rebels massed behind Bull Run Creek. The Confederate force of 21,000 was commanded by none other than P.G.T. Beauregard, the conqueror of Fort Sumter. The Confederate password for the day: "Our Homes."[40]

The armies glared at each other from across the shallow creek. Insults flew thick and fast, and challenges, too. "You damned black abolitionists, come on!" a Confederate shouted, waving his musket over his head.[41]

The Yankees came.

Back at the White House, Lincoln waited for news from the front. He knew a battle was raging, because he could hear the rumble of distant artillery. Willie and Tad also heard the noise, and saw the worry in their elders' eyes. "Pa says there's a battle in Virginia," Willie told a friend. "That's big cannon going off that sounds like slamming doors."[42]

The Confederates gave ground steadily. The spectators cheered and exchanged champagne toasts. "Bully for us! Bravo!" they cried.[43] McDowell had whipped the rebels! Jeff Davis would soon be hanging from a sour-apple tree! The war was over!

They were wrong. Thomas Jackson's 4,500-man unit still held its position on the side of a low hill. Noticing this, another general called to his retreating troops, "There is Jackson, standing like a stone wall! Rally behind the Virginians!"[44] *Like a stone wall!* The name stuck. "Stonewall" Jackson was on his way to becoming a legend. Stonewall held his position for about an hour, which was long enough for rein-

Union soldiers await treatment after a battle. Civil War weapons caused frightful wounds, which often made it necessary to amputate an arm or leg. The man at the far left appears to have lost a hand.

forcements to arrive. The Confederates then swept forward in a fierce counterattack.

The Union line collapsed. Soldiers ran away, pushing and shoving one another in a desperate effort to escape. One fellow saw a rabbit bolt from a nearby bush. "Git out of the road, gosh dern you," he shouted, "and let somebody run that knows how."[45] The spectators fled, too, leaving a trail of champagne bottles and picnic baskets. Some Johnny Rebs had a feast.

The Battle of Bull Run, or Manassas, was small compared to later fights.[46] It claimed a total of 4,878 killed, wounded, and missing, among them 2,896 Union men and 1,982 Confederates. "Missing" meant that a soldier had missed roll call after the battle. He had either deserted, been captured, or been blown into unrecognizable pieces.

Bull Run was worse than anyone had dared predict. When the war began, men enlisted believing it was going to be a glorious adventure. They were naive. Most of them, having never heard a shot fired in anger, much less seen a person killed, could not imagine death in battle. At worst, they thought it came quickly and painlessly, with a neat hole through the heart. Real war, however, was anything but neat. It was dirty, nasty, and degrading.

Work details buried the dead in shallow trenches. Since it was summer, they handled bloated corpses amid clouds of flies. Workers wrapped handkerchiefs around their mouths, but they could not keep the flies out of their eyes, ears, and noses. One of Stonewall Jackson's men found the remains of a friend. "I sat down by him and took a hearty cry," he wrote his folks. After a few minutes, however, it dawned on him that crying was not soldierly. "Thinks I, 'It does not look well for a soldier to cry,' but I could not help it. I then stuck his gun in the ground by his side, marked his name, company, and regiment on a piece of paper, pinned it to his breast, and went off."[47] Civil War soldiers did not have dog tags. If a dead soldier had no identification papers in his pockets, or if nobody recognized him, he went into an unmarked grave. His family never learned his fate.

The wounded faced a worse ordeal than battle. "And such wounds!" wrote a Bull Run veteran. "Some with both legs shot off; some with a thigh shot away; some with both legs broken; others with horrid flesh wounds. . . . I saw one man with a wound in his back large enough to put in my fist. He was fast bleeding to death. They lay so thick around me that I could hardly step between them, and every step was in blood."[48] Often soldiers walking over a battlefield heard the wounded cry out, begging for the "mercy" of a bullet or a bayonet thrust. Some soldiers obliged, though we can never know how many. "Mercy killing" was still killing, and therefore unlawful. Anyone convicted of killing the wounded, even out of kindness, might face a firing squad.

Survivors described field hospitals as torture chambers. Not that surgeons wished to cause pain; it was simply a reality, an essential part of soldiering. The only painkillers were chloroform and ether, but these might be scarce, forcing a surgeon to operate while his assistants held the patient down. A Civil War rifle fired a one-ounce bullet that shattered bones and made a large, jagged hole. Anyone hit in the arm or leg usually had the limb removed to avoid blood poisoning. Amputation was quick, avoiding unnecessary loss of blood. A skilled surgeon could remove a limb in three minutes.

At least the Confederates had field hospitals nearby, since they held the battlefield. The retreating Yankees had to move their wounded in ambulances, springless wagons that shook and bounced every inch of the way. For two days, the wretched army streamed past the White House in a pouring rain. Exhausted men dropped in the muddy streets or stumbled along like drunkards. The commander in chief stood at a window, watching it all.

Shock over the disaster spread in the North as quickly as joy spread in the South. The Confederate Congress in Richmond ordered a day of thanksgiving. Johnny Reb put his own words to a popular song, "Oh! Susanna":

> *I come from old Manassas with a pocket full of fun—*
> *I killed forty Yankees with a single-barrelled gun;*
> *It don't make a niff-a-stifference to neither you nor I,*
> *Big Yankee, little Yankee, all run or die.*[49]

The Illinois ape would soon be running for his life! The war was over! The Confederacy had won its independence!

Robert E. Lee knew better. Lee was a realist, a person who saw things as they are, not as he wished them to be. He had read the Independence Day address that Lincoln had given to a special session of Congress two weeks before Bull Run. "That man," as he called the President, had character. A single defeat, however decisive, would not make him back down. It seemed unlikely that he would *ever* allow the Confederacy to go its own way.

Then, as in later generations, Lincoln's critics challenged his determination to preserve the Union at all costs. The Declaration of Independence says that governments derive their powers from the consent of the governed. Well, critics argued, Southern people no longer wished to be governed by the United States. If they wanted their own country, why not just let them go? Why shed oceans of blood in the name of national unity?

Lincoln's speech dealt with these questions in simple terms. The conflict, he insisted, was not about an insult to the flag or any of the other things nations usually fought about. Nor was it about slavery. If Lincoln can be said to have had "one big idea," it was the sanctity of democracy under the rule of law. For Lincoln, the Union embodied the experiment in self-government begun in 1776. And self-government, if it means anything, means free elections and majority rule. In a democracy, the ballot replaces the bullet. Losers abide by the outcome, knowing it can be reversed in a future election. That is the civilized way of doing things, for the verdict of the bullet is final. The bullet kills forever or scars for life. Nothing can ever undo its effects.

By defending the Union, Lincoln believed, patriots were defending more than a land called the United States of America. They were defending fundamental ideals of right and justice. Their sacrifices proved "that when ballots have fairly, and constitutionally, decided, there can be no successful appeal . . . to bullets . . . teaching men that what they cannot take by an election, neither can they take it by a war—teaching all, the folly of being the beginners of a war."[50]

By "election," he meant not simply his own victory at the polls, but the principle that the people as a whole must have the final say on all public issues. Lincoln believed that when the Southern states joined the Union, they committed themselves to its laws. Having done so, Southerners could not later choose to abide by some laws and reject others as they pleased. Thus, Confederates were using bullets to violate the law of the land—indeed, to destroy the nation itself. Lincoln could not tolerate such a situation. As the duly elected chief executive, he was President of all the people. Therefore, he felt justified—no, compelled—in using force to put down an unlawful rebellion.

The Civil War, therefore, was no ordinary conflict. It was "a People's contest," a struggle for the future of humanity. In 1861, the United States was the world's only democracy, a model for peoples everywhere. Europe's privileged classes sneered at democracy as "mobocracy"—mob rule. For them, ordinary men and women were too stupid and weak-willed to rule themselves. They needed an aristocracy—the rule of the best—to govern them. A Confederate victory, therefore, would not only destroy the United States, but set back the cause of democracy worldwide.

The President would never yield, never compromise, never weaken in his resolve to restore the Union. America's fiery trial had only just begun.

4 THE FIERY TRIAL

Fellow-citizens, we cannot escape history. . . . The fiery trial through which we pass, will light us down, in honor or dishonor, to the latest generation. We say we are for the Union. The world will not forget that we say this. We know how to save the Union. . . . In giving freedom to the slave, we assure freedom to the free — honorable alike in what we give, and what we preserve. We shall nobly save, or meanly lose, the last best, hope of earth.

ABRAHAM LINCOLN, DECEMBER 1, 1862

Abraham Lincoln decided that his only course was to wage war on a grand scale. The day after Bull Run, he called for another 500,000 volunteers and named George B. McClellan their commander. A short, muscular man, McClellan had a boyish face that made him look younger than his thirty-four years. The only Union general to win any victories in 1861, he had driven the Confederates out of western Virginia earlier that month.[1] Although the fighting had not been severe, the press dubbed him the "Young Napoleon of the West," America's answer to the French emperor. He seemed the ideal replacement for the ailing Winfield Scott. When the President asked if the job might be too much for him, he declared, "I can do it all."[2]

It surely seemed that way. McClellan took the raw recruits who poured into Washington and shaped them into a magnificent fighting force: the Army of the Potomac. Soldiers loved their "Little Mac." As he galloped by on a sleek black stallion, regiments dropped what they were doing and cheered themselves hoarse. During training exercises, soldiers set the pace by singing: "McClellan's our leader, he's gallant and he's

strong! For God and our country, we're marching along!"[3]

Marching along, yes; but never very far from the parade ground. Summer gave way to fall, fall to winter, and still McClellan did not take the offensive. The President, puzzled, thought there must be good military reasons for delay. After all, the Young Napoleon *was* a brilliant officer, and he only a small-town politician. He decided to keep quiet until he knew more about making war.

Lincoln borrowed military books from the Library of Congress—books by experts written for West Point cadets. Careful reading and common sense did the rest. The books enabled him to see the struggle in ways that escaped most of his generals. Trained in the details of war making, they had overlooked the obvious. The President, however, learned just enough to see the "big picture" without getting bogged down in the fine points.

Strategy, he learned, is the art of setting long-range goals; *tactics* is the science of reaching those goals by force of arms. Lincoln drew a simple conclusion: the Union must reduce Confederate advantages while using its own advantages to the fullest.

The Confederacy had two major advantages. First, it controlled an area twice that of any European country except Russia. Second, it enjoyed interior lines of communication, the ability to shift troops freely within its own territory. Lincoln imagined the Confederacy as a gigantic wheel with an outer rim connected by spokes to an inner hub. To win the war, Union forces must move inward from the rim. Yet that was easier said than done. Since the defenders held the hub, or interior, they could block any advance by shifting troops along the spokes, or railroad lines. Although Southern railroads were in poor condition, they went to all the right places.

Union advantages in manpower and supplies meant little if the Union attacked only one point at a time. Lincoln's strategy was to apply pressure to several points at once, pinning down the defenders and preventing them from helping one another. When Union forces found a weak spot, they must break through with overwhelming force. Their object must be to destroy the opposing army, not occupy territory—unless it held a vital facility like a railroad center or seaport. The President's tactics called for hitting hard, fast, and often. Most important, they required fighting generals, risk takers who would settle for nothing less than total victory.

The Young Napoleon was no risk taker. Behind the dashing warrior image stood a timid man who dreaded any action likely to result in heavy losses. He loved his soldiers and did not wish to hurt them, an admirable quality in a civilian but dangerous in a general. Casualties are an inevitable part of battle, and to think otherwise is to ignore the realities of war. Moreover, before McClellan would take action, every buckle and button had to be fastened—that is, every preparation made and every difficulty provided for, an impossibility given the ever-changing nature of battle. These failings would make McClellan the worst general ever to command an American army in wartime. A pompous man who despised anyone who voiced an opinion different from his, he saw himself as God's gift to the Republic.

The President topped his hate list. Lincoln never stood on formality; if he wanted to discuss an idea, he dropped in unannounced at headquarters. This outraged McClellan. The notion that a general should discuss military affairs with a civilian was ridiculous to him. And such a civilian! Why, the President had no dignity, no sense of the "proper" way of doing things! McClellan wrote his wife that Lincoln was a self-taught "idiot," a "well-meaning baboon," and "the original Gorilla."[4] The President was not fit to lick the boots of an officer and a gentleman.

McClellan's rudeness matched his snobbery. On November 13,

OPPOSITE: *General George B. McClellan was a brilliant organizer but poor at following through. On more than one occasion, he had the Confederates at his mercy, only to let them escape. This picture was taken about 1863 by Mathew B. Brady, a leading photographer. Brady accompanied the Union armies, taking thousands of photographs that became the basis for the pictorial history of the Civil War.*

1861, Lincoln, Secretary of State Seward, and an aide called at his Washington home. The butler said the general was at a wedding and should be back within the hour. So they went into the parlor to wait. When McClellan returned, the butler told him about the visitors. Too bad! Without saying a word, he strode past the door and went upstairs to bed. Seward and the aide sputtered with anger. Lincoln brushed the incident aside, saying "I will hold McClellan's horse if he will only bring us success."[5]

The Young Napoleon brought no success. He spent the winter of 1861 making plans, which he kept to himself. He did not trust the commander in chief to keep a secret, fearing he would tell Tad, who would shout it from the White House rooftop. Meanwhile, the First Family settled into life in wartime Washington.

Their home was not as cozy as the one in Springfield. The White House stood between four government departments—State, Treasury, War, Navy—all reached by paths that crisscrossed the White House lawns. John Nicolay, Lincoln's chief secretary, described the mansion as "ill-kept and dirty," a dull, dingy, "dilapidated old shanty" unworthy of a proud nation. Lincoln called it "this damned old house."[6]

It was not a healthy place. The livery stables along Pennsylvania Avenue gave off disgusting odors. Rats infested the basement and squeaked as they rummaged in the walls. Germ-carrying insects flew through the unscreened windows. "The gas lights over my desk," John Nicolay wrote his fianceé, "are burning brightly and the windows of the room are open, and all bugdom outside seems to have organized a storming party. . . . The air is swarming with them, they are on the ceilings, the walls and the furniture in countless numbers, they are buzzing about the room, are butting their heads against the window panes, they are in my clothes, in my hair, and on the sheet I am writing on."[7] In summertime, the First Family retreated to a twelve-room "cottage" at the Retired Soldiers' Home on a wooded hillside in the suburbs.

Willie and Tad kept a menagerie of dogs, cats, rabbits, ponies, and a turkey named Jack, all of which attracted fleas and flies. Tad's pet goats, Nanny and Nanko, stank to high heaven. The goats wandered through

OPPOSITE: *The President and his private secretaries John Nicolay (left) and John Hay (right). Both men later wrote the first multivolume biography of their chief and published an edition of* The Complete Works of Abraham Lincoln. *Hay later became U.S. ambassador to Great Britain and secretary of state. In 1901, he negotiated the treaty providing for the construction of the Panama Canal.*

the White House corridors, and Nanny, Tad's favorite, slept on his bed at night. It is not surprising that the Lincolns repeatedly suffered bouts of fever and diarrhea. Once the family got sick from eating Potomac River fish. But so did everyone else. The polluted river supplied Washington with fish and its undertakers with customers.

The President's day began early. Seldom rising later than 6:00 A.M., he padded around the White House in carpet slippers and a red flannel nightshirt that came down to his knees. If he had a moment to spare, he dressed and walked to the Avenue to buy a newspaper. Accustomed to "doing" for himself, he might also take a few minutes to sew a button on a shirt or polish his boots. A congressman once found him bent over with a rag and polish. "Mr. Lincoln," he said sternly, "gentlemen do not black their own boots." Mr. Lincoln replied: "Whose boots *do* they black?"[8]

After a breakfast of eggs and coffee, Lincoln visited the War Department telegraph office to read the latest messages from the front. He walked alone or with anyone he happened to ask along for company. By 8:00 A.M. he was in his second-floor office in the East Wing of the White House. The "shop," as he called it, was a large room with a marble fireplace, a desk, two sofas, and an oak table. Like his old law office, it was a marvel of disorder, with stacks of papers on every flat surface. The Oval Office was a library that he seldom used.

From 9:00 to 10:00 A.M., Lincoln went over the mail. His secretaries had already sorted it, selecting only certain letters for his attention. Of these, he answered a few in person, writing in longhand

and signing them *A. Lincoln*; he signed his full name only to the most important documents. The secretaries—John Nicolay and John Hay—answered the other letters as he directed, signing their own names. At ten o'clock sharp, they opened the office door to visitors.

Unlike today's presidents, whose every waking moment is programmed weeks in advance, Lincoln did not keep to a tight schedule. He did, however, spend up to three-quarters of his time with visitors. "Well, friend, what can I do for you?" he would ask each in turn. They told him.

Besides the usual job seekers, visitors came for all sorts of reasons. They begged Lincoln for favors, criticized him, gave him advice, told him how to win the war, preached to him, prayed *for* him, and asked to pray *with* him on bended knee. Sometimes his patience wore thin. One blazing summer afternoon, for example, a fellow kept nagging him for a favor. Try as he did to be polite, he could not make the fellow take no for an answer. He began to fidget, turning away to stare out the window at the Potomac River. Finally, his temper flared. "Now, my man, go away!" he snapped. "I cannot attend to all these details. I could as easily bail out the Potomac with a spoon."[9]

These sessions exhausted him physically, but he would not have missed them for the world. Lincoln felt it his duty to meet the people, not stay cooped up in the White House. His "public opinion baths," as he called them, allowed him to gauge the country's temperament and adjust his actions to its changing moods. Nowadays, presidents hire professional polltakers for that purpose.

Lincoln immersing himself in a "public opinion bath." Whenever possible, the President met ordinary citizens in his office to learn firsthand their opinions on the issues of the day. Nowadays, they usually hire experts to take polls.

Lincoln ate lunch at 1:00 P.M., usually a biscuit, a glass of milk, and a plate of fruit. Another three hours of work and visitors followed; then he took a carriage ride with Mary, his only daily recreation. Yet this, too, was a form of work, since they usually stopped at one of Washington's twenty-five military hospitals; the largest was Lincoln General Hospital. Strolling into a ward, he would go from bed to bed, shaking hands and making small talk. During one visit, he noticed a Pennsylvanian taller even than he. Lincoln's face lit up and he joked about their heights. "Hello, comrade," he said, grinning from ear to ear. "Do you know when your feet get cold?"[10]

Supper was at six o'clock, a meal of soup, meat, and potatoes, followed by homemade apple pie. One night a week, except in summertime, the First Family held a public reception in the East Room of the White House. People flocked to the mansion to shake the President's hand and perhaps ask for a favor. He took it all in stride, trying to look interested. The novelist Herman Melville, author of *Moby-Dick*, attended such a reception. Lincoln, he recalled, shook hands mechanically, "like a man sawing wood at so much per cord."[11]

If someone brought a child, however, his expression instantly changed. He became alert, and his face glowed with joy. "Hurrah for Mist' Linthon!" a youngster lisped. "Hurrah for Mister You!" Lincoln replied, sweeping the boy off the ground and raising him high above his head. The President beamed when a little girl called out after he kissed her cheek, "Why, he is only a man after all!" Another girl had not known what to expect when she came up to the big man. He sat down, took her on his lap, and chatted with her as if he had all the time in the world. "Oh, Pa! He isn't ugly at all; he's just beautiful!" she called across the room.[12]

Eventually, Lincoln slipped away to his office to review the sentences of military trials, or courts-martial. Military law was extremely harsh, a carryover from the old European armies, where men were often kidnapped into military service. Courts ordered common offenders—gamblers, drunks, thieves—strung up by their thumbs or tied up for hours in painful positions. Serious crimes—striking an officer, sleeping on post, cowardice, desertion—carried the death penalty. To set an example, thousands of soldiers were forced to watch the grisly spectacle. The condemned man rode to execution in a wagon, seated on his own coffin. Then, as drummers beat a long roll, a firing squad or hangman carried out the sentence. Only the commander in chief could overrule a court-martial decision.

Those late-night sessions showed Lincoln at his best. The President put himself in the shoes of the condemned man and his loved ones. Soldiers were not robots, but human beings with feelings and fears. How did it feel to see friends blown apart? What would he, the commander in chief, have done in a similar situation? What would his own execution mean to Mary and the boys? Questions like these demanded honest answers.

Lincoln confessed to being "pigeon-hearted," although he never said so in public. "The fact is I am a great coward," he told a friend. "I have moral courage enough, I think, but I am such a coward, physically, that if I were to shoulder a gun and go into action, I am dead sure that I should turn and run at the first fire—I *know* I should."[13]

The President used any excuse to save a life. He pardoned hundreds of cowards, claiming "it would frighten the poor devils too terribly to shoot them." He saved a fourteen-year-old runaway by scrawling a question on the court record: "Hadn't we better spank this drummer boy and send him back home?"[14]

Lincoln called deserters his "leg cases." Blame the legs, but do not kill their owner, he insisted: "If God gives a man a cowardly pair of legs, how can he help their running away with him?"[15]

Any woman with a baby in her arms held a passport to life. White House servants knew that, whatever her man's crime, Lincoln never rejected a plea for mercy if he saw an infant. "It was the baby that did it, madam," a butler said as one wife left, tearful but clutching a pardon for her husband. A pardon, however, did not always mean freedom. Lincoln ordered some men returned to their outfits, others to do hard labor in the Dry Tortugas, some tiny islands a hundred miles off the Florida coast.[16]

Around 1:30 A.M., he turned off the gaslight in his "shop" and made a final trip to the telegraph office. The duty officer expected him and had placed the messages in a desk drawer. Having read his way through the pile to the one he had read first, Lincoln would say: "Well, I have got down to the raisins."

Raisins? What on earth did telegrams have to do with raisins? Clerks wondered about it until one found the courage to ask.

Lincoln was happy to explain. Once upon a time, he knew a little girl in Illinois who went on an eating binge. Did she ever eat! She stuffed herself with soup, meat, salad, potatoes, vegetables, ice cream, cake, and raisins by the fistful. Then she began to vomit. And vomit. At last the raisins came up. "Well," she said, turning to her mother, "I will be better now, I guess, for I have got down to the raisins."[17]

His chores finished, the President crawled into his nine-foot-long bed, its wooden headboard carved with flying birds and bunches of grapes. Yet he did not necessarily expect a full night's sleep. There was often business that could not wait until morning, and officials might appear at any hour with urgent messages. Therefore, the First Lady slept in a separate room.

Lincoln enjoyed seeing his boys enjoy themselves. Willie and Tad used the White House as a playground. Joined by Bud and Holly Taft, a judge's sons, they hitched their pet goats to chairs and chased "rebels" through the halls like Roman charioteers. One day the White House roof served as the deck of a pretend-warship, another day as a pretend-fort complete with wooden cannons and broken pistols, gifts from Secretary of War Edwin M. Stanton. The attic became a circus tent: five cents a performance, and everyone welcome, including the servants. Each boy wore a long dress and smelled of Bloom of Youth perfume, looted from the First Lady's wardrobe. Tad began with his favorite song:

Old Abe Lincoln a rail splitter was he,
And he'll split the Confederacee.[18]

Julia Taft brought her brothers to the White House each morning. A proper lady of sixteen, she blushed whenever the President called her a "flibbertigibbet," his name for a lovely girl in a snow-white dress with long curls and a radiant smile.

A keen observer, Julia later recalled those days in *Tad Lincoln's Father,* the best firsthand account we have of Lincoln and his younger sons in wartime. The President, she wrote, liked to join in the fun. She once heard a terrific racket coming from inside a room. Opening the door,

William Wallace ("Willie") Lincoln died in the White House on February 20, 1862, at the age of eleven. A sensitive child, he was a fast learner who memorized railway timetables and wrote poetry. Mathew Brady took this photograph in 1861.

she saw Lincoln and the four boys wrestling on the floor. Although each boy held an arm or a leg, they could not pin him down. "Julie, come quick and sit on his stomach," Tad cried. She would do no such thing, and shut the door. She did join the listeners when Lincoln gathered the boys on his lap in an easy chair to tell scary stories. Somehow she always found herself drawn into the group by a long arm that seemed to reach across the room.[19]

Tad's soldier doll, Jack, kept falling asleep at his post. The boys held a court-martial, found Jack guilty, and sentenced him to be shot. Following "paw's" example, however, they always found a reason for a last-minute pardon. Finally, Jack dozed off once too often. Now his only hope was a presidential pardon. So the boys burst into Lincoln's office during a meeting. Cabinet members frowned, but their boss played along. On official White House stationery he wrote: "The doll Jack is pardoned. By order of the President. A. Lincoln."[20]

The fun ended early in 1862. Tad and Willie fell ill, probably with typhoid fever. Tad recovered, but Willie could not shake the infection. He tossed and turned in bed, unable to sleep or hold down food. His parents took turns comforting him and putting wet towels on his forehead. Willie would rally, relapse, and then rally again. Yet the rallies grew fewer, the relapses longer and more frequent. Willie died on February 20, after a two-week illness.

Leaving the bedside, Lincoln burst into tears. Regaining his composure, he went to tell Tad that his brother would never play with him again.

The First Lady took it harder. Too upset to attend the funeral, Mary sat in her darkened room, wailing like a tormented soul in hell. She seemed to be losing her mind. One day, her husband took her to a window and pointed to a distant building: an insane asylum. "Mother, do you see that large white building on yonder hill?" he asked. "Try to control your grief, or it will drive you mad, and we may have to send you there."[21]

Those words started the healing process. Although Mary never got over the loss of her son, she learned how to find relief in constructive action. Out of her own misery there grew a deep sympathy for the misery of others. She "adopted" other mothers' boys, bringing food, flowers, and comfort to army hospitals. Soldiers spoke of the First Lady as an angel in disguise, and named Camp Mary Lincoln in her honor.

Elizabeth Keckley, a former slave who had bought her freedom with her earnings as a dressmaker, became the First Lady's closest friend in Washington. A warm, gentle person, "Lizzie" had recently lost her own son, so she understood Mary's feelings. Lizzie washed and dressed Willie's body before the funeral and held his weeping mother in her arms. Active in black causes, she encouraged her friend to become active, too. Mary collected money for needy blacks, sent them food, and found them jobs. To the President, Lizzie was always "Madame Keckley," a grand lady.[22]

Elizabeth Keckley was Mary Lincoln's dressmaker and friend. Born a slave, she learned to be a fine seamstress. In 1855, she bought her own and her son's freedom for $1,200, contributed by her customers. Her son died in battle during the Civil War, which further deepened her friendship with the First Lady.

As Willie lay dying, war was exploding across the land. Out in Tennessee, a stubby little man named Ulysses S. Grant won the nickname "Unconditional Surrender" by capturing two key forts. Come spring, he would defeat the Confederates at Shiloh in southern Tennessee, while a fleet led by David Glasgow Farragut forced the surrender of New Orleans, the Confederacy's largest city.

In Washington, the Young Napoleon finally revealed his plan. Unrolling his maps, he showed Lincoln that strong enemy forces still held Manassas Junction. Rather than fight his way overland, he intended to bypass their defenses. He would use Union naval power to make a surprise landing on the Virginia Peninsula between the York and James Rivers, then move against Richmond seventy miles to the northwest. Once ashore, he expected his 107,000 men to break through the city's "back door." The President approved the plan, despite fears that the move might weaken Washington's own defenses.

Four hundred vessels had assembled on the Potomac when an urgent telegram interrupted a Cabinet meeting on March 8, 1862. It told how, that very morning, the Confederate navy had sent the *Merrimac,* the world's first "ironclad," against a Union squadron cruising off the Peninsula. Built low, her sides covered by iron plates, she mounted ten heavy guns. The wooden warships never had a chance. The *Merrimac* withdrew at sundown, leaving two vessels sunk and a third severely damaged.

Cabinet members rushed to the window, expecting to see the monster steaming up the Potomac. The President, however, knew help was on the way. Several months earlier, during the *Merrimac*'s construction, a black woman had escaped from Norfolk with news of the secret weapon. Lincoln ordered the navy to build its own ironclad, the *Monitor,* at the Greenpoint Shipyard in Brooklyn, New York. The *Monitor* deserved her nickname, "Tin Can on a Shingle." Almost level with the water, like a flat shingle, her "tin can" was a revolving turret with two heavy guns. Unlike every other warship, whose guns fired from either side of the vessel, the turret allowed the *Monitor* to bring her guns to bear from any angle.

Next morning, March 9, the *Monitor* arrived off the Peninsula. The *Merrimac* came after her with guns blazing. Sailors compared the experience to being under a

The Virginia Peninsula

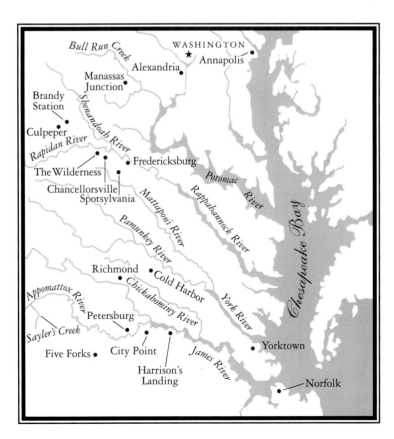

The battle between the Monitor and the Merrimac off Hampton Roads, Virginia, March 9, 1862. This was a decisive turning point in sea warfare. For the first time in history, ironclad vessels powered by steam engines clashed. From that day forward, the wooden warship was doomed.

bell struck by sledgehammers. BABAM-CLANG. BABAM-CLANG. Each blow set their teeth on edge and made their ears ring. Nevertheless, neither vessel seriously damaged the other; armor-piercing shells would not exist for another generation. The battle ended in a draw. The *Merrimac* withdrew to Norfolk. A week later, the Union army landed at the tip of the Peninsula.

The Confederates retreated to Yorktown without a fight. Had McClellan moved quickly, he could easily have overrun the 15,000 defenders, whose commanders had orders to pull out at the first sign of a major assault. Yet that sign did not come.

Like any other general, the Young Napoleon needed "order-of-battle" information, a list of enemy units operating in his sector and their strength. A network of spies, including a black group called the "Friends of Uncle Abe," sent him daily reports. Unfortunately, the reports were wrong. Even today, no one can say why so many agents should have been so wide of the mark. They put rebel strength at 120,000 men!

A bolder general would have sent patrols to verify the reports. McClellan took them at face value, because they confirmed his own fears. Rather than fight a battle, he dug in for a siege. Every day he dashed off a batch of telegrams demanding more men, more horses, more guns, more ammunition—more *everything!*

Lincoln sent everything he could. The buildup continued for weeks, and still McClellan refused to move until "ready." Finally, the great day arrived. He ordered a bombardment to begin at dawn on May 4, but it never took place. The Confederates knew when to get going. They had abandoned their positions the night before the scheduled attack and continued their retreat. When Billy Yank took their positions, he found dozens of logs painted black to resemble cannons. Confederate "defenses" had always been a fake.

The President decided to see things for himself. On May 6, he landed at Fortress Monroe, thus becoming the first commander in chief to visit a combat zone. His appearance did not impress the soldiers, though they appreciated the visit anyhow. As Lincoln was reviewing troops on horseback, they noticed that he wore long underwear despite the heat and humidity. A private wrote his folks:

> Whether intentionally or unintentionally, Mr. Lincoln had been provided with a small . . . horse about fourteen hands high. The President's legs looked longer than ever, and his toes seemed almost to touch the ground. He wore the same solemn suit of black that he always assumed, a tall silk hat, a little the worse for wear, with a long, full skirted black coat. He had neglected to strap down his pant legs while riding, and, as most of the time he was kept at a jog trot, his pants began to draw up until finally, first one white drawers leg, then the other, began to be conspicuous. . . . The hard trot settled his tall . . . hat on the back of his head, until it had rested upon his ears, which were large and somewhat projecting, and it looked as if it had been purposely jammed down into that position. Altogether he presented a very comical picture, calculated to provoke laughter along the entire length of the lines, had it not been for that sad, anxious face so full of melancholy.

"But the boys liked him," a comrade added. "All have faith in Lincoln. . . . God bless the man and give answer to the prayers for guidance I am sure he offers."[23]

The President soon made a startling discovery. Although Norfolk lay across the bay from Fortress Monroe, Union forces had not tried to capture it. How stupid! He and Secretary of War Stanton sailed along the coast to find a suitable landing place for the assault force.

Two days later, May 8, the Yankees landed against light opposition. Moments before they reached Norfolk, the *Merrimac*'s crew blew up the vessel. Never again would the Confederates seriously challenge Union naval power. Lincoln's decision to take Norfolk also opened the James River to Union ironclads as far as Drewry's Bluff, eight miles below Richmond.

While the President waited for news from the landing force, an officer entered his room on other business. He found Lincoln seated at a table, looking as sad as any human being could look. "I dream of my boy Willie," he said as the tears came.[24]

The Young Napoleon advanced to the outskirts of Richmond, where he paused to await reinforcements. Meanwhile, Stonewall Jackson routed Union forces in the Shenandoah Valley to the north. Flanked by mountain ranges on either side, the Shenandoah, or Valley of Virginia, was like a spear pointed at the Union capital. Fearing an attack, Lincoln ordered McClellan's reinforcements back to Washington. Jackson retreated down the Valley, as planned. The whole operation had been a trick, and Lincoln had fallen for it.

Had McClellan moved quickly, he probably would have captured Richmond with the forces available. By delaying, however, he allowed Confederate General Joseph E. Johnston to attack when a flooded river cut the Union army in two. In the Battle of Seven Pines, May 31–June 1, 1862, the Young Napoleon barely held his ground, while Johnston nearly died of a bullet wound.

General Thomas J. Jackson as he appeared in 1863, a few weeks before his death at the Battle of Chancellorsville. Known as "Stonewall" because of his skill and determination, his loss was a serious blow to the Confederacy.

Until Seven Pines, Robert E. Lee had been the Confederate president's military adviser. A desk general, Lee had always yearned for action. Now he took over Johnston's command, naming it the Army of Northern Virginia. The Young Napoleon misjudged his opponent and was glad that Lee had left his desk. He thought the Virginian *"too* cautious & weak" when faced with danger.[25]

That description fit McClellan, but never Lee. Johnny Reb called Lee "Marse Robert," for "Master Robert." Normally a sweet-tempered man, Lee was as tough as they come in the line of duty. He summarized his military thinking in eleven words: "If you can accomplish the object, *any* risk would be justified."[26] Here was the risk taker Lincoln needed, only he fought on the other side.

Marse Robert began an all-out effort to drive the Yankees away from Richmond. In the Seven Days' Battles, a series of clashes from June 25 to July 1, the armies pounded each other savagely. McClellan lost his nerve. After burning supplies worth millions of dollars, he retreated to Harrison's Landing on the James River. Although Confederates hailed Lee as the "savior of Richmond," he knew better. The Seven Days cost the Confederacy 20,141 and the Union 15,849 men killed, wounded, and captured. Since the Union force was so much larger, it could easily absorb such losses. Defeat lay in its commander's mind, not on the battlefield. The Army of the Potomac was still a deadly fighting machine.

McClellan's demands increased, and when he did not get exactly what he wanted, when he wanted it, he whined and blamed others for his failure. The government had betrayed the army! If only those "fools" in Washington met his demands, he could easily whip Lee! The President, he wrote his wife, was "an old stick—and of pretty poor timber at that."[27]

Lincoln doubted that anything could put backbone into the general. "If I gave McClellan all the men he asks for they could not find room to lie down," he sighed. "They'd have to sleep standing up."[28] There was no point sending more troops to sit on the mudflats along the James River.

In August, Lincoln ordered the army back to the Washington area. Lee, however, was still ready—no, eager—to take risks. The withdrawal was well underway when Lee struck again, this time at a 65,000-man force camped near Manassas Junction. On August 29, he drew General John Pope into the Second Battle of Bull Run (Second Manassas.) McClellan refused to send help, although he had thousands of well-armed men nearby. It almost seemed as if he *wanted* Pope defeated.

Lincoln replaced the defeated generals. Pope went west to guard the frontier against the Sioux Indians. McClellan lost command of the Army of the Potomac. But if the Young Napoleon could not fight himself, he still knew how to rebuild a shattered army. The President wanted him to reorganize Pope's force while he searched for a new army chief.

Lee had other plans. Instead of waiting for an attack in Virginia, he took the offensive. Early in September 1862, his troops splashed across the Potomac into Maryland. Acting with his usual boldness, he divided the army into three strike forces. Lee commanded the main force, while Stonewall Jackson raced ahead to capture Harpers Ferry; Jackson's men moved so fast they called themselves "foot cavalry." Another contingent headed for Hagerstown, Maryland, near the Pennsylvania border. Taken by surprise, and still without an army chief, Lincoln gave McClellan his old command.

OPPOSITE: *Confederate General Robert E. Lee. One of the greatest fighting generals in history, he and his Army of Northern Virginia gave President Lincoln sleepless nights for nearly four years.*

McClellan proceeded at his usual snail's pace, until a soldier found an envelope in a deserted Confederate camp. Left behind by a mysterious "somebody" who has never been identified, the envelope contained a full set of Lee's plans. Confident of victory, McClellan moved faster, forcing Lee to concentrate his forces at Sharpsburg, Maryland, between the Potomac River and Antietam Creek, a shallow stream east of town.

On September 17, the armies squared off for an epic battle. With their backs to the Potomac, 35,000 rebels faced 87,000 Yankees massed across the Antietam. McClellan hurled four assaults against their line. So many guns were firing at once that it was impossible to hear single shots. Soldiers were engulfed by the continuous crash, rumble, and roar of artillery. Swarms of rifle bullets sawed down trees and leveled fields of corn like huge scythes. Blood turned the ground to reddish-brown mud and made the grass slippery as ice. In one place, Confederate bodies lay in even ranks as if resting in parade formation. Elsewhere, a Johnny Reb saw dead Yankees heaped "thick as autumn leaves."[29]

The assaults might easily have broken the Confederate line. However, Lee found an unlikely ally in the Union general. By attacking each section of Lee's line separately, rather than hitting everywhere at once, McClellan allowed him to shift troops from quiet areas. Even then, Lee expected to be crushed. He was losing so many men so quickly that he feared a breakthrough at any moment. But when a breakthrough nearly came on the Confederate right, McClellan, always cautious, held back his reserves, 20,000 men who had not fired a shot that day. His refusal saved the Army of Northern Virginia.

Lee recrossed the Potomac next morning, his exhausted men singing "Carry Me Back to Old Virginny." Antietam (Sharpsburg to Confederates) saw the bloodiest twenty-four hours of the Civil War, and the bloodiest day in American history. Combined casualties numbered 22,712, of whom 3,654 lost their lives, or four times the losses suffered by American forces on D day, when the Allied forces invaded Europe in World War II. On that day, June 6, 1944, Americans faced Germans armed with quick-firing artillery, machine guns, and automatic rifles.

Lincoln urged McClellan to pursue the weakened Confederates. If he could corner them, he might end the war in a single blow. Yet that was not to be. Fearful as ever, the Young Napoleon let the enemy escape.

Confederate soldiers killed at the Battle of Antietam on September 17, 1862. This photograph, one of a series made by Mathew Brady's assistants, was part of an exhibit in his New York gallery. Such realism was new to the American public. In its review of the exhibit, The New York Times *said: "Mr. Brady has done something to bring to us the terrible reality and earnestness of the war. If he has not brought bodies and laid them in our door-yards and along {our} streets, he has done something very like it."*

Whenever Lincoln ordered him to get going, he found ingenious excuses for staying put, like the sore tongues of his cavalry horses! "I have just read your dispatches about sore-tongued and fatigued horses," an angry President wired back. "Will you pardon me for asking what the horses of your army have done since the battle of Antietam that fatigues anything?"[30]

Lincoln's respect for the rebel commanders grew, while he lost the last shreds of respect for his own general. Seeing a picture of Lee, he called him "a noble, noble, brave man." He admired Stonewall Jackson as "a brave, honest" soldier, adding "If only we had such a man to lead the armies of the North, the country would not be appalled by so many disasters." As for McClellan, he had an incurable disease: "the slows." In November, the President dismissed him for good. Lee hated to lose McClellan. He had always understood him so well, and he feared Lincoln would continue to make changes until he found someone Lee did not understand.[31]

Lincoln and McClellan discuss military affairs in the general's headquarters tent at Antietam on October 2, 1862. It was to be their last meeting. Notice the American flag. Back then, Old Glory was not treated as a "sacred" symbol. The general used it as a tablecloth; the President put his stovepipe hat on it.

Antietam was the critical battle of the Civil War *and* a turning point in American history. Although a draw militarily, it changed the course of our country's life forever. On September 22, as burial squads went about their grisly work, the President sent an official document to the newspapers. Its title: the Preliminary Emancipation Proclamation.

From the day the Civil War began, abolitionists had been urging Lincoln to declare it a crusade for freedom. Frederick Douglass led the way with a series of hard-hitting statements. Freedom for the slave, he wrote in the July 1861 issue of *Douglass' Monthly*, was not only what God wanted, but a military necessity. To fight the rebels without liberating their slaves was both foolish and costly. "The very stomach of this rebellion is the negro in the condition of the slave," he insisted. "Arrest that hoe in the hands of the negro, and you smite rebellion in the very seat of its life. . . . The negro is the key to the situation—the pivot upon which the whole rebellion turns."[32]

Douglass knew what he was talking about. Slaves formed the backbone of the Confederate labor force. Not only did blacks grow most of Johnny Reb's food, they put weapons into his hands. Behind the fighting lines, black miners dug iron ore for black gunsmiths to turn into guns. At the front, every unit had black "servants" to cook food, drive wagons, carry stretchers, and tend the wounded; half the nurses in Confederate army hospitals were black. Slaves dug trenches, filled sandbags, built forts, loaded cannons, and brought water to the troops during battle.

The war changed some Billy Yanks into abolitionists. During the Peninsular campaign, many saw the Peculiar Institution for the first time. It turned their stomachs. As they advanced, they found whipping posts, slave jails, and mulatto girls carrying mulatto babies. They met youngsters with scarred backs, and heard how those scars got there. An Indiana private listened in stunned silence to the story of a fifteen-year-old. "To hear this child tell about the thrashing he has received from a brutal master and the chains and weights he has carried in the field," he wrote his family, "is enough to make a man feel like it would be God's service to shoot them [rebels] down like buzzards."[33] Incidents like this made soldiers see black people not as brutes but as human beings like themselves.

Other soldiers—perhaps a majority—had little sympathy for the slave as a person. Nevertheless, they hated slavery with a fury that grew as the war continued. Slavery supported those "fellers" who were killing and maiming their friends. Slavery, then, became a deeply personal matter and not a question of human rights. Billy Yank realized that the sooner it ended, the sooner the war would end and he could go home. His officers agreed. In occupied areas, local commanders sheltered runaways in their camps. In border state Missouri, General John C. Frémont freed slaves whose masters favored the rebellion.

Lincoln canceled these actions, warning that nobody should attack slavery without his permission. More, he enforced the Fugitive Slave Law to the letter. Commanders received orders to return fugitives without delay. In Washington itself, jails filled with runaways awaiting transfer to their owners. Slave catchers kidnapped free blacks on Pennsylvania Avenue itself, claiming them as fugitives. One poor man broke away, only to be seized while running up the steps of the Capitol with chains on his legs.[34]

Abolitionists blasted the President as a hypocrite. Frederick Douglass led the way, expressing "disgust" at Lincoln and his "spineless" policy. Lincoln's reply was that, yes, he hated slavery—always had, always would. Yet, as President, he must set aside his personal beliefs for the greater good. He had taken a solemn oath to defend the Constitution. The South had left the Union and was making war on it. Very well; he would fight the rebels with every means at his disposal. However, since the Constitution protected slavery, so must he.

On the military side, Lincoln had reason for caution. The border slave states remained in the Union—just barely. Should he try to free the slaves, he feared they would too secede. The nation could not survive such a disaster. With Maryland in rebel hands, it would be impossible to hold Washington. Kentucky, however, was the true prize, a two-edged sword that could cut either way. Rebel armies could use the Bluegrass State as a springboard for invading Illinois, Indiana, and Ohio. In Union hands, Kentucky exposed Tennessee and its seven Confederate neighbors to attack. A popular saying put it this way: "Lincoln would like to have God on his side, but he must have Kentucky."[35]

The Peninsular campaign caused Lincoln to change his mind. The setback proved that Frederick Douglass had been right all along. It was not enough simply to fight the Confederate armies. To win the war, Lincoln must reach behind those armies to the people who kept them in the field. On July 13, less than two weeks after the Seven Days' Battles, he took aides into his confidence. "We have played about our last card," he said during a carriage ride, "and must change our tactics or lose the game."[36] A desperate situation required a desperate solution. The commander in chief's duty was to save the Union at any cost. If slavery must die so the Union might live, then so be it. He intended to free the slaves as a military necessity. He had no constitutional power to free the slaves in states loyal to the Union. But in the rebellious states, he could act to seize enemy resources.

Early one morning, Lincoln came to the War Department telegraph office and asked for some writing paper. Then he sat at a table and began to work. It was slow going. Major Thomas T. Eckert, the officer in charge, recalled: "He would look out of the window a while, and then put his pen to paper, but he did not write much at once. He would study between times and when he had made up his mind he would put down a line or two, and then sit quiet for a few minutes. After a time he would resume his writing. . . ."[37] On that first day he did not fill a whole sheet of paper. When he left, he asked Major Eckert to keep the paper locked in a desk drawer; Eckert could read it, if he wished, but must not show it to anyone or discuss its contents. The President returned during the following days. On some days he wrote a line or two, and put question

marks in the margins. He was "tasting" every word to make sure it said exactly what he meant.

On July 22 Lincoln read a draft of the Emancipation Proclamation to his Cabinet. It said that unless the rebellious states returned to the Union by January 1, 1863, their slaves "shall be then, thenceforward, and forever free." Secretary of State Seward urged him to delay issuing it until Union forces won a decisive victory. Otherwise, he warned, emancipation would seem like a desperate gamble by a defeated government. The President agreed. He would use the extra time to prepare the North for the big change.

Lincoln understood the difference between a President and a king. A king commands his "subjects," while a President leads free citizens. A democratic leader may have to take people in directions they may not wish to go, but which he believes correct. He does this by listening to them, calming their fears, and gaining their trust. Emancipation would be the supreme test of Lincoln's leadership abilities.

Being a leader often entails having to offend some people to win or keep the support of others. In 1862, this meant offending black people—who could not vote—and reassuring whites—who could. Given the realities of Northern racism, Lincoln dared not be seen as sympathetic to black people. For example, on August 14, 1862, a group of

Titled "Abe Lincoln's Last Card, or Rouge-et-Noir," this cartoon appeared in the English magazine Punch *on October 18, 1862. Blind to the true meaning of the Emancipation Proclamation, many Englishmen saw it only as the last desperate act of a devilish gambler—Lincoln—faced with certain defeat.* Punch *spoke for England's nobility, who wanted to see America's democratic experiment fail.*

black leaders visited the White House. Lincoln gave them a long speech, urging them to persuade their followers to resettle in places like Haiti and Central America. "See our present condition," he said, "the country engaged in war!—our white men cutting one another's throats. But for your race among us there could not be war, although many men engaged on either side do not care for you one way or the other. Nevertheless, I repeat, without the institution of Slavery and the colored race as a basis, the war could not have an existence. It is better for us both, therefore, to be separated."[38] Lincoln said this while a draft of the Emancipation Proclamation lay in his desk drawer!

The leaders were furious. Frederick Douglass denounced Lincoln for "his pride of race and blood, his contempt for negroes and his canting hypocrisy."[39] In meetings throughout the North, free blacks scorned the idea of settling elsewhere. Why should they leave? Wasn't America their country, too? Didn't they have as much right to live there as any white person? Surely the facts spoke for themselves. Blacks were actually *more* American than most whites. At the time of the Civil War, barely 1 percent of black people had been born overseas.[40]

The White House meeting, however, was part of a carefully thought-out strategy. Knowing the importance of political positioning, Lincoln had used it to address a wider audience than the black leaders. By saying what he did, he sent a subtle message to millions of white Americans. They need not worry about *him!* Their President did not favor blacks. Yes, he hated slavery; he had never hidden that fact. But whatever he did in his official capacity, it had nothing to do with his personal feelings. They could rest assured that he would act only in the nation's best interests.

Lincoln spoke more directly in response to demands by the New York *Tribune,* an influential newspaper, that he abolish slavery without delay. He used the *Tribune's* criticism to pre-

Before becoming Lincoln's secretary of state, William Henry Seward was a U.S. senator from New York, a prominent lawyer, and an outspoken abolitionist. In 1867, he negotiated the purchase of Alaska from Russia for a mere $7.2 million. Called "Seward's Folly," it turned out to be one of the wisest purchases ever made by the U.S. government.

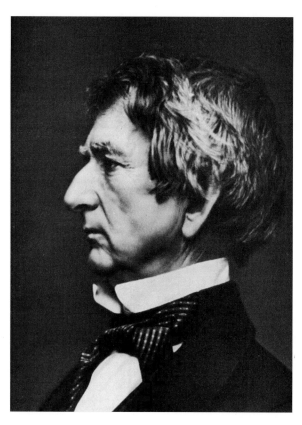

The first reading of the Emancipation Proclamation to President Lincoln's Cabinet, after an engraving of a painting by Francis B. Carpenter, 1866. While working on the picture, the artist lived in the White House for six months, during which time he observed the First Family in its daily life.

pare the nation further. "My paramount object in this struggle *is* to save the Union," he said in a public letter, "and is not either to save or to destroy slavery. If I could save the Union without freeing *any* slave I would do it, and if I could save it by freeing *all* the slaves I would do it; and if I could save it by freeing some and leaving others alone, I would do that. What I do about slavery, and the colored race, I do because I believe it helps the Union."[41] In other words, he would not ask Americans to fight for black freedom as such. Yet nobody should be surprised if he freed blacks to save the Union.

Antietam had been enough of a "victory" to justify the President's next move. On September 22, he called a special Cabinet meeting. He told members that, while the armies had been massing for battle, he had vowed to take victory as God's signal to issue the proclamation. Well, Lee had retreated. "God had decided this question in favor of the slaves."[42] Next day, the Preliminary Emancipation Proclamation appeared in Northern newspapers. The Confederacy had one hundred days to accept its terms or pay the consequences.

Would Lincoln sign the final proclamation? That became *the* question as the year 1862 drew to a close. The Republicans had suffered setbacks in the fall elections, and party leaders worried that their chief had gone too far on the slavery issue. Moreover, McClellan's replacement, Major General Ambrose E. Burnside, had crossed into Virginia with 125,000 men, only to be defeated at Fredericksburg. On December 13, he sent waves of infantry against rebel troops posted behind a stone wall outside the city. The result reminded a Georgia farmer of "an immense hog pen and them all killed."[43] Burnside lost over 12,600 men to Lee's 5,300.

News of Fredericksburg hit the President like a ton of bricks. "If there is a worse place than Hell, I am in it," he cried.[44] He fired Burnside and began the search for yet another commander. With this further setback, the pressure against signing the proclamation intensified. Yet he stood firm.

There were few festivities that New Year's Eve. Everywhere friends of emancipation held prayer services and vigils. Washington's black community held a "Big Watch-Meeting" in a church. Those who came never forgot the pastor's order not to pray standing up or on one knee. Everyone must "get down on *both knees* to thank God Almighty for his freedom and President Lincoln too."[45]

New Year's Day dawned, and still no word from the White House. During the afternoon, Lincoln spent three hours in the East Room, shaking hands with a line of well-wishers that stretched to the front door and beyond. His right arm ached.

During a break, he slipped away to his office, where the Cabinet waited to witness the signing. Never had he felt so sure he was doing the right thing. And seldom had he felt so nervous. The President apologized for his trembling hand and hoped they would not mistake an unsteady signature for hesitancy. Then he slowly wrote *Abraham Lincoln* at the bottom of the document. When he finished, he stood up straight and stared at the paper a moment. "If my name ever goes down in history, it will be for this act," he said.[46]

Henry M. Turner, a black minister, ran along Pennsylvania Avenue with a copy of the proclamation. He tried to read it to a gathering of blacks, but was so winded he handed it to a friend. At the words "thenceforward, and forever free," the crowd exploded with joy. "We're free now, bless the Lord! They can't sell my wife and child any more, bless the Lord!" a runaway slave cried. "No more that! no more that! no more that, now! President Lincoln has shot the gate!" Thousands of blacks surrounded the White House to cheer Lincoln and tell him that if he would "come out of that palace," they would hug him to death.[47]

That day fixed Lincoln's image in black people's minds for a century. Blacks adored him. His picture hung in their homes, schools, and churches. He became their Moses, their Great Emancipator sent by God to break the chains of bondage.

By the 1960s, however, many African-Americans saw him differently. Angered by America's continuing racism, they said the older generations had been naive. Malcolm X, for example, denounced Lincoln as a racist who "did more to trick blacks than any other man in history."[48] His Emancipation Proclamation had applied only to Confederate slaves, not those in the border states and enemy territory occupied by Union troops. Thus, where Lincoln could have freed slaves, he did not. And where he wanted to free them, he could not. Black people, therefore, had no reason to love him.

Frederick Douglass would have disagreed. Always quick to criticize the President, he also gave credit where it was due. Although the proclamation had not gone far enough, Douglass asked blacks to applaud "this righteous decree."[49] Given the realities of American racism, Lincoln had worked a miracle. "From the genuine abolition view, Mr. Lincoln seemed tardy, cold, dull, and indifferent, but measuring him by the sentiment of his country—a sentiment he was bound as a statesman to consult—he was swift, zealous, radical, and determined."[50]

Lincoln's action had been a giant step down a long road. There was no time from his inauguration in 1861 to New Year's Day, 1863, when the Confederates could not have saved the Peculiar Institution by returning to the Union. The Emancipation Proclamation, as the former slave said, had "shot the gate." It shut the door to compromise, insuring a fight to the finish.

This cartoon appeared in Harper's Weekly *on January 3, 1863. By then, Northerners were losing patience with Lincoln's inability to win the war. Columbia asks the President: "Where are my 15,000 sons—murdered at Fredericksburg?" Lincoln replies: "This reminds me of a little joke." Columbia cuts him short, saying: "Go tell your joke at Springfield."*

For the first time, the United States government had committed itself to freeing slaves. With a stroke of the pen, the President destroyed the worth of "property" valued at over three billion dollars. Wherever his armies went, they tore slavery out by the roots. His proclamation also gave the Civil War a new aim. It became a struggle for Union *and* freedom, or rather a new Union freed of slavery's curse and living up to the promise of the Declaration of Independence. News of the proclamation spread quickly among the slaves. Southern newspapers printed articles about it, which people with stolen educations read at secret gatherings. Overhearing whites discuss it among themselves, others passed the news along their "grapevine" telegraph. In certain isolated areas, whites first learned about it from their own slaves.

Music carried the message of freedom. The old spirituals had asked God for deliverance:

> *Go down, Moses,*
> *Way down in Egypt land.*
> *Tell old Pharaoh*
> *Let my people go.*

Now Lincoln, the modern-day Moses, had done just that, as we learn from this song:

> *Abe Lincoln freed the nigger*
> *With the gun and the trigger,*
> *And I ain't a-going to get whipped anymore.*
> *I got my ticket*
> *Leavin' the thicket,*
> *And I'm headin' for the Golden Shore!*[51]

Blacks did not wait to be given their freedom; they took it by themselves. Hundreds fled to the Union lines each day, bringing their masters unexpected hardship. It was not just a matter of losing a valuable investment. Hardship came in countless small ways. The Virginia woman who burst into tears did so not because her slaves had deserted, but because she had never learned to cook. Another Virginian noted that runaways had become *the* topic of conversation in the neighborhood. One day her little daughter, Nannie Belle, and her friend, Sallie, were playing "ladies." Sallie pretended to be an adult visiting a neighbor. "Good morning, ma'am, how are you today?" she asked. Nannie Belle replied with a sigh: "I don't feel very well this morning. All of my niggers have run away and left me."[52]

Those blacks who stayed behind—and a majority did—acted in ways that would have cost them dearly before the proclamation. Slaves openly violated the curfew, insulted their masters, and demanded wages. Masters, fearing open rebellion, became less demanding.

Finally, the proclamation helped Lincoln personally. Throughout his adult life, he had loved a political system based upon freedom, but which protected human slavery. The conflict in values made him miserable.

Not anymore. Now he could visit Duff Green's Row, a camp for runaways on Capitol Hill. He could let the tears flow as they sang "I Thank God I'm Free at Last" and other spirituals.[53] The Emancipation Proclamation put him at peace with himself. By freeing the slaves, Abraham Lincoln also freed himself.

5 NEW BIRTH OF FREEDOM

. . . We here highly resolve that these dead shall not have died in vain —that this nation, under God, shall have a new birth of freedom. . . .

LINCOLN, GETTYSBURG ADDRESS, NOVEMBER 19, 1863

By 1863, the Civil War had spread far behind the fighting lines. Besides the Confederate armies, the Union fought what the President called "the enemy in the rear," Northerners loyal to the South. At the very least, these rebels in civilian dress hurt the war effort by urging men not to enlist in the army. At their worst, they became enemy spies, burnt bridges, tore up railroad track, and cut telegraph wires. In the border states, young men like Jesse James joined guerrilla bands to terrorize Union sympathizers.

Lincoln believed the danger so great that he became the first President to limit civil rights in wartime. Using his emergency powers under the Constitution, he suspended the writ of habeas corpus, which protects a citizen from arrest without being told the reason or being held beyond a reasonable time without being charged. When that proved inadequate, he put Secretary of War Stanton in charge of internal security.

Edwin M. Stanton was a fussy little man with gold-rimmed spectacles and perfumed whiskers that reached to his chest. Friends called him the "Great Energy." The President dubbed him "Mars," after the Roman god of war. Hardworking and hard-fisted, he was a stickler for discipline, and no aide wanted to be around when bad news came from the front. Stanton pursued anyone suspected of opposing the war effort. He declared martial law in areas behind the front, allowing army officers to jail civilians without a jury trial. His detectives eavesdropped on conversations, paid informers, and searched private homes without warrants. His special agents closed down over thirty newspapers, arresting nearly a hundred publishers, editors, and reporters. Stanton's men arrested and imprisoned a total of 15,000 people for "unpatriotic" activities.[1]

Secretary of War Edwin M. Stanton was a tough-minded, able administrator whose bluntness made him countless enemies among the nation's military and political leaders. Lincoln, however, put up with his gruff manner and sharp tongue for the sake of the country.

Lincoln supported these actions. We must not forget the special nature of the Civil War. There had never been anything like it in America, and there were no guidelines for dealing with opposition during a rebellion that threatened the nation's very existence. The President placed the importance of keeping the union intact above individual rights. When, for example, Ohio Democrats denounced the arrest of a party leader for encouraging desertion, he lost his temper. "Must I shoot a simple-minded soldier boy who deserts, while I must not touch a hair of a wily agitator who induces him to desert?" he snapped. "I think that in such a case, to silence the agitator, and save the boy, is not only constitutional, but . . . a great mercy."[2] Such people were cowards, Lincoln thought, and he would not allow them to hide behind the same laws they wished to destroy. In short, the Constitution was not a suicide pact.

Although Lincoln hated bloodshed, he believed any weapon that shortened the war would save more lives than it claimed. Always on the lookout for new weapons, he welcomed inventors to the White House. Most had silly schemes, like giving soldiers "canoe-shoes" to cross streams without getting their feet wet. An Illinois man showed his "cross-eyed gun," a rifle with barrels going off to the right and left for use by cross-eyed soldiers. Another fellow brought a "bulletproof" vest made of iron links wired together. Lincoln promised to approve the device if it passed a simple test: the inventor must wear it on a shooting range. The fellow bowed and left the room.

Thaddeus Lowe's observation balloons were instant hits with the President. So was John D. Mills's contraption with a hand crank. Invited to turn the crank, Lincoln saw cartridges drop into a cylinder revolving in front of a firing pin. Amazed at this early-model machine gun, he dubbed it the "coffee-mill gun," because it resembled a coffee grinder. Although the gun did poorly in action, it signaled a revolution in weapons technology. Within fifty years, machine guns would be spraying battlefields at a rate of five hundred bullets a minute.

The exploding rifle bullet, another Lincoln favorite, would later be outlawed as too cruel for use even in warfare. Designed to burst after penetrating a victim's body, it caused massive wounds and agonizing pain. Christopher M. Spencer's repeating rifle also won presidential approval. The Civil War soldier normally carried a single-shot muzzle-loader; that is, he had to ram a fresh bullet down the barrel after each shot. The Spencer rifle, however, was a seven-shot breech-loader. It fired seven bullets stored in the breech, a chamber at the rear of the gun. After trying the weapon himself—he usually tested guns on open ground behind the Washington Monument—Lincoln ordered ten thousand Spencer repeaters for the cavalry.

The President demanded improved mortars, short-barreled cannon for dropping shells into trenches. He got them—iron monsters that fired hundred-pound shells from railroad flatcars. The explosions left survivors trembling. "They kill and wound more men with Mortar Shell than any other way for the last few weeks," a Johnny Reb wrote. "They throw them up and Drop them Right into the trenches when they Explode and tare to pieces all around them." Besides explosive shells, Lincoln gave orders to shoot incendiary shells into Confederate cities. These "fire shells," as he called them, had been tested on the White House lawn.[3]

Weapons, however, are useless without men to use them. And here the President had a serious problem. By 1863, the people's enthusiasm for fighting had vanished. No longer a short, glorious adventure, the Civil War had become a grinding ordeal with no end in sight. Enlistments declined. Desertions increased. Losses could be made up only by forcing men into the ranks.

Eight weeks after Lincoln signed the Emancipation Proclamation, Congress passed the first draft law in American history. The law made every able-bodied male from age twenty to forty-five eligible for military service. It was not popular. "Lincoln! Tyrant!" protesters shouted. "Lincoln! Slave driver!" Rather than be drafted, thousands of men headed for the western frontier, beyond the reach of the law. In several cities, mobs stoned recruiters and burnt draft offices.

African-Americans were another source of manpower. American blacks had a long tradition of military service. In colonial days, "free men of color" joined the British army. During the French and Indian Wars, and again during the American Revolution, black men wore red coats. Some became "chosen men," special assault troops selected for their courage and skill with the bayonet. The English general Lord Dunmore recruited an "Ethiopian Regiment" whose members had "Liberty to Slaves" inscribed on their belt buckles. On the American side, at least a dozen black patriots fought at Bunker Hill.[4]

During the War of 1812, one in six American sailors was a free black or a runaway slave. Always short of men, the navy cared little about a recruit's past life. Commodore Oliver Hazard Perry singled out his black crewmen for commendation during the Battle of Lake Erie, describing them as "absolutely insensible to danger." At the Battle of New Orleans in 1815, General Andrew Jackson, a slave owner himself, had an all-black battalion. Fine soldiers, they helped shoot down the flower of the British army, veterans who had defeated Napoleon. Federal law later barred blacks from serving in the army, though not in the navy. An old salt noted that in battle everyone is covered with gunpowder and looks alike—looks equally black.[5]

Free blacks saw the Civil War as their fight. The day after Lincoln's call for volunteers in 1861, blacks in New York City, Boston, and Philadelphia reported for duty. Frederick Douglass urged them on. The road to citizenship, he said, crossed the battlefield. "Once let the black man get upon his person the brass letters, U.S.; let him get an eagle on his button, and a musket on his shoulder and bullets in his pocket, and there is no power on earth which can deny that he has earned the right to citizenship in the United States."[6]

But the government wanted no black soldiers. Officials argued that blacks were inferior. On the one hand, they said, blacks lacked the discipline required of fighting men. On the other hand, their spirit had been crushed by centuries of slavery. Taught to "know their place" and behave meekly, they lacked the courage and initiative to stand up to a determined foe. Such racism ignored the facts of history. Oddly enough, it also conflicted with Southern fears that black people, given the chance, would fight like tigers.

President Lincoln shared these beliefs. He once told White House visitors that he doubted blacks would make good soldiers. "If I were to arm them," he said, "I fear that in a few weeks the arms would be in the hands of the rebels."[7]

Necessity, however, forced him to change his mind. Desperate for more fighting men, he used the Emancipation Proclamation as a recruiting tool. Not only did it free slaves in enemy territory, it allowed blacks to enlist in segregated units commanded by white officers.

At first, most Billy Yanks hated the idea of serving with blacks. "Pukey Abe's proclamation," they snarled, had turned the war for the Union into "an abolitionist war." Hundreds deserted, and thousands threatened to desert if they ever saw a black in uniform. In certain outfits, soldiers rioted against black recruits, wounding many and occasionally killing a few. At Ship Island, Mississippi, gunners on a warship were ordered to support three black units ashore. The gunners fired on the blacks instead of the enemy, mowing down their own men. A few angry soldiers kidnapped black "comrades" and sold them into bondage.[8]

Gradually, however, Billy Yank accepted the inevitable. Most soldiers, no matter how they felt about black people, wanted to end slavery so they could go home. They also realized that bullets are color-blind.

"Sambo's Right to Be Kilt," an army poem recited in an Irish brogue, put the case bluntly:

> *Some tell us 'tis a burnin shame*
> *To make the naygers fight;*
> *An' that the thrade {trade} of bein' kilt*
> *Belongs but to the white;*
> *But as for me, upon my soul!*
> *So liberal are we here,*
> *I'll let Sambo be murthered instead {of} myself*
> *On every day of the year.*
>
> *On every day of the year, boys,*
> *And in every hour of the day;*
> *The right to be kilt I'll divide with him,*
> *An' divil a word I'll say.*
>
> *Though Sambo's black as the ace o' spades,*
> *His finger a trigger can pull*
> *And his eyes run sthraight on the barrel-sights*
> *From under his thatch of wool.*[9]

Lincoln's recruiters fanned out across the North and the occupied areas of the South. Joining the army changed black men completely. Army recruiters described the ragged, hangdog appearance of former slaves— no fault of their own but of the state in which slave owners kept them. It did not take long, however, to transform not only the way they looked but their spirit. The process began with an army haircut that left only a half-inch of closely cropped hair on their skulls. After their dirty rags went into the fire and they had a bath in near-boiling water, they received a clean blue uniform. Recruits could hardly believe the change in themselves. "This was the biggest [thing] that ever happened in my life," said Elijah Marrs after his first roll call. "I felt like a man with a uniform on and a gun in my hand. I felt freedom in my bones."[10]

It took courage to be a black in blue. To discourage runaway slaves from enlisting, Confederates threatened to sell their families to harsh

A few of the nearly 200,000 black men who fought for the Union during the Civil War. These men belonged to the 107th Colored Infantry stationed at Fort Corcoran, one of the units defending Washington.

masters in distant states. In May 1863, the Confederate Congress ordered captives sold into slavery or executed according to the laws of their states. Like John Brown, their white officers would be hung for inciting rebellion.

In July, an outraged President Lincoln issued his own order. Titled the "Executive Order of Retaliation," it promised that for every Union soldier killed in violation of the laws of war, a Confederate prisoner of equal rank would be executed. And for every Union soldier enslaved, a Confederate soldier would be put to hard labor.

The Confederate government backed down. Ordinary Johnny Rebs, however, did not. Although the vast majority never mistreated prisoners, black or white, a trigger-happy minority killed them in cold blood. Rebels shot captured blacks while "attempting to escape." At Fort Pillow, Tennessee, in April 1864, troops under General Nathan Bedford Forrest massacred scores of black prisoners, including the wounded. After a skirmish with a black outfit, a North Carolina soldier wrote his mother that "several [were] taken prisoner & afterwards either bayoneted or burnt. The men were perfectly exasperated at the idea of negroes opposed to them & rushed at them like so many devils."[11]

Each atrocity gave birth to another, as blacks answered in kind. Black units occasionally fought under a black flag, a warning that they would take no prisoners or ask mercy for themselves if captured. At Fort

Blakely, Alabama, a Union officer reported "the niggers did not take a prisoner, they killed all they took to a man." Shooting Confederate prisoners became so common that Chaplain Henry M. Turner, the preacher who had raced along Pennsylvania Avenue with the Emancipation Proclamation, complained bitterly about these crimes.[12]

Blacks earned their comrades' respect in the only way soldiers can: through courage. On June 7, 1863, Confederates attacked Union outposts near Vicksburg, Mississippi. The defenders, two newly formed black regiments, threw back the attacks with bayonet charges. A month later, Union forces struck Fort Wagner, a Confederate position at the entrance to Charleston harbor. The Fifty-fourth Massachusetts Regiment, a black outfit from Boston, led the assault against massed artillery and rifles. The Confederates broke the assault with heavy losses, then buried the regiment's white colonel, Robert Gould Shaw, in a ditch "with his niggers." Shaw's father thought it an honor to have his son lie among so many brave men.[13]

In actions like these, blacks unmasked the lie of racism. And because of them, many a Billy Yank changed his mind. He began to see blacks as real soldiers, worthy brothers in arms. "Now," one wrote, "the man who declares that a man possessing devotion to his cause, fidelity and soldierly pride can't make a soldier, is simply a hopeless ass."[14]

The President reminded critics that blacks were risking their lives for the Union. "You say you will not fight to free negroes. Some of them are willing to fight for you," he said. On the day of victory, "there will be some black men who can remember that, with silent tongue, and clenched teeth, and steady eye, and well-poised bayonet, they have helped mankind" go forward. *That* was something to be proud of, a priceless gift to future generations. Blacks repaid the compliment. Whenever Lincoln visited black units, they cheered him with "The Lord save Father Abraham!"[15]

Officially, 186,017 blacks served in the Union armies, or 10 percent of the total force. Unofficially, the number may have exceeded 220,000, since light-skinned mulattoes often enlisted in white units. Whatever the number, blacks took part in 449 battles, thirty-nine of them major fights, and seventeen won the Congressional Medal of Honor for valor "above and beyond the call of duty." A total of 68,178 black soldiers died in action, of wounds, or of disease. An additional 29,000 blacks, or 25 percent of all seamen, served aboard Union warships. Four black sailors received the Congressional Medal of Honor. Thanks to the Emancipation Proclamation, at least 80 percent of African-American servicemen were former slaves.[16]

Until 1864, most blacks served in the Western armies under Ulysses S. Grant. Meanwhile, the Army of the Potomac faced the Army of Northern Virginia. Billy Yank knew Johnny Reb was a good soldier, but felt that he himself had not had the chance to show his true worth. The problem was leadership. It seemed that the rebels could do nothing wrong, while Billy Yank's own generals could do nothing right.

The President agreed. Having fired McDowell, McClellan, Pope, and Burnside, in January 1863 he turned to Joseph, or "Fighting Joe," Hooker. A West Point graduate and veteran of the Mexican War, Hooker, age forty-eight, had been in every battle from the Peninsular to

Second Manassas and Antietam. Six feet tall, blond, and blue-eyed, he had a rosy complexion, caused, some said, by drinking too much whiskey. Although he boasted loudly, nobody doubted his ability. General Hooker led from the front, encouraging his men by example. Like the Young Napoleon, he despised Lincoln, calling him "a played-out imbecile."[17] The country, he claimed, would do better under a military dictator.

Soon after making that remark, Fighting Joe was called to the White House. The expression on Lincoln's face showed it would not be a nice day. After some blunt remarks, the President handed him a letter and left the room. The latter said Hooker deserved his promotion as head of the Army of the Potomac. "And yet," it continued, "I am not quite satisfied with you. . . . I have heard, in such a way as to believe it, of your recently saying that both the Army and the Government needed a Dictator. Of course it was not *for* this, but in spite of it, that I have given you the command. Only those generals who gain successes, can set up dictators. What I now ask of you is military success, and I will risk the dictatorship. . . . And now, beware of rashness. Beware of rashness, but with energy . . . go forward, and give us victories."[18] Lincoln's rebuke stung Hooker, and he vowed to make good.

Hooker found his army camped along the Rappahannock River opposite Fredericksburg. Morale had reached an all-time low due to repeated defeats and supply shortages. Soldiers moped about camp, shivering in the damp cold for lack of warm clothing. Everyone seemed to have a runny nose, and few had escaped without a case of dysentery, a severe form of diarrhea that killed more soldiers than any other illness. Men drowned their sorrows in "rotgut" and "white lightning," cheap whiskey sold by civilian merchants called sutlers. Garbage littered the area, and latrines were filled to overflowing. Rats swarmed in the camp streets and the sleeping huts, flimsy wooden structures with dirt floors. Hundreds of men deserted each day.

Fighting Joe rose to the challenge. The moment he arrived, he ordered a thorough cleanup. Soldiers, and occasionally officers, stood knee-deep in muck with shovels, burying garbage as punishment for some offense. The sutlers vanished. Wagon trains rolled in with warm uniforms and fresh food. To cure homesickness, a major cause of desertion, the general issued two-week furloughs. Men knew that failure to return on time meant a court-martial and hard labor. If they deserted, no one else in their unit could go home. Anybody who did that to a comrade better not cross his path again!

Hooker's efforts paid off. Visitors saw the results in various ways. Soldiers treated one another with more respect. Gambling declined and drunkenness practically disappeared. Fighting Joe became a hero to his men. No only had he improved their living conditions, he gave them back their self-respect. During inspections, they cheered, threw their caps in the air, and sang:

OPPOSITE: *Although the odds were heavily in his favor, Union General Joseph ("Fighting Joe") Hooker suffered a disastrous defeat at the Battle of Chancellorsville. The disaster so unnerved the President that the secretary of war feared he might commit suicide.*

Tad Lincoln and his father, Washington, February 5, 1865. Although there is a book on the table and "paw" is holding a book, Tad was a slow learner and could not read until the age of twelve. This photograph was taken by Alexander Gardner ten weeks before the President's assassination.

For God and our country
We're marching along.
Joe Hooker is our leader;
He takes his whiskey strong.[19]

Lincoln spent the first week of April with the Army of the Potomac. Since the visit was also a "vacation," he brought along his wife and youngest son.

Father and son had drawn closer since Willie's death. Tad missed his brother and, sensing his father's unhappiness, turned to him for companionship. The boy might burst into a room, leap onto his father's lap, plant a kiss on his cheek, and rush away without a word. A closed door never stopped Tad, who interrupted important meetings with three quick taps followed by two slow bangs—Morse code for the number three. Lincoln always let him in, explaining "I promised never to go back on the code." The President ignored the stares of the men seated around the table and heard the boy out. Tad might have good reason for interrupting, like the time he promised a weeping woman that "paw" would send her wounded son home on leave. He did.[20]

An hour with Tad was like a day's rest. Whenever Lincoln had a chance, he romped up and down the White House hallways with Tad, playing horse and blindman's bluff. Putting on his stovepipe hat, he would take Tad's hand and go for a stroll. Tad's favorite destination was Joseph Stuntz's toy shop on New York Avenue. Mr. Stuntz had served in the European wars under Napoleon. Crippled by a leg wound, he now carved lifelike toy soldiers and told endless stories about the emperor. Lincoln bought Tad whatever he chose. "I want to give him all the toys I did not have and all the toys that I would have given the boy who went away," he told the shopkeeper.[21]

Yet there was nothing like the real article. Tad was fascinated by anything that had to do with the enemy. Any general who gave him a Confederate souvenir became a friend for life. Most of all, Tad wanted to see live rebels. So two staff officers took him and his father down to the Rappahannock shore. Peering through a spyglass, they saw what two days of shelling had done to Fredericksburg. Union artillery had turned the beautiful old city, one of George Washington's favorite spots, into a burnt-out ruin.

Confederate gunners also saw them. The "graybacks," as Tad called them, shouted that they had "whupped" the Yankees "right good." An officer heard the commotion and joined the gunners for a better look. Nobody could have mistaken the tall man on the opposite shore. Here was the chance of a lifetime, a chance to blow the enemy's supreme commander to kingdom come. But this officer was a gentleman. Rather than shoot at defenseless people, he took off his hat, bowed deeply, and left.

Lincoln strolled through the camps and visited the hospital tents, stopping to speak to nearly everyone. Fighting Joe had rolled out the red carpet in his honor, and a day seldom passed without a parade. One day, 17,000 horsemen clattered before the commander in chief, the largest cavalry force ever assembled in the New World. Another time, tens of thousands of infantry marched past the reviewing stand like a moving forest of bayonets, followed by four hundred cannons whose wheels churned the field into brown mush. Guests noted the President's reaction. Whenever officers saluted, he merely touched the brim of his hat. He returned the salutes of ordinary soldiers by removing his hat and holding it over his heart.

Lincoln and Hooker discussed the upcoming offensive. It was not going to be easy, the President believed. The Army of the Potomac numbered 135,000 men, more than double the Army of Northern Virginia. General Lee, however, had built twenty-five miles of trenches and strong points along the Rappahannock. Given enough ammunition, his men boasted, they could kill anyone who got within fifty yards of their line. Just let the "Lincolnpoops" come!

Fighting Joe had no intention of falling into the trap. Instead, he planned to slip behind Lee, drive him out of his defenses, and fight him in the open. While a small decoy force crossed the Rappahannock below Fredericksburg, his main force would leave camp under cover of darkness and cross further upstream. Swinging southward past Chancellorsville, it would march through the Wilderness of Virginia, seventy square miles of dense forest and winding streams, taking Lee by surprise.

Lincoln liked the plan. It was a good plan, but he had seen good plans before. McClellan's Peninsular plan had been excellent. So had Burnside's Fredericksburg plan. The problem was not in the plan, but in its execution. Fighting Joe worried him. The general could not keep his mouth shut. Forever bragging about his army, "the finest army on the planet," he stated that his only fear was that Lee would turn tail and run before it went into action. "My plans are perfect," he said, "and when I start to carry them out, may God have mercy on General Lee, for I will have none."[22]

Lincoln found this the most depressing thing about Hooker. The general's confidence bordered on recklessness. He always said "when I get to Richmond" and "after I have taken Richmond," never "if."[23] Yet *if* was the word to use when going against the team of Robert E. Lee and Stonewall Jackson. With them, any mistake was likely to be fatal.

Before returning to Washington, Lincoln gave Fighting Joe a lesson from nature. "The hen," he noted, "is the wisest of all of the animal creation, because she never cackles until the egg is laid."[24] That was sound advice, and a stern warning against overconfidence. Unfortunately, the general lacked the hen's wisdom.

Confederate scouts detected the Union troop movements, and Lee guessed their objective. Instead of retreating or waiting to be hit from behind, he struck first. During the Battle of Chancellorsville (May 1–4) that followed, Hooker's plan collapsed. Although his army outnumbered Lee's, numbers meant little in the Wilderness. Artillery and cavalry were no match for determined men shooting from behind trees. Infantry columns became lost in the undergrowth and smoke, downing their comrades with "friendly fire." Exploding shells ignited brushfires in which hundreds of wounded men died.

Fighting Joe went to pieces. He had expected General Lee to flee in panic, but when the Confederate defied the odds and attacked, Hooker lost his nerve. Like the Young Napoleon, he held back his reserves, giving Lee the victory that had eluded him at Antietam.

Chancellorsville cost Lee about 13,000 men, or 22 percent of his army killed, wounded, and missing. Hooker's losses numbered 17,000, or 13 percent of his force. These losses may seem small compared to those of twentieth-century battles, where casualties have soared into the tens of thousands. Nevertheless, the percentages tell a different story. Modern armies number hundreds of thousands, even millions, of fighting men. For them, a two-day loss of even 10 percent is an utter disaster. During the Civil War, armies often lost 20 percent within a few hours. Fighting Joe's only consolation was that Stonewall Jackson's own men had shot him by mistake. Surgeons amputated Jackson's left arm, and he was recovering when pneumonia set in. He died on May 10.

Lincoln knew a battle was raging, but had no idea of its progress. For security reasons, Hooker had clamped a news blackout on the combat area. Reporters were kept out entirely or prevented from leaving if they happened to be with the army when it broke camp. All the President could do was haunt the telegraph office and wait for a message.

On May 6, two days after Chancellorsville, Noah Brooks, a reporter for California's *Sacramento Union,* visited the White House with a friend. The two men were sitting in a room when the door opened and in walked the President. Lincoln's face was ash-gray, the color of the wallpaper. His hand shook as he held out a telegram. "Read it," he said in a loud voice. "News from the army." In cold, military language, the telegram announced the disaster. As Brooks read, Lincoln clasped his hands behind his back and paced back and forth across the room. "My God! My God!" he muttered. "What will the country say! What will the country say!" He left after a few minutes, still muttering.[25]

He went to the War Department to see Secretary Stanton. "Mars" was stunned; he had never seen the President so depressed. "My God, Stanton, our cause is lost!" he cried, his body trembling and beads of sweat forming on his forehead. After a moment, he added, "If I am not about early tomorrow, do not send for me nor allow anyone to disturb me." Those words sent a chill up Stanton's spine. Fearing Lincoln would drown himself in the Potomac, he told him to buck up and, for heaven's sake, try to get some sleep.[26]

Although Chancellorsville was a stunning victory, the greatest of Lee's career, he had only defeated a weak-willed opponent. The Army of the Potomac still existed. Given time for replacements to arrive and for supply dumps to be refilled, it would return even stronger. Only next time, Lee would face it without Stonewall Jackson. In days to come, he would sorely miss his chief lieutenant.

The reason lay on the banks of the Mississippi River a thousand miles to the west. There Ulysses S. Grant was proving to be a stubborn enemy. Like Lee, he believed that wars are won by fighting—*hard* fighting. He lived by a simple maxim: "When in doubt, fight!"

In the fall of 1862, Grant began a nine-month campaign to take the Confederacy's last stronghold on the Mississippi River. After the fall of New Orleans, Union forces controlled the river from its mouth to Vicksburg, Mississippi. Built on high bluffs overlooking the eastern bank, Vicksburg was a natural fortress, made stronger by thousands of troops and scores of cannons. Jefferson Davis called it "the nailhead that holds the South's two halves together." Abraham Lincoln agreed. "Vicksburg is the key," he said. "The war can never be brought to a close until that key is in our pocket."[27]

Vicksburg joined the Confederacy's western states—Texas, Arkansas, Louisiana—to its eastern states. It was a vital crossing point for Texas cattle, English rifles smuggled through Mexico, and mercury, a mineral used in manufacturing bullets. Arkansas supplied grain and hogs; Louisiana, sugar and rice. From Vicksburg, rickety trains carried these supplies to the Confederacy's eastern armies. Thus, if Vicksburg were taken, it would be only a matter of time before the Confederacy collapsed.

When Grant began his advance, Lincoln knelt in prayer. Although he seldom attended church, he believed God shaped human affairs according to a righteous plan. "I have been praying to Almighty God for Vicksburg," he confessed. "[I have] wrestled with Him, and told Him how much we need the Mississippi, and how it ought to go unvexed to the sea . . . and I reckon He understands the whole business from 'A to Izzard'. . . . We are going to win at Vicksburg. . . . I can't tell how soon. But I believe we will . . . and be in line with God's law besides."[28]

As Union forces closed in on Vicksburg, Jefferson Davis called an emergency Cabinet meeting. The majority wanted to rush troops to the danger spot without delay. Robert E. Lee did not. Sending reinforcements, he insisted, would weaken his army just as the enemy was recovering from Chancellorsville. Besides, the problem was more serious than Vicksburg.

By 1863, nobody in his right mind claimed that one rebel could whip five Yankees. Even if one could, it would not change the war's outcome. President Lincoln was replacing his losses through the draft, by enlisting blacks, and with European immigrants. The South, however, had to rely on the men it had when the struggle began. Unable to replace its losses, it was left weaker with each victory. Lee argued that the South must deliver a knockout blow while it still had the strength. He wanted to invade the North, cripple the Army of the Potomac, and capture Washington, Philadelphia, and New York. Public opinion would then force Lincoln to make peace on Confederate terms. The invasion would be a gamble, but the Confederacy's only hope of survival. The Cabinet agreed.

The Army of Northern Virginia crossed the Potomac at Harpers Ferry during the second week of June 1863. Marching through Maryland, it entered Pennsylvania toward the end of the month. Johnny Reb marched like a conqueror, though he looked like a tramp. He was usually barefoot, his dirty uniform in tatters; still, his rifle gleamed in the sunlight. Marse Robert, that sly fox, had given him two smashing victories within six months. Three was a lucky number, wasn't it? Nothing, it seemed, could break his winning streak.

Yet something *was* different. Fredericksburg and Chancellorsville had been fought on Confederate soil, and Antietam in friendly Maryland. Now, for the first time, Johnny Reb had invaded the North proper. Pennsylvania was Yankeeland to the core, the home of the Declaration of Independence and the Liberty Bell. Rebels had few friends in the Keystone State.

Pennsylvanians did not hide their feelings. In town after town, Johnny Reb passed through streets decorated with Old Glory and lined by crowds singing "The Star-Spangled Banner." A private recalled how refined women greeted his unit with sour looks and loud catcalls. "One female had seen fit to adorn her ample bosom with a huge Yankee flag, and she stood at the door of her house, her countenance expressing the greatest contempt for the barefooted Rebs; several companies passed her without taking notice; but at length a Texan gravely remarked, 'Take care, madam, for [our] boys are great at storming breastworks when the Yankee colors is on them.' " The patriotic lady fled in panic.[29]

Lincoln welcomed Lee as a cat welcomes a bird flying near its paw. "We cannot help beating him," he said, bursting with confidence.[30] Each day's march brought Lee further from his supply bases in Virginia. The Army of the Potomac had only to cut his supply line and beat him with its overwhelming numbers.

On June 28, a spy brought Lee disturbing news. Lincoln had replaced Hooker with a tough campaigner. George Gordon Meade was a friend from way back. Meade, age forty-eight, had served with Lee in the Mexican War. A native of Pennsylvania, the general stood six feet tall, had a high forehead, a big nose, and a fiery temper. Apparently he was incapable of smiling—soldiers described his expression as that of someone with a toothache biting into a hard apple. Staff officers dreaded having to report a mistake to Meade, whom they called a "damned old goggle-eyed snapping turtle."[31]

The armies met at a town near the Maryland border. Founded by James Getty in 1780, Gettysburg by 1863 had grown to a population of 2,300. Next to farming and building carriages, shaping young minds was Gettysburg's chief industry. Three colleges located in or near the town attracted students from neighboring states.

From July 1 to the 3rd, Gettysburg was the scene of a battle that became the greatest ever fought in the New World. Meade's 101,000 men held a two-mile line along Cemetery Ridge just south of town. To the west, Lee's 70,000 men occupied Seminary Ridge, named for the Lutheran seminary at its crest. The ridges over-looked a gently rolling valley of peach orchards, wheat fields, and hay meadows.

General George Gordon Meade. A stubborn man with a hair-trigger temper, he led the Army of the Potomac to victory at the Battle of Gettysburg in July 1863.

The Confederates struck first, and might have won easily, had Stonewall Jackson been there to take advantage of a breakthrough just north of the town. He was not, and the attack stalled. Meade rushed fresh troops to the danger spot, and the Union line held. On the second day, Lee tried to break the Union left in repeated assaults, all failures. Men tore at one another with animal ferocity. A farmer found two dead officers lying side by side, each with a bloody sword in his hand. Else-where, a Virginian and a Pennsylvanian lay with their hands around each other's throats. Yet even in battle, there was room for humor. Hit in the leg, Confederate General Richard ("Bald Dick") Ewell never flinched. "It don't hurt a bit to be shot in a wooden leg," he sang out.[32]

On the third day, Lee ordered a mass attack on the center of the Union line. It began with a thunderous artillery barrage to soften up the target. Hundreds of Yankees died, but their comrades held their fire. Meade was bluffing, and Lee took the bait. Thinking the Yankees were about to give way, he hurled 15,000 men at Cemetery Ridge. Since General George E. Pickett commanded the lead units, the assault is known as "Pickett's charge."

A swarthy man of medium height and powerful build, Pickett, age

A harvest of death. The bodies of Confederate soldiers await burial at Gettysburg. Since Civil War soldiers did not have name tags, thousands of men went to their graves anonymously, and their families never learned of their fate.

thirty-eight, wore his perfumed hair shoulder length. A Virginian by birth, he had been sent as a teenager to Illinois to read law in an uncle's office. There he met a rising lawyer named Abraham Lincoln. They became friends, and, after a while, he told the older man a secret: he found the law dull as dishwater. He did not want to be a lawyer but a soldier. Lincoln used his influence to get him an appointment to West Point. "I should like to have a perfect soldier credited to our dear old Illinois," he wrote the seventeen-year-old.[33]

Pickett became a good soldier, though not a perfect one. As he neared Cemetery Ridge, every Union rifle and cannon opened fire, sending a storm of hot metal crashing through his ranks. Soldiers fell, riddled with bullets. Shells exploded in the midst of tightly packed units, sending heads, arms, and legs flying into the air. Pickett's charge was a disaster. His main effort defeated, and with Union defenses holding firm, Lee decided that enough was enough. Next morning, July 4, he ordered his army to fall back to the Potomac.

Gettysburg set telegraph keys clicking. Across the North, newsboys shouted the headlines: VICTORY! VICTORY! EPIC BATTLE! REBELS ROUTED! Reporters noted how the news made civilians "very jolly." Stay-at-homes envied Meade's brave lads, thinking it glorious to be numbered among his "fallen heroes."

Had the fallen heroes been able to speak for themselves, they might have been less jolly. Gettysburg was a human tragedy of gigantic proportions. In three days of fighting, Lee's army suffered 22,638 casualties, compared to 17,684 for Meade's army. Pickett's charge alone claimed 6,467 in dead, wounded, and captured.

The July heat made the dead almost unrecognizable as human beings. A Confederate prisoner who helped in the burials left a vivid description of the scene. "The sights and smells that assailed us were indescribable—corpses swollen to twice their original size, some of them actually burst asunder with the pressure of foul gases and vapors. . . . The odors were nauseating and so deadly that in a short time we all sickened and were lying with our mouths close to the ground, most of us vomiting profusely."[34] Not all were buried. For years afterward, farmers kept finding the remains of men overlooked by the burial squads.

The wounded outnumbered Gettysburg's population by ten to one. Everything with a roof—homes, shops, churches, schools, stables, barns, storage sheds—became a hospital. Three hundred surgeons operated for five days straight, and each day orderlies dumped wagonloads of amputated limbs into burial pits near the town. Only a few feet from her front door, recalled a teenager named Tillie Alleman, "I noticed a pile of limbs higher than the fence."[35]

Dorothea Dix, the Union's chief of female nurses, earned the nickname "Dragon Dix" because she would not let "delicate" youngsters attend the wounded. They went anyhow. And they rose to the occasion. After assisting at scores of operations, Cornelia Hancock felt older than her twenty-three years. "I feel assured I shall never feel horrified at anything that may happen to me hereafter," she wrote her family in New Jersey. Gettysburg had made her mature quickly.[36]

Back in Washington, Lincoln waited anxiously for news from the front. When it came, he felt that God had answered his prayers. First, a telegram from Meade announced victory at Gettysburg. Four days later, on July 8, Grant reported the fall of Vicksburg. Besides the city, he had captured an entire Confederate army and its equipment: 31,600 prisoners, 172 cannons, 60,000 rifles. The President read the message, grinned, and said: "The Father of Waters again goes unvexed to the sea."[37] Now it was up to Meade. He had only to destroy the battered Army of Northern Virginia and the war would be over.

Lee retreated westward, slowed by heavy rains and a seventeen-mile wagon train filled with wounded soldiers. Floodwaters prevented the Confederates from crossing the Potomac. Trapped between the swollen river and the pursuing Yankees, Lee gave orders to dig in. If he had to go down, it would not be without a fight.

Lincoln urged Meade to attack at once. But Meade ordered the Army of the Potomac to dig in, too.

Lincoln became more desperate with each passing day. Why didn't Meade fight? Had Meade lost his nerve? Was Meade another McClellan? Another Hooker? The President had lots of questions, but no answers. Furious at the delay, he suspected treason.

Viewed from the White House, victory appeared a simple matter of advancing with determination. Viewed from Meade's headquarters, however, things were not simple at all. Long marches and hard fighting had left the army exhausted. Billy Yank had been going for weeks on little more than nervous energy. Now, with the battle over, he suffered a physical and emotion letdown. He was, as a private explained, "plumb wore out." So was his general. What with his constant activity before and during the battle—holding staff meetings, issuing orders, directing troop movements—Meade had not changed his clothes, eaten a warm meal, or washed for eleven days. He itched, and he stank, too. Groggy with fatigue, he had gotten by on two or three hours of sleep a night; on some nights, he did not sleep a wink. He wrote his wife that he had aged more during those days than in the last thirty years.[38]

Meade had yet another reason for caution. Johnny Reb was still a dangerous opponent. During questioning, prisoners seemed absolutely devoted to their cause. Asked if his men had had enough of fighting Yankees, an officer snarled: "We will fight them, sir, till hell freezes over, and then, sir, we'll fight them on the ice."[39] General James

Longstreet, Lee's second-in-command, wanted the Yankees to attack. The rebel position was so strong, he believed, that the battle would be a Gettysburg in reverse. We will never know, because Meade did not put Longstreet's idea to the test.

On July 14, the White House learned that the water level of the Potomac had dropped, allowing Lee to escape without losing a man. The President was devastated. Years later, Robert Lincoln, who had come home from Harvard University for the summer vacation, recalled that day. He had gone into his father's room, only to find him slumped over a table with his head cradled in his arms. For the first time in his life, Robert saw his father cry. Asked the reason, Lincoln answered that a God-given opportunity to end the war had been lost.[40]

After Gettysburg and Vicksburg, fighting slackened for the remainder of 1863. The armies rested, regrouped, and prepared for future battles.

Meanwhile, the citizens of Gettysburg fought their own special battle. Because Army burial squads had done such a poor job, summer rains uncovered thousands of graves. Wherever one turned, decomposing bodies lay exposed, forcing people to go about carrying smelling salts and handkerchiefs dipped in vinegar. The putrid odors made people faint, clung to clothing, and caused food to taste rotten. Nobody could recall a summer with so many flies.

A citizens' committee decided to buy land for a National Soldiers' Cemetery on the battlefield. After the governors of eighteen Northern states whose men had fought and died collected the necessary money, workers started laying out the new cemetery and reburying the dead. The cost: $1.59 per body.

The dedication ceremony was scheduled for the third week in November. Printed invitations went to thousands of public figures in the North. Although the President received an invitation, it was merely a courtesy; no one expected him to leave the capital except to see his generals or inspect the army. However, when he accepted, it seemed rude not to ask him to make "a few appropriate remarks." Edward Everett, a former governor of Massachusetts and America's leading orator, had agreed to deliver the main address.

Lincoln wanted to give a short speech not only to honor the dead, but to drive home the message of the Emancipation Proclamation: that the Civil War was a struggle for human freedom and equality. He began by jotting down ideas and phrases as they came to mind. One evening, he went to a performance at Ford's Theatre, only a short ride from the White House. He sat alone in a private box, unseen by the audience below, collecting his thoughts as he watched *The Marble Heart*, the story of a sculptor whose statues come to life. A popular actor named John Wilkes Booth played the leading role. The President admired Booth's acting style.

The day before Lincoln's departure for Gettysburg, Tad became seriously ill. Mary begged her husband not to go at such a critical time. Since Willie's death, she was more worried than ever. Lincoln understood her concern, but insisted on going anyhow. He had promised to speak and could not back out at the last moment.

The presidential train reached Gettysburg at sunset on November 18. Workers had decorated the station with American flags and black bunting. As he walked to the waiting carriage, Lincoln saw coffins arranged in neat rows on the station platform; hundreds of families were taking loved ones home for burial. He passed through the solemn crowd, a somber expression on his face.

After dinner at the home of David Wills, his host and Gettysburg's leading citizen, Lincoln went upstairs to put the finishing touches to his speech. At midnight, an aide brought a telegram from the First Lady. Moments later, the guard outside his bedroom got the surprise of his life. Suddenly the door swung open and the President stepped into the hallway in his nightshirt. "That telegram was from home," he announced. "My little boy is very sick, but is better."[41]

Morning. November 19, 1863.

The procession of honor guards and dignitaries got underway at 10:00 A.M., its destination Cemetery Hill at the northern end of Cemetery Ridge, where the Confederate advance had been halted on the first day of the battle. Lincoln rode a horse so small that his feet nearly touched the ground. Nearing the battlefield, he saw the skeletons of horses and the remains of trees splintered by gunfire. Civilians out to make a quick dollar displayed souvenirs—buttons, bullets, bayonets,

The procession to the cemetery where Lincoln delivered the Gettysburg Address.

canteens, shell fragments, cannonballs, army caps, bloodstained rags—on tables.

At the foot of Cemetery Ridge, a general leaned over in his saddle and pointed upward. "Think, Mr. President, of the men who held these heights," he said. Lincoln sat quietly a moment, studying the lay of the land. "Yes," he replied, "but think of the men who stormed those heights."[42] He considered George Pickett a friend and was proud to be the countryman of the brave soldiers he had led.

Edward Everett spoke for two hours, comparing the Union dead to the heroes of ancient Greece. Between 15,000 and 20,000 people surrounded the speakers' platform. After a while, unable to hear or bored with the speech, many lost interest and wandered off to tour the battlefield. By doing so, they risked their lives with every step. Unexploded shells still lay just below the surface of the ground; they would continue to kill the unwary for another sixty years. Souvenir hunters dig up live shells even today. Although caked with dirt and rust, they are still deadly.

Everett finished at two o'clock. Ward Hill Lamon, the master of ceremonies, stepped forward and cried, "The President of the United States." Lincoln rose, put on his spectacles, and began reading from a handwritten sheet of paper. The Gettysburg Address consists of ten sentences totaling 271 words.

Lincoln (circled) seated on the speaker's stand prior to delivering the Gettysburg Address. The man standing to his left, wearing a sash and top hat, is Ward Hill Lamon, the President's friend and self-appointed bodyguard.

Four score and seven years ago our fathers brought forth on this continent, a new nation, conceived in Liberty, and dedicated to the proposition that all men are created equal.

We are now engaged in a great civil war, testing whether that nation, or any nation so conceived and so dedicated, can long endure. We are met on a great battlefield of that war. We have come to dedicate a portion of that field, as a final resting place for those who here gave their lives that that nation might live. It is altogether fitting and proper that we should do this.

But, in a larger sense, we can not dedicate—we can not consecrate—we can not hallow—this ground. The brave men, living and dead, who struggled here, have consecrated it, far above our poor power to add or detract. The world will little note, nor long remember what we say here, but it can never forget what they did here. It is for us the living, rather, to be dedicated here to the unfinished work which they who fought here have thus far so nobly advanced. It is rather for us to be here dedicated to the great task remaining before us—that from these honored dead we take increased devotion to that cause for which they gave the last full measure of devotion—that we here highly resolve that these dead shall not have died in vain—that this nation, under God, shall have a new birth of freedom—and that government of the people, by the people, for the people, shall not perish from the earth.[43]

Lincoln folded his paper and returned to his seat. A photographer had set up his camera, but it all happened so quickly that he could not snap the shutter in time. The entire speech lasted two minutes.[44]

The audience sat still. No one applauded. No one said a word. Not a sound came from that vast throng. Everyone was shocked, confused, and disappointed. They had expected more, *much* more, and did not know what to make of the speech. After a few moments, comments like "Did he finish?" and "Is that all?" rippled through the audience.

Many journalists blasted Lincoln, denouncing the Gettysburg Address as "dull," "dishwatery," "silly," "flat," and "vulgar." Other journalists, however, praised it as a work of genius. Although the speech failed as oratory, they called it a masterpiece of literature. They were right. The Gettysburg Address must be read to be appreciated.

Its elegant phrases—"a new nation, conceived in Liberty," "all men are created equal," "a new birth of freedom"—went beyond the Emancipation Proclamation itself. They clearly defined the struggle as a crusade for humanity and democratic values. Without Lincoln's words, Gettysburg would have been merely another Civil War slaughterhouse. With them, Lincoln called for a rededication to the ideals of the Declaration of Independence. In 1863, as in 1776, equality was still worth fighting for, and freedom for *all* people still worth dying for. Those who lay in soldiers' graves at Gettysburg had died for a noble ideal. In doing so, they had proven once again that freedom is not free.

6 A QUIET LITTLE FELLOW

He's the quietest little fellow you ever saw. . . . The only evidence you have that he's in any place is that he makes things git! Wherever he is, things move!

ABRAHAM LINCOLN, 1864

The art of war is simple enough. Find out where your enemy is. Get at him as soon as you can. Strike at him as hard as you can and as often as you can, and keep moving on.

ULYSSES S. GRANT, 1864

A soldier came up to Lincoln during one of his excursions with Tad. "I'm from Indianny!" he said proudly, holding out the rough hand of a farmer.

"So am I," the President replied, shaking hands warmly. "I almost wish I was back there again."

"That's jest what I was a-wishin' myself, but instid of that I've got to go back to camp. Ain't they a-workin' ye pretty hard, Mr. Lincoln?"

"I reckon they are."[1]

That was an understatement. By 1864, the job was devouring the man in the White House. The constant worry. The strain of always having to make vital decisions. The guilt of knowing that every decision brought misery and death. Lincoln hated it. It was torture.

Photos taken in 1861 and 1864 show dramatic changes. The earlier Lincoln appears robust, healthy, and clear-eyed. Three years later, the cheeks are hollow and the face furrowed by deep worry lines. White House visitors described his complexion as pale, his eyes showing "profound sadness." The President complained of insomnia, an inability to sleep; and when he did fall asleep, guards heard him moaning through the bedroom door. His hands and feet seemed always to be cold. He had searing, pounding headaches. "If to be head of Hell is as hard as what I have to undergo here," he groaned, "I could find it in my heart to pity Satan himself." He told a congressman, "This war is eating my life out."[2]

Lincoln needed a general who could lift the burden from his shoulders. He needed a man who could not only devise plans, but stick to them without making impossible demands or excuses for setbacks. That was a tall order, as nearly three years of fighting had shown. By 1864, however, the President had found his man: "Unconditional Surrender" Grant.

Grant, age forty-two, was easy to ignore in a crowd. A plain-looking man, he stood five feet eight inches tall, weighed 135 pounds, had a high forehead, light brown hair, and gray eyes. After graduating from West Point and serving as a captain in the Mexican War, he left the army rather than face charges of being drunk on duty. A failure at everything except as a husband and father, he spent the seven years before the Civil War doing odd jobs to feed his family. Things grew so desperate that he swallowed his pride and became a clerk in his father's leather goods shop in Galena, Illinois.

The war turned Grant's life around. Although he held no strong opinions on slavery, he considered secession illegal. Answering Lincoln's call for volunteers after Fort Sumter, he reenlisted and quickly rose to brigadier general. Such rapid promotion would have been impossible in the old army, where lieutenants waited twenty years to become captains. In 1861, however, trained officers were so scarce that anyone with a West Point diploma automatically qualified for high rank.

Those who saw Grant for the first time wondered if there had not been a mistake. His rumpled uniform and unpolished boots resembled a laborer's outfit, not a general's. Nor did he carry himself like a soldier. Grant had stooped shoulders and walked with a shuffle, a cigar clamped tightly between his teeth. A shy man, he blushed whenever anyone used bad language. The general never raised his voice, and the strongest words in his vocabulary were "by jinks," "by lightning," and "by thunder." Grant was tone deaf, and knew only two songs: "One is Yankee Doodle, and the other isn't."

Yet this gentle man had toughness and grit. A brother officer said it best: "He habitually wears an expression as if he had determined to drive his head through a brick wall, and was about to do it."[3] Nothing rattled Grant. He might be roused from a deep sleep by news of an enemy attack and instantly issue a stream of precise orders. No rush, no fuss, no excitement. The more frantic things became, the calmer he grew—a strange inner calm in which he seemed not to be part of the action, but viewed it from far away. Once he set a goal, he never wavered, never doubted, never turned back. Oddly enough for a fighting general, he could not stand the sight of blood. Blood made him woozy; his meat had to be broiled dry as shoe leather.

Alcohol was Grant's only weakness. He drank not for pleasure, but out of loneliness and boredom, particularly when separated from his wife for long periods. But if his "Dear Julia" was nearby, he never touched the stuff. So she and at least two of their four children traveled with the army whenever possible. They lived in everything from tents and barns to plantation Big Houses. The Grant children were not strangers to the sounds of battle. Papa's soldiers, many with children of their own, adored them. Combat veterans watched their language around Grant's "young 'uns."

During the Vicksburg campaign, officers jealous of his quick rise spread rumors that Grant was drinking again. At first, Lincoln brushed the rumors aside with a joke. If whiskey allowed Grant to win battles, then, he said, he would send a barrel of the general's favorite brand to each of his commanders. When congressmen demanded Grant's dismissal, Lincoln insisted, "I can't spare this man; he fights."[4]

Senator Ben Wade, however, did not let the matter drop. During a visit to the White House, he said that Lincoln absolutely *must* fire him—or else! "You are on your way to hell, sir," the Ohio Republican snarled. The President looked Wade straight in the eye, an impish smile crossing his lips. "Senator," said he, "that is just about the distance from here to the Capitol, is it not?"[5] Lincoln made a lifelong enemy, since the senator never forgave a rebuke. Yet he had also made his point. Grant stayed.

In February 1864, Lincoln asked Congress to revive the rank of lieutenant general. The army's highest rank, it had been held by only two

Mathew Brady took this picture of Ulysses S. Grant outside his tent at Cold Harbor, Virginia, in 1864. Despite severe losses at the Battle of Cold Harbor, Grant retained the President's confidence. The First Lady, however, called him a "butcher."

men: George Washington on a permanent basis, and Winfield Scott as an honorary title. Congress obliged, and the President named Grant to the post.

Grant traveled to Washington to receive his commission. On March 8, he checked into Willard's Hotel with his thirteen-year-old son, Fred. After dinner, he walked the two blocks to the White House. He walked alone, in almost pitch-darkness, toward the flickering lights. The First Family was holding its weekly reception, so he took a place at the end of the receiving line, like an ordinary guest. Up ahead he could see the President, towering over everyone else. Lincoln looked awkward in formal evening dress, with a collar a size too big and a clumsily tied necktie. Already they had something in common: messiness.

"Why, here is General Grant!" said Lincoln, spying him from across the room. "Well, this is a great pleasure, I assure you!" They had never met, but he had seen Grant's picture in the newspapers.[6]

The President's words set off a mob scene. People had heard so much about the general that they could not contain their excitement. They cheered, shouted, and pressed around the hero. Women jostled one another for the chance to introduce themselves, and more than one had the train of her silk dress trampled in the stampede. It got so rowdy that Secretary of State Seward made Grant stand on a sofa to give everyone a better look. Bashful and blushing, his face beet-red, Grant shook the hands that reached out from every direction. Beads of sweat rolled down his face, and the veins in his neck bulged. "For once at least the President of the United States was not the chief figure in the picture," a guest recalled. "The little scared-looking man who stood on the crimson-covered sofa was the idol of the hour."[7]

Next morning, Grant received his commission at a formal ceremony. Afterward, Lincoln took him aside for a private conversation, the first of many. Grant remembered every detail of their talk, and described it in his *Personal Memoirs* twenty years later. The President explained that he had hoped to leave the war to the generals. Their bungling, however, had forced him to become involved in military affairs. All he wanted— all he *ever* wanted—was somebody to take responsibility and call on him for help as needed. The general asked if the President had any special instructions. Lincoln replied that the country expected Grant to take Richmond. Could he? Yes, he could, Grant replied, and would, if he had the troops.[8]

Grant began by visiting the Army of the Potomac camped around Brandy Station, Virginia. Reining in his horse outside General Meade's tent, he saw a huge flag on a pole topped by a golden eagle. "What's this?" he asked a staff officer. "Is Imperial Caesar anywhere about?"[9] There was no need for an answer; bystanders got the message from the tone of Grant's voice. This messy little man meant business. He had decided to make his headquarters with their army. Although Meade would still be in charge of its daily affairs, Grant would direct its operations as part of a larger plan.

Known as the Grand Plan, this was an updated version of Lincoln's earlier strategy. The President explained it by using an Irish folktale set to verse, but with one change:

> *There wanst was two cats in Kilkenny,*
> *And aitch thought there was one cat too many;*
> *So they quarreled and fit,*
> *And they gauged and they bit,*
> *Till excepting their nails,*
> *And the tips of their tails,*
> *Instead of two cats there warn't any.*

The change, he said, was that "our cat has the longest tail."[10]

Lincoln and Grant understood the importance of having the longest tail—that is, the largest army. By 1864, the Union's eastern and western armies had won solid victories, but not solid enough to end the war. This was because they fought separately, never as part of a team with a unified plan. Now those days were gone forever.

The Grand Plan called for the armies to attack everywhere and at once. As Lincoln had suggested in 1861, this would prevent the Confederacy from shifting troops from one front to the other. Victory would not come easily or cheaply. Yet an aggressive strategy promised to be the most economical. Invade, fight, retreat, invade again: it made no sense to continue the vicious cycle. Better to push ahead, take losses,

and finish the war. Never again would a Confederate army be allowed to escape.

Grant gave his commanders their assignments. The Army of the Potomac, 120,000 strong, would attack the 64,000-man Army of Northern Virginia. "Lee's army will be your objective point," he told Meade. "Where Lee goes, so will you go."[11] It would be good if Meade took Richmond, but not essential. For while Meade pressed Lee, other Union forces would take the offensive in the Deep South.

Lincoln's determination to hold Kentucky at any cost was about to pay off. Already Grant had used it as a staging area for advances into Mississippi and Tennessee. The capture of Vicksburg had cut the Confederacy in half. A second invasion, this time from Tennessee, would slice off another chunk of enemy territory. Major General William Tecumseh Sherman had orders to invade Georgia with 100,000 men. Outnumbering the defenders by two to one, he would plunge into the enemy heartland, destroying its resources as he went. While Meade kept Lee busy in Virginia, Sherman would chop the Confederacy into pieces behind his back.

Grant turned the Union armies into well-oiled fighting machines. Hundred-car freight trains chugged into base camps loaded with beans and bullets, uniforms and shoes, tents and medical supplies. Rear-area units that had never seen combat found themselves at Brandy Station. Veterans lined the roads, glad to see them exchange their "soft pads" for hard ground. Certain cavalry outfits turned in their horses for infantry rifles, which pleased the veterans no end. Infantrymen told how a mule brayed as former "hoss" soldiers slogged into camp. A dust-covered trooper turned and said: "You needn't laugh at me—you may be in the ranks yourself before Grant gets through with the army."[12]

In Washington, you did not have to be a genius to know something big was coming. The signs were visible everywhere. Military hospitals took deliveries of fresh supplies and new coffins—piles of them kept under canvas tarpaulins. Troops constantly marched through town, bound for Brandy Station. One day, Lincoln watched thousands of them from the balcony of Willard's Hotel. Clouds gathered and lightning flashed. Rain fell in sheets. Everyone got soaked to the skin. Aides urged the President to go indoors. He refused. "If *they* can stand it, I guess I can," he said as the scorched, bullet-torn flags passed along Pennsylvania Avenue.[13]

The Grand Plan called for Grant to cross the Rapidan River a few miles below Lee's defenses. Like Fighting Joe Hooker, he intended to pass through the Wilderness and slip between Lee and Richmond, forcing the Confederates to abandon their positions and fight in the open.

Wednesday, May 4, 1864. After breaking camp, the Army of the Potomac crossed the river on several floating bridges built by military engineers. Besides its men, the army had 274 cannons, 56,000 horses and mules, 835 ambulances, and 4,300 supply wagons. A reporter estimated that if the wagons were arranged in single file, they would stretch seventy-five miles.

Lee was waiting. For days his scouts had observed Yankee bridge-building and troop movements. Already a plan had formed in his mind. He would make history repeat itself. Just as Grant was retracing Fighting Joe Hooker's route, Lee meant to fight another Chancellorsville. He would let the invaders get entangled in the Wilderness, then hit them with all he had.

The Yankees got across the river without opposition. That in itself gave veterans the jitters. It was *too* easy, they thought, so unlike the aggressive Lee. Where was he? What was he up to? Whatever it was, it could not be anything good for them.

After an all-day march, they camped on the old Chancellorsville battlegrounds. Exactly a year and a day since that battle, the place gave

OPPOSITE: *One of General Grant's "artillery parks" at City Point, Virginia, in 1864. The cannonballs in the foreground are hollow and filled with gunpowder. Ignited by a fuse, they are meant to explode over their targets, showering the men beneath with sharp metal fragments. Behind them are mortars, short-barreled cannons that throw explosives or heavy iron balls at steep angles. In the background are dozens of long-barreled cannons, able to fire exploding shells more than half a mile.*

Skeletons found in the Wilderness during Grant's invasion of Virginia in 1864. All the remains shown here are those of soldiers killed in the Battle of Chancellorsville the previous spring.

Billy Yank the creeps. Stonewall Jackson's arm was supposed to be buried nearby, surely a bad omen. Like Gettysburg, the ground was strewn with broken equipment and bodies unearthed by rain. Cavalry horses pawed at bones wrapped in rotting scraps of blue cloth. Skulls, bleached white, shone in the moonlight. On a spot thirty feet square, soldiers counted fifty skulls, their eyeless sockets staring into space. A soldier kicked a skull into the midst of a group gathered around a cooking fire. "That is what you are coming to," he said "and some of you will start toward it tomorrow." He meant to be funny. Nobody laughed.[14]

The Confederates launched a surprise attack at daybreak. For two days, May 5–6, great armies grappled amid raging forest fires. Survivors called the Battle of the Wilderness "an Indian war on a grand scale." It is a good analogy. As in an Indian war, small, isolated bands of men fought countless actions. Blinded by the smoke and brush, units shot in the enemy's general direction, hoping not to hit their own men.

U.S. Grant sat under a tree, his back propped against the trunk. Bullets chipped the bark above his head and sent branches crashing down around him. Explosions shook the ground. The general just sat there, calmly smoking a cigar and writing orders in his clear, delicate hand. Send a reserve regiment here! Put a gun battery into action over there! Find the enemy! Hit him fast, hit him hard, and hit him often! Fight!

Folks in Washington waited impatiently for news. Once Grant had crossed the Rapidan, no word could get through, thanks to Confederate cavalry patrols. Anxious congressmen called at the White House to beg for the tiniest shred of information. If anyone knew anything, they supposed, it must be the commander in chief.

Lincoln knew nothing. "I can't tell you much about it," he joked. "You see, Grant has gone into the Wilderness, crawled in, drawn up the ladder and pulled in the hole after him, and I guess we'll have to wait till he comes out before we know just what he's up to."[15] But the suspense was agony. The President scarcely slept for two nights. He paced the floor with his hands clasped behind his back, black rings under his eyes. Although impatient to hear from the front, he dreaded the news. So many generals had disappointed him that, inwardly, he braced himself for yet another failure.

On the night of May 7, Henry Wing, a reporter for the New York *Tribune,* knocked at the White House door. Wing had come from Grant's headquarters with a personal message for the President. The butler hurried him into Lincoln's office.

Wing's journey to Washington was an adventure in itself. The reporter dared not travel in his fine civilian suit, much less in a Yankee uniform, for fear of rebel patrols. So, putting on shabby jeans and wooden-soled shoes, he disguised himself as a Confederate messenger and headed for the capital seventy miles away. Sure enough, he met Confederate scouts and rode with them until they grew suspicious—so suspicious they decided to hang him as a spy. Wing dived into a stream and swam to the opposite bank, bullets whipping the water inches from his head. At Manassas Junction, he hitchhiked to the capital on an army locomotive.

Grant! You come from General Grant! Lincoln pulled the reporter into his office and took him to the map table. Now explain!

After describing the situation, Wing repeated Grant's message. "General Grant told me to tell you, from him, that, whatever happens, there is to be no turning back."

Then it happened. Suddenly, the reporter felt two bony arms enclosing his body like iron bands. They drew him closer, closer, until he felt a wet kiss on his face.[16]

As Wing was being kissed, Grant's troops were leaving the Wilderness. Veterans knew the way even in the dark; it was Fighting Joe Hooker's retreat route. Again they had fought bravely. And again their general had lost his nerve—or so they thought. But when they reached a crossroads, they saw military police directing the columns to the right. To the right! To the south! They were not retreating, after all, but going deeper into Confederate territory. Their spirits rose. Soldiers burst into a black spiritual, "Ain't I Glad I'm Out of the Wilderness!" Then they knew it: there would be no turning back until the war ended and they could go home. The Army of the Potomac finally had the leader it deserved.

Lee did not feel like a winner. True, he had hurt the Yankees badly; Grant's losses totaled 17,666, compared to 7,750 Confederates killed, wounded, and missing. Yet victory is not simply a matter of piling up bodies. Although Lee's losses were far fewer than Grant's, they were higher than he could afford. The North's "Kilkenny cat" still had the longest tail. Worse, Lee had wanted a replay of Chancellorsville to cripple the enemy for the rest of the year. Here, too, he failed. Grant had taken his hardest blows and come back for more, something no opponent had ever done. The quiet little fellow had seized the initiative. From now on he would make the moves, while Lee could only react. Lee would continue the fight with his usual skill and daring; after all, he *was* General Lee. But he knew deep down that the Wilderness had been a turning point. It was the beginning of the end for the Confederacy.

As Grant moved South, Lee followed, keeping his army between the invaders and Richmond. The move became a continuous running battle. "My sainted Love," a Johnny Reb wrote his sweetheart. "If the Yankee cusses will let me alone, I will write you. U.S. Grant is a 'bull-dog,' and Meade a match for the devil. No matter how deep we get into the woods, the Yanks are sure to find us. They fight more fiercely than I have ever seen them before. They build strong works [field defenses], and then our brave officers order us to charge them. We have done so, and have gotten hell every time. My dear, you will excuse this language, for if you were here you would say hell, too. Do not blame me, my sainted love, but I really wish I was out of this army and joined to you by the holy bond of matrimony. I must close; the Yankees are coming."[17]

The armies would pause for a full-scale battle, rest a few days, and then continue southward. On May 12, at Spotsylvania Court House, Grant broke the Confederate line in a dawn attack, only to have Lee send reinforcements to plug the gap. At Cold Harbor, on June 3, Grant sent human waves twenty-eight feet deep against rebel trenches. Sheets of flame and lead literally blew the attackers away. The main assault lasted twenty minutes. Union dead covered five acres of ground so thickly that you could have walked on them without touching the earth. The cost: ten thousand casualties—five hundred a minute, ten a second. "It was not war; it was murder," said one of Lee's aides.[18] Still Grant kept on moving. On June 13, he crossed the James River and attacked Petersburg, a rail center twenty miles south of Richmond. Again Lee sent reinforcements, saving the city and blocking the Union advance. Grant was stuck. Unable to push ahead, he dug in for a siege.

From Wilderness to Cold Harbor, from May 5 to June 3, Grant lost some 60,000 men, nearly the entire strength of Lee's own army; Lee lost 25,000 men. The wounded poured into Washington. In the hospitals, it seemed as if the cutting and sewing would last forever. Well-stocked hospitals ran short of medicines and bandages. Surgeons collapsed from fatigue. "I tell you, young man," a frustrated surgeon growled at an assistant, "I'd rather be in *Hell*—with a broken *back*—trying to eat *soup*—out of a *bottle*—with a *fork*—than in this damned hole!" Yet duty came first. The surgeon stayed at his post.[19]

Unlike our twentieth-century Presidents, none of whom ever saw the wounded fresh from the battlefield, Lincoln saw them every day. Lines of ambulances passed his windows at all hours. On his rides from the White House to the Soldiers' Home, his carriage gave ambulances the right-of-way at street corners. Lincoln could not help looking inside and hearing the pitiful moans. "Those poor fellows," he would exclaim. "I cannot bear it. This suffering, this loss of life is dreadful." The artist Francis B. Carpenter was living in the White House while painting a picture of Lincoln reading the Emancipation Proclamation. Carpenter recalled how, as the President posed, he had "the saddest face I ever saw. There were days when I could scarcely look into it without crying."[20]

On May 13, Lincoln rode across the Potomac to visit the hospital at Arlington House, Robert E. Lee's former estate. Out in Mary Lee's garden, he found dead soldiers in their coffins awaiting burial. Nothing could be done, however, because the military cemetery in Washington was full. So Lincoln ordered the dead buried amid the flower beds and fruit trees. Graves were dug, prayers read, and the first bodies lowered

A Confederate soldier killed during the siege of Petersburg in 1864. The wooden devices are movable barricades made of logs studded with sharpened sticks.

into the ground that would be called Arlington National Cemetery, the final resting place for thousands of America's war dead from then on.

The nation wept. People had expected casualties, but nothing like these. Many, including the First Lady, blamed Grant. The general needlessly killed young men, she stormed—might even kill her dear Robert if she let him enlist, which she would not. "He is a butcher and is not fit to be at the head of an army," she told her husband. "Yes, he generally manages to claim a victory, but such a victory! He loses two men to the enemy's one. He has no management, no regard for life. . . . I could fight an army as well myself. According to his tactics, there is nothing under the heavens to do but march a new line of men up in front of the rebel breastworks to be shot down as fast as they take their position, and keep marching until the enemy grows tired of the slaughter. Grant, I repeat, is an obstinate fool and a butcher."[21]

"Well, Mother, supposing we give you command of the army," Lincoln replied. "No doubt you would do better than any general that has been tried."[22]

Lincoln trusted Grant and vowed to support him despite the critics, or how loudly Mary scolded. Grant must proceed with the Grand Plan. The President's advice was short and simple: "Hold on with bull-dog grip, and chew & choke, as much as possible."[23]

The siege of Petersburg was in full swing when Lee sent 15,000 men to attack Washington. Although forty forts ringed the city, Grant had taken away the bulk of their troops. Lee did not expect to seize the capital; even if it fell, his force was too small to hold it for more than a few days. The idea was to throw Grant off balance, possibly force him to abandon the siege.

News of the rebel approach threw Washington into a panic. Raw recruits and "walking wounded," soldiers able to leave their hospital beds, filed into the forts. Government workers traded their pens for guns and drilled on vacant lots. Grant debated whether to go in person, but decided it would be exactly what Lee wanted. In the Southerner's place, he would have done the same thing. Instead, he sent 13,000 men under Major General Horatio G. Wright.

The rebels appeared on July 11. Next day, they tested the city's defenses. Their heaviest blow fell at Fort Stevens, north of the capital and only four miles from the Soldiers' Home, where the First Family was escaping the summer heat.

Lincoln and his wife came to see the fight for themselves. Mary kept under cover, peering out only occasionally. Her husband, however, stood on the wall beside General Wright, a perfect target in his black suit and stovepipe hat. It was the first (and only) time a President of the United States exposed himself to enemy gunfire. And for the first (and only) time, a President saw men killed in action.

"The Dictator," a giant mortar mounted on a railroad flatcar. U.S. Grant used scores of heavy mortars during the siege of Petersburg.

As Lincoln watched, an army surgeon fell within five feet of him. General Wright turned white as a sheet. "Mr. President," he said firmly, "I know you are the commander of the armies of the United States, but I am in command here, and as you are not safe where you are standing, I order you to come down."[24]

Order the President to come down! Never! "The Commander in Chief of the Army mustn't show any cowardice in the presence of his soldiers, however he may feel," Lincoln replied.[25] He had vowed never to show fear, and he meant to keep that vow, rebel bullets or not. He stayed put.

A soldier fell dead three feet away, a bullet in his brain. That did it. A twenty-three-year-old captain clutched Lincoln's arm and dragged him under cover, crying "Get down, you fool!"

The commander in chief got down. Their attack broken, the rebels retreated.

"Goody-bye, Captain Holmes," Lincoln said afterward. "I'm glad to see you know how to talk to a civilian." Captain Holmes was Oliver Wendell Holmes, Jr., a lawyer by profession and a future justice of the U.S. Supreme Court.[26]

With Grant stalled in Virginia, Lincoln hoped for better news from the Deep South. General Sherman, the commander there, was a colorful character. A tall, wiry redhead of forty-four, Sherman had a razor-sharp mind, strong opinions, and a wicked temper. Soldiers described him as a bundle of nervous energy who never sat still for more than two minutes and needed less than four hours' sleep a night. "If he walked, talked or laughed, he walked, talked or laughed all over. He perspired thought at every pore."[27] Nicknamed "Uncle Billy," Sherman despised black people and thought slavery the best thing that ever happened to them. Yet he despised rebels more, and would do anything to smash the Confederacy.

Sherman invaded Georgia three days after Grant crossed into Virginia. His objective was the city of Atlanta, a railroad center with factories and warehouses vital to the Confederate war effort. Uncle Billy advanced cautiously, fighting as little as possible, and then only on ground of his own choosing. Rather than attack strong positions, he slipped around them, forcing the defenders to fight or retreat. They retreated.

Johnny Reb held him in awe. "Sherman gits on a hill," a prisoner explained, "flaps his wings and . . . yells out, 'Attention! Creation! By kingdoms right wheel! March!' And then we git!"[28]

Only once, at Kennesaw Mountain, did he order a head-on assault. It cost 2,500 men in less than an hour. Sherman stayed calm—at least outwardly. He wrote his wife: "I begin to regard the death and mangling of a couple thousand men as a small affair, a kind of morning dash."[29] Inwardly, however, he felt awful. Yet he learned quickly and never repeated a mistake. Sherman pushed ahead, seeking battle on his own terms, until he reached Atlanta late in July. There he stalled. As in Petersburg, Atlanta's railroads supplied the defenders with food and ammunition.

Those hot summer days were the darkest of the war for the Union. So far, the Grand Plan had failed. Rebels held the jaws of Lincoln's bulldogs open at Petersburg and Atlanta. Victory was further away than ever, and peace seemed an impossible dream.

Americans had grown weary of war. You could read their mood in the bold type of newspaper headlines: STOP THE WAR! NO MORE KILLING! END THE SLAUGHTER! MAKE PEACE NOW! You could hear it in the words of popular songs like "When This Cruel War Is Over," "Brother, Will You Come Back?" and "Tell Me, Is My Father Coming Back?" People grew misty at the words of "Weeping, Sad and Lonely," *the* hit of 1864. Soldiers sang it on the march, and women gathered around pianos to sing it at home:

> *Dearest love, do you remember*
> *When we last did meet,*
> *How you told me that you loved me,*
> *Kneeling at my feet?*
> *Oh! how proud you stood before me*
> *In your suit of blue,*
> *When you vow'd to me and country*
> *Ever to be true.*
>
> *Weeping, sad and lonely,*
> *Hopes and fears how vain!*
> *Yet praying,*
> *When this cruel war is over,*
> *Praying that we meet again.*[30]

Time was running out for the sixteenth President. The United States was still a democracy, and 1864 an election year.

Lincoln had been wrestling with certain questions for months. First question: Should there be an election? Advisers urged him to postpone the contest while the war lasted. An election, they argued, would divide the country further, playing into the enemy's hands.

The President agreed, but felt that more important issues were at stake. Not only did the Constitution mandate a presidential election every four years, the Civil War was about the future of democracy—free government by a free people. And democracy requires that the people express their will, even in the worst times. Although having an election carried risks, Lincoln felt bound to uphold the basic principle of democracy. Moreover, an election would show the world that a democracy could survive despite a desperate civil war.

Second question: Should he, Abraham Lincoln, run for a second term? He thought so. Not that he loved a job he said was killing him. It was a matter of duty: he simply saw himself as the best man to end the war and build a just peace. Lincoln knew he faced major obstacles. Seeking another term meant breaking with tradition. No President had won reelection during the previous thirty years. Worse, he faced a growing resentment—no, *hatred*—toward himself and his wife.

Never before, or since, has a First Lady been as hated as Mary Lincoln. It was a kind of sport to make fun of the "vulgar" woman from the West. Newspapers printed gossip about the First Lady's bad taste and crude manners. She read descriptions of herself as a dumpy woman who wore low-cut dresses and masses of artificial flowers on her head. "The weak-minded Mrs. Lincoln," a critic sneered after a White House reception, "had *her bosom* on exhibition, and a flower pot on her head, while there was a train of silk, or satin dragging on the floor behind her several yards in length." Rumor had it that she did not love her husband and was planning to run away with a Russian count.[31]

Rival politicians, Republicans and Democrats alike, attacked the First Lady as a way of reaching her husband. Lincoln's critics charged her with being "two-thirds slavery and the other third secesh."[32] As we know, four of her brothers and three brothers-in-law served in the rebel army. Brothers Samuel and Alexander died in action, as did brother-in-law Ben Hardin Helm, a Confederate general. Mary felt sad for them and their families but was glad they had died. She wished all her Confederate relatives would be killed or captured. "They would kill my husband if they could, and destroy our government—the dearest of all things to us," she explained.[33]

The ignorant and the vicious never saw the First Lady as a patriot, because they did not want to see. Instead, they added up the "facts" and decided that she gave military secrets to the enemy. There *were* female spies in Washington, like Rose O'Neal Greenhow and Belle Boyd, attractive women skilled at coaxing secrets from congressmen and army officers. Mary Lincoln, however, never revealed a secret.

Each day the postman delivered the hate mail, scores of obscene letters left unsigned by cowards. The First Lady did not know how to defend herself. The wounded soldiers she visited knew her as a kind, caring woman. She did not brag or pretend to be a saint, as did the Washington society ladies who made sure everyone knew about their "good deeds." Mrs. Lincoln visited hospitals alone or with Elizabeth Keckley, never thinking to invite a reporter who would write a flattering story. So when the insults became unbearable, she locked herself in her room and cried bitterly.

Ever since Willie's death, Lincoln had feared for her sanity. If the smear campaign continued, he felt, Mary might go insane. To prevent that tragedy, he was willing to do anything, even swallow his pride. One day, he stood before the Senate Committee on the Conduct of the War. Slowly, sadly, the commander in chief gave a formal statement: "I, Abraham Lincoln, President of the United States, appear of my own volition before this Committee of the Senate to say that I, of my own knowledge, know that it is untrue that any of my family hold treasonable communication with the enemy." Having said his piece, he quietly left the room. Embarrassed committee members sat speechless. Then, by a silent understanding, they dropped all discussion about whether the First Lady was a traitor.[34]

Republicans had doubts about Lincoln himself. Senator Ben Wade, for example, called him "poor white trash" and tried to organize a movement to dump him in favor of some other candidate. Party leaders described him as "ignorant," "thickheaded," "idiotic," "a vulgar joke," and "a rail-splitting buffoon."[35] Their main concern, however, was that he had become so unpopular that his defeat would drag down other Republican candidates. His only chance was to beg Jefferson Davis for peace and drop the Emancipation Proclamation, they said. That would be such a "small" price to pay for ending the war, reuniting the nation, and saving lives, they claimed.

The President disagreed. The Union needed its black soldiers more than ever, he insisted. Besides, returning blacks to bondage would be dishonorable. "I should be damned in time & eternity for so doing," he said. "The world shall know that I will keep my faith to friends & enemies, come what will."[36] Lincoln could afford to lose the presidency, but never his integrity and self-respect.

Democrats blamed Lincoln for causing the war, ruling as a dictator, freeing the slaves, and prolonging the war unnecessarily. At their August convention in Chicago, they adopted a platform calling for a negotiated peace, even if that meant recognizing Confederate independence. The party's candidate, General George B. McClellan, rejected the peace plank, vowing to continue the struggle rather than sacrifice the Union and insult the memory of his slain comrades. But he also promised to do what the President found impossible: reject emancipation as a condition of reconstruction.

By August 23, Lincoln had become convinced that he could not win a second term. On that date, he wrote a brief memorandum on the situation: "This morning, as for some days past, it seems exceedingly probable that this Administration will not be re-elected. Then it will be my duty to so co-operate with the President elect, as to save the Union between the election and the inauguration; as he will have secured his election on such ground that can not possibly save it afterwards."[37] Thus, Lincoln was all but certain that losing the election meant losing the war and the Union with it. Nevertheless, if that was what the American people wanted, he must abide by their wishes.

The 1864 election was the most vicious in United States history. Democrats used every device to portray Lincoln as a demon. Party speakers called him "Abe the Widowmaker." He was a "Simple Susan," a "living dead man," a "filthy storyteller," a "fiend," "beast," "monster," "murderer," and "dictator." Banners urged voters to "Crush the Tyrant

Lincoln Before He Crushes You." Opposition workers appealed to Northern racism in harsh, poisonous language. They described Lincoln's followers as "the negro-loving, negro-hugging worshippers of old Abe." Crowds at Democratic rallies sang a takeoff on "When Johnny Comes Marching Home," a popular tune:

> The widow-maker soon must cave,
> Hurrah, hurrah,
> We'll plant him in some nigger's grave,
> Hurrah, hurrah.[38]

In Meadville, Pennsylvania, a landlord found an inscription scratched on a windowpane: "Abe Lincoln Departed this Life . . . By the effects of Poison." John Wilkes Booth had occupied the room the night before.[39]

Lincoln prided himself on being a forgiving man. He believed life too short to be wasting it in quarrels and harsh words. If someone

There was strong opposition to Lincoln's seeking a second term on both sides of the Atlantic. The cartoon titled "Mrs. North and Her Attorney" appeared in the September 24, 1864, issue of Punch, *the English humor magazine. It shows the President nervously hunched over his desk, while a woman dressed in mourning—for the Union dead—says: "You see, Mr. Lincoln, we have failed utterly in our course of action. I want peace, and so, if you cannot effect an amicable arrangement I must put the case in other hands."*

stopped attacking him, he never bore a grudge. But when it came to a political brawl, he could take care of himself. In 1864, as in 1860, he did not give campaign speeches or make political appearances. Instead, he handed out government jobs to buy the support of local politicians and ordered federal employees to aid his party—or else. Scores of workers in the Brooklyn Navy Yard lost their jobs for favoring the opposition. Lincoln even imposed a "war tax" of 5 percent on workers in the War, Treasury, and Post Office departments to help pay campaign expenses. Although such actions are illegal today, they were perfectly legal in the nineteenth century.

Lincoln's firmest supporters were black people, who could not vote, and soldiers, who might have reason for voting against him. After all, he had given them Grant and the Grand Plan, the Wilderness, Cold Harbor, and Petersburg. Billy Yank knew that a vote for Lincoln was a vote for more war—fought by himself. Nevertheless, he could see no other way to end the struggle with dignity. It was a matter of pride and patriotism. A Democratic victory would be a Confederate victory in disguise. A Democratic peace would be peace with shame. Too many men had already died. Ending the war the Democratic way would insult their sacrifice and their memory. No—from Billy Yank's point of view, the war must continue until final victory.

Different men said this in different ways. "I am in favor of Electing the man whom the rebels hate, and that man is Abraham Lincoln," an Illinois sergeant wrote his wife. An Indiana sergeant agreed: "One reason I love Old Abe is because the enemies of our country both North and South hate him with a hatred that is strong, deep, fierce, and irreconcilable." Still others put new words to "Yankee Doodle":

OPPOSITE: This famous drawing, "Long Abraham Lincoln a Little Longer," appeared in Harper's Weekly *on November 26, 1864, only a few days after he won election to a second term. It gave humorous expression to the relief many loyal people felt that the war would end in a Union victory.*

> *We've got a Grant from Abraham*
> *To beat the Rebels hollow*
> *And when we have a man to lead*
> *Why we're the boys to follow.*
> *And of our gallant Sherman now*
> *We feel a little prouder*
> *Because he's made a lively Hood*
> *By stirring Rebs with powder.*[40]

The boys in blue rescued their "Uncle Abraham." On August 5, Admiral Farragut led his fleet into Mobile Bay, closing Alabama's main seaport and forcing its surrender the following day. On August 21, Grant sent Major General Philip H. Sheridan into the Shenandoah Valley with 45,000 troops and orders to burn the place from end to end. On September 2, Sherman telegraphed the White House: "Atlanta is ours, and fairly won!" Uncle Billy had fooled everyone. Rather than besiege Atlanta, he cut the railroad south of the city, forcing its defenders to retreat or starve. On October 19, Sheridan destroyed a large Confederate force at Cedar Creek and went on to burn the valley. By the time he finished, the lovely Shenandoah, the "breadbasket of the Confederacy," lay in ruins. At Petersburg, Lee's troops tightened their belts.

These victories proved that the war was not the hopeless failure Democrats claimed. The Union armies were on the march again. Victory was not only possible, but probable. All voters had to do was allow Lincoln to finish the job.

They did. Within hours of the polls' closing on Election Day, November 8, the President had decisively won a second term. Final tallies showed 2,213,635 votes for Lincoln, 347,183 more than he received in 1860. This time he won 55 percent of the vote, compared to 40 percent four years earlier. The Young Napoleon got 1,805,237 votes, carrying only the states of Kentucky, Delaware, and New Jersey. Best of all, Billy Yank voted for Lincoln in overwhelming numbers. Sherman's army gave him 86 percent of its vote.

Soldiers cheered when they learned of Lincoln's victory. "At a point where the lines came within a few yards of each other," a private wrote from Petersburg, "our men heard a voice from behind the rebel breastworks. 'Say, Yank.' 'Hilloa, Johnny.' 'Don't fire, Yank.' 'All right, Johnny.' 'What are you 'uns all cheering for?' 'Big victory for our side.' 'What is it, Yank?' 'Old Abe has cleaned all your fellers out up North.' 'You don't say so, Yank?' 'Fact, gobbled the whole concern; there are no peace men enough left in the whole North to make a corporal's guard.' "[41]

On election night, the President slept soundly for the first time in months. He would never know that he had a secret protector. Ward Hill Lamon, his bodyguard four years earlier, had become marshal of the District of Columbia. Lamon had a feeling that somebody might try to kill his friend now that he was reelected. So, as Lincoln slept, Lamon armed himself with two pistols and a bowie knife and spent the night curled up on a blanket outside the bedroom door. At daybreak, before the President awoke, he quietly rolled up the blanket and slipped away.

7 RICHMOND AT LAST

I looked down the street and to my horror beheld Negro cavalrymen yelling:
"Richmond at last!"

FANNY WALKER, APRIL 4, 1865

Even as Lincoln slept on election night, the Union war machine was gearing up for the final campaign. Shortly after the fall of Atlanta, Sherman sent Grant a secret message. If Washington approved, he intended to march his army clear across Georgia, from Atlanta to the sea, nearly three hundred miles to the south. Normally, such a march carried great risks, because every mile he advanced would stretch his supply line, making it easier to be cut by enemy forces operating in the rear. Sherman, however, felt confident. His soldiers were veterans, tough, experienced fellows used to winning. Sherman planned to detach 30,000 men to deal with the enemy at his back, while he advanced with the remaining 62,000 men.

A believer in "hard war," Sherman meant to turn his army into a gigantic eating machine. Apart from guns and ammunition, most supplies would be taken from enemy civilians and the rest destroyed. By this tactic, he hoped to kill two birds with one stone: keep supplies from the Confederate army and make things so difficult for ordinary Southerners that they would force their leaders to surrender. Lincoln

While Grant pounded Lee in Virginia, William Tecumseh Sherman threatened the Confederate rear by hammering his way through Georgia and the Carolinas. Brilliant and high-strung, Sherman was, a friend noted, "a man of immense intellectuality, but his brain is like a splendid piece of machinery with all the screws a little loose."

and Grant gave the plan their blessing.

Sherman left Atlanta on November 15, 1864. Except for a handful of citizens who remained behind, the population had already been forced to abandon their homes and seek shelter elsewhere in the Confederacy. As the army set out, the city burst into flames. Sherman had intended to burn everything of value to the enemy. Some of his men, however, got "careless" with matches and torched dozens of public buildings and private homes. A strong breeze did the rest. By the time the fires died out, much of Atlanta lay in ruins.

Sherman's men believed in their leader. He was, to them, a superman, all-powerful and all-knowing. When ordered to do anything that seemed impossible, they shrugged and said: "Well, *he* can't make a mistake." Several burning bridges in the rear of a column, cutting off its only means of retreat, had the same effect. "Guess, Charley, Sherman has set the river on fire," a private muttered. "Well, if he has, I reckon it's all right," Charley replied.[1]

The army advanced in four columns along a front twenty to forty miles wide. Groups of scouts called "bummers" left the columns each morning with wagons and pack mules. Their job was to "forage on the enemy," a polite term for looting. Meanwhile, specialists in railroad destruction went about their task. Crews tore up lengths of track, set them across a pile of wooden ties, and built a fire. The red-hot rails were then bent around trees to form "Sherman neckties" and "Sherman hairpins," useless chunks of iron that could be straightened only in a steel mill. "We had a gay old time," a New Yorker boasted. "Destroyed all we could not eat, stole their niggers, burned their cotton & gins, spilled

their sorghum, burned & twisted their R. Roads and raised Hell generally."[2]

Sherman, though a racist, freed more slaves than any other Union
general. He freed them not for their sakes, but to hurt the enemy. Nevertheless, blacks saw his coming as the answer to their prayers. "Marse
Lincoln done remember us!" they cried as Sherman's columns swept
past the plantations. To them, the blue soldiers may have seemed nothing less than the army of the Lord, and their general a redheaded, red-
bearded Moses with a flaming sword of justice. Wherever Sherman
appeared, blacks danced and sang, crowded around to touch his horse
and boots, and held up infants to see this "Angel of the Lord," as one
called him.[3]

Blacks fell in behind the marching columns. From old-timers hob-
bling on canes to infants in their mothers' arms, they turned their backs
on slavery. An Illinois artilleryman watched as ever-growing numbers of
people followed the army "like a sable cloud in the sky before a thunder
storm. . . . Some in buggies, costly and glittering; some on horseback,
the horses old and blind, and others on foot; all following up in a right
jolly mood, bound for . . . freedom."[4] A total of 25,000 blacks joined

*As slaves flee the
plantations, General
Sherman's "bummers"
tear up railroad track
and burn Confederate
property on their march
across Georgia to the
sea.*

Sherman's columns. Most eventually dropped out due to fatigue, hunger, and sickness, but 7,000 completed the march.

Blacks aided "the Lincoln soldiers" in countless ways. Men became laborers for a few cents a day or a square meal, and women did camp chores. The Confederates had few secrets these people did not know. Where does this road go? Is there a shortcut around that fallen bridge? Are supplies hidden nearby? Do rebel cavalry patrol the woods yonder? When? How many? An officer need only ask the right question to get the right answer. "Let those who choose to curse the negro curse him," a veteran recalled, "but one thing is true . . . they were the only friends on whom we could rely for the sacred truth in Dixie. What they said might be relied on, so far as they knew; and they knew more and could tell more than most of the poor white population."[5]

Yankees could also rely on blacks in areas far from Sherman's line of march. Any Union soldier who escaped from a Confederate prison camp knew he could count on help from any black person. All he had to do was knock on the door of a slave cabin to find shelter, food, and a guide to lead him to safety. Participants in this "underground railroad" knew the risks: whipping, sale, even death. Yet no fugitive ever told of a black who refused to help. Nor was any Yankee ever betrayed to a search party. "If such kindness will not make one an Abolitionist," noted an escaped prisoner, "then his heart must be made of stone."[6]

On December 22, a telegram arrived at the White House. It announced Sherman's Christmas gift to the nation: the city of Savannah, Georgia. The march to the sea had ended in complete success. At a cost of 2,200 casualties, largely from sickness, Sherman destroyed every bridge, tunnel, locomotive, railroad station, factory, warehouse, cotton gin, and flour mill in his path. Besides crippling a major part of the rebel war-making capacity in Georgia, he had seized 21 million pounds of food worth $100 million. Of this sum, his army ate $20 million worth and burnt the rest.

Yet this was just the beginning. Sherman's next move was a continuation of the Grand Plan. During the march to the sea, Georgians had begged his men to treat South Carolina with equal harshness, since "they started it."[7] Billy Yank was only too glad to oblige. Had it not been for South Carolina, that "hellhole of secession," there might never have been a war. She had supported secession for generations, led her sister states out of the Union, and fired on Fort Sumter. Now she must pay.

On January 3, 1865, Sherman swung northward from Savannah. While Grant hammered Petersburg, Sherman would march through the Carolinas to strike Virginia from the west. Despite winter cold and rain-swollen streams, he made a steady ten miles a day. It was no picnic, but his soldiers, sensing final victory, overcame every obstacle. If a swamp blocked their way, black and white axemen made "corduroy" roads; that is, they felled trees, cut off the branches, and arranged the logs side by side, like the ridges in corduroy fabric. Forests not needed for corduroy were set ablaze, the fires raging out of control for days after the army passed.

Burning towns marked the army's path. The worst destruction was in Columbia, the South Carolina state capital. In a deliberate act of re-venge, Sherman's boys torched the Capitol building and library contain-ing thousands of precious books. After the flames died down, seventeen-year-old Emma LeConte walked among the ruins. Nothing on Main Street was as she remembered. No matter where she turned, it was the same story: utter desolation. "The wind moans among the black chimneys and whistles through the gaping windows. . . . The market is a ruined shell . . . its spire fallen in and with it the old town clock whose familiar stroke we miss so much." Seeing "Secessia," the great bell that had rung each state out of the Union in 1861, broke her heart. It lay half buried in mud and ashes.[8]

News of the campaign reached Lee's army at Petersburg. Many of his troops hailed from Georgia and South Carolina. They took Sherman's actions personally. Calling themselves "Lee's miserables," since lack of supplies made them so miserable, they had the added burden of worry-ing about their families. Worry hit them harder than any battle defeat. It gnawed at their souls, undermining their fighting spirit. A soldier explained: "i hev conkludud that the dam fulishness uv tryin to lick shurmin Had better be stopped. we hav bin gettin nuthin but hell & lots uv it ever sinse we saw the dam yanks & I am tirde uv it. Thair thicker an lise on a hen and a dam sit ornraier."[9]

This Johnny Reb's spelling was poor, but his meaning is clear. The

Confederacy was dying; and the sooner Southerners realized it, the better for everyone. Each night, at least a hundred men deserted. Thousands of deserters lived in small bands in the mountains, seceders from secession. Most were veterans no one would have dared accuse of cowardice. Yet even they had lost hope.

Sherman took Charleston on February 18. Unfortunately, retreating rebels had set fire to the cotton warehouses and the flames leaped out of control, burning much of the downtown area. Still, the conquerors were in high spirits. A few weeks after the city's capture, they celebrated with a parade. Marching bands led the way, followed by gaily decorated floats. One float depicted a mock slave auction. "How much am I offered for this good cook?" the auctioneer cried. "She is an excellent cook, gentlemen." As bystanders called out their bids, black women burst into frantic shouts. Forgetting it was all in "fun," they wailed: "Give me back my children! Give me back my children!" Slavery was nothing to joke about.[10]

The President had already taken steps to prevent future sales of American children. Lincoln saw his election victory as a mandate to finish the work of the Emancipation Proclamation. There had been questions about its legality from the outset. Few doubted that the commander in chief could free slaves as a wartime measure. But could he free them forever?

Slave owners appeared to have the law on their side. According to American law, a person cannot lose his freedom or property without a trial. Yet no Confederate had ever stood trial for treason. The issue, however, went beyond the American legal system. Under international law, property seized in wartime must be returned afterward. In the War of 1812, for example, the British freed thousands of slaves and took them to the West Indies. After the war, the United States demanded either the slaves' return or payment according to their value. The British paid. Lincoln also feared that the courts, Congress, or another President might later discard the Emancipation Proclamation. The only remedy was a constitutional amendment abolishing slavery across the land, not merely in the rebel states.

*The passage of
the Thirteenth
Amendment as
depicted in the
February 18, 1865,
issue of* Frank Leslie's
Illustrated News-
paper.

The Thirteenth Amendment did exactly that. Although it easily passed the Senate, it ran into trouble in the House of Representatives, where the Democrats held more seats. Operating in private, Lincoln made all sorts of deals to get the needed votes. The deals involved such things as releasing rebel prisoners related to Democratic congressmen and awarding government contracts to certain companies. Thus, the President bought Democratic votes with political favors and taxpayer dollars. Said Thaddeus Stevens of Pennsylvania, "The greatest measure of the nineteenth century was passed by corruption, aided and abetted by the purest man in America."[11]

On January 31, as Sherman was punching his way across South Carolina, the amendment passed by only three votes more than the required two-thirds majority. For a moment all was quiet. Then House Republicans went wild. "Strong men embraced each other with tears," an onlooker wrote. For a full ten minutes, "the galleries and aisles were bristling with standing, cheering crowds. The air was stirred with a cloud of women's handkerchiefs waving and floating; hands were shaking; men threw their arms about each other's necks, and cheer after cheer, and burst after burst followed."[12]

"With malice toward none." On March 4, 1865, the President read his second inaugural address from a podium outside the U.S. Capitol. The actor John Wilkes Booth was in the audience that day.

The news traveled swiftly by telegraph. Abolitionists felt relieved. Blacks gathered to pray and celebrate. Churches rocked to the words of a spiritual: "Sound the loud timbrel o'er Egypt's dark sea,/Jehovah has triumphed, His people are free."[13] The Lord, acting through Abraham Lincoln, had ended American slavery, and there could be no turning back.

Lincoln's second inauguration took place on Saturday, March 4, 1865. It was a somber, rainy day, with three inches of mud coating the streets of Washington. At noon, the state carriage started down Pennsylvania Avenue from the White House, escorted by cavalry and infantry. Scores of men with empty sleeves and pants legs, veterans of the Army of the Potomac, lined the route. No matter where the President turned, he met reminders of war's human costs.

Arriving at the Capitol, Lincoln took his place on the inauguration platform. Below, a sea of raised umbrellas spread before him. Then, suddenly, the scene changed. As he walked to the podium, the rain stopped, the sun came out, and the umbrellas snapped shut. The President began reading from a large sheet of paper printed in two columns. His voice, a soldier recalled, "was not heavy or coarse, but singularly clear and penetrating, with almost a metallic ring."[14] His words carried to the far edges of the crowd.

Lincoln's second inaugural address is a masterpiece. Brief and to the point, it deals with the war's meaning in words that still stir the emotions.

When the war began, said Lincoln, each side prayed for victory, since each believed it had justice on its side. God could have stopped the killing instantly, but did not—*would* not! Allowing the war to continue was His way of punishing Americans, both North and South, for the sin of slavery. Despite human hopes, it would go on until the evil was washed away. "Fondly do we hope—fervently do we pray—that this mighty scourge of war may speedily pass away. Yet, if God wills that it continue, until . . . every drop of blood drawn with the lash, shall be paid by another drawn with the sword, as was said three thousand years ago, so still it must be said 'the judgments of the Lord, are true and righteous altogether.' "[15]

Now slavery was abolished. Both sides had passed through the cleansing ordeal, and soon, God willing, the Confederacy would live only in memory. Americans must turn to peace, not in a spirit of vengeance but in a spirit of forgiveness. Lincoln concluded: "With malice toward none; with charity for all; with firmness in the right, as God gives us to see the right, let us strive on to finish the work we are in; to bind up the nation's wounds; to care for him who shall have borne the battle, and for his widow, and his orphan—to do all which may achieve and cherish a just, and a lasting peace, among ourselves, and with all nations."[16]

When the applause died down, Chief Justice Salmon P. Chase administered the oath of office. Lincoln then kissed the Bible and left the platform. As he turned to leave, he may have glanced up at the hundreds of invited guests standing behind a railing to the right. Among them was a handsome young man in a stylish suit and a silk top hat. We will never know if Lincoln noticed him. John Wilkes Booth, however, could not take his eyes off Lincoln. He had gotten his pass from a girlfriend, the daughter of a senator.

That evening the White House blazed with lights. Well-wishers formed a slowly moving line stretching from the Avenue, across the lawn, through the front door, into the East Room, and past the President. Lincoln shook the hands of an estimated six thousand people. He smiled at politicians and army officers, the rich and powerful, the poor and humble. All were welcome. Most were jolly and well behaved. Vandals, however, cut floral designs out of lace curtains for souvenirs and stole whatever fit into their pockets.

The only black guest arrived when the festivities were already in full swing. As Frederick Douglass stepped from his carriage, two policemen ordered him to leave. The White House was for white people, they snapped. Now go away!

Refusing to take no for an answer, Douglass asked a guest to tell the President he was outside. Word soon came that Mr. Lincoln wanted Mr. Douglass shown in at once.

"Here comes my friend Douglass," the President said, extending his hand. "Douglass, I saw you in the crowd today listening to my inaugural address. There is no man's opinion that I value more than yours. What do you think of it?"

"Mr. Lincoln, it was a sacred effort."

"I am glad you liked it!"[17]

They never met again.

Ten days later, Lincoln had a terrifying experience. He awoke to find that his body refused to obey his mind. He would prop himself up on his elbows, only to fall back with his head on the pillow. No matter how hard he tried, he could not get out of bed. Mary sent for Dr. Robert K. Stone, the family physician. His diagnosis: "Exhaustion, complete exhaustion."[18] Unless Lincoln took a vacation, and soon, Dr. Stone refused to be responsible for the outcome.

Notified of Lincoln's condition, General Grant made him an offer he could not refuse. By telegraph, he invited the President to visit the Petersburg front to see the end of the war. With Sherman cutting his way across North Carolina, it was time to smash the Army of Northern Virginia. The visit, Grant knew, would raise Lincoln's spirits and get him away from the hubbub of Washington. Oddly enough, the only place for the President to relax during those hectic days was at the front.

On March 23, Lincoln, Mary, and Tad sailed aboard the *River Queen*, a passenger ship rented by the government. Next morning, City Point, Virginia, hove into view. Located at the junction of the York and Appomattox Rivers, this tiny tobacco port had become Grant's main supply base. As the vessel neared shore, passengers saw the docks crowded with troop transports and supply ships. Beyond, reaching to the horizon, lay army camps, hospitals, warehouses, repair shops, and ammunition dumps. A military railroad connected City Point to the Petersburg siege lines ten miles to the southwest.

Captain Robert Lincoln joined his father for breakfast ashore. It had taken a lot of convincing, but his mother had finally allowed him to join the army, provided he stayed out of harm's way. At the President's request, Grant gave him a place on his staff as a tour guide for visiting dignitaries. Combat officers kept their opinions about his "soft" job to themselves.

Robert mentioned "a little rumpus up the line" earlier that morning. In reality, that rumpus had been a desperate gamble to save the Confederacy. For several weeks, Lee had known that time was running out. While Grant's 130,000 well-fed, well-clad men held his 50,000 hungry, ragged troops at Petersburg, Sherman was closing in from the west. Lee's only hope was to leave Petersburg, join forces with the army in North Carolina, whip Sherman, and then turn on Grant. To do this, however, he had to throw Grant off balance long enough for his army to escape. So before dawn on March 24, he seized Fort Stedman, a key Yankee position, in a surprise attack. Again Grant showed his toughness. Rather than pull back, as Lee expected, he blasted the fort with artillery and sent in waves of infantry.

After retaking Fort Stedman, Grant invited the President to tour the area. Lincoln accepted; he had seen the rebels driven from Washington, but had never been on a battlefield so soon after a fight. From a window of a slow, jolting railroad car, he looked out on a scene of utter devastation. He passed through acres of smoking ground plowed by shells and covered with shattered trees and broken weapons. Broken men, too. Lincoln saw one soldier with a bullet hole between his eyes and another with both arms torn away. He watched burial squads at work and surgeons tending the wounded, both blue and gray.

As he toured the fort, Captain John S. Barnes, a naval aide, described his own adventure. Barnes had been carrying water to wounded Confederates when he found a redheaded boy lying in a pool of blood. "Mother! Mother!" the boy called. Barnes asked where he was hit. The boy turned around, showing where a bullet had torn away part of his skull, then fell back dead. It was too much for the President. "Mr. Lincoln's eyes filled with tears and his voice was choked with emotion, and he repeated the well-known expression about 'robbing the cradle and the grave.' "[19]

Next day, March 25, Lincoln sailed up the James River for a military review, joined by his wife and Julia Grant. Rounding a bend, they found the shore crowded with thousands of troops looking not the least bit soldierly. They were General Sheridan's men, returning to base after burning the Shenandoah Valley. Naked troopers whooped as they splashed in the icy water, while others tended their horses or sat on the riverbank, talking and smoking pipes. When they heard that the presidential party was watching them, they cheered. Some jumped up and down in their birthday suits.

Sheridan came aboard the *River Queen* to pay his respects. Nicknamed "Little Phil," he was a short fellow with coal-black hair, long arms, stubby legs, and a rosy complexion. Next to Grant and Sherman, he was probably the Union's most valuable commander. Certainly he was the feistiest; where other generals ordered their men forward, Little Phil shouted "Follow me!" Staff officers always knew where to find him: in the thick of the fight. "General Sheridan," said Lincoln, gazing down, "when this peculiar war began I thought a cavalryman should be six feet four, but I have changed my mind—five feet four will do in a pinch."[20] Do in a pinch! That bit of understatement was one of the highest compliments the commander in chief ever paid an officer.

Lincoln rode to the review on horseback, while the ladies followed in a carriage a few minutes behind. Thousands of troops had been standing in parade formation for hours. Their commander, Major General

Edward Ord, said that, although they had missed lunch, the review should be delayed until the ladies arrived. Lincoln would not hear of it; he would never stand between Billy Yank and a square meal. The President rode along the lines with bands playing, flags waving, and soldiers presenting arms. Mrs. Ord, a famous beauty, rode beside the guest of honor.

What began as a pleasant outing for Lincoln ended in an ordeal. As Mary drew near, she was shocked to see him with another

woman by his side. She began to rant and rave. "What does that woman mean by riding by the side of the President?" she screamed in jealous rage. "Does she suppose that *he* wants *her* by the side of *him?*" Moments later, the unsuspecting Mrs. Ord trotted over to the carriage. That was a mistake. The First Lady gave her such a tongue-lashing that she burst into tears.[21]

Julia Grant tried to soothe the angry woman, only to be insulted as well. Turning on her, Mary snarled: "I suppose you think you'll get to the White House yourself, don't you?"[22]

Julia, a modest, soft-spoken person, said the idea had never crossed her mind.

"Oh, you had better take it if you can get it," said the First Lady. " 'Tis very nice."[23]

Hearing the commotion, Lincoln rode up to the carriage and dismounted. "Mother—now, mother—do be quiet!" he pleaded.[24] Instead of calming her, his words sparked another outburst. She turned her anger against her husband, insulting him before a group of officers. The President turned and walked away. Mary's tantrum showed again that she was a sick woman. Always high-strung, she had been through so much—Willie's death, relatives and friends killed in the war, the smear campaign—that she finally seemed to be losing her mind.

The son of Irish immigrants, General Philip ("Little Phil") Sheridan commanded the cavalry corps of the Army of the Potomac. A bold, daring soldier, he never shirked danger, leading cavalry charges in person. After the war, he went West to direct the campaign against the Indian tribes on the Great Plains.

The First Lady returned to Washington to "rest." For the next two days, March 26–27, her husband tried to relax. He and Tad explored the countryside on Cincinnati and Jeff Davis, horses lent by General Grant. During camp visits, Lincoln joked with the men and explained the fine points of woodchopping; they gathered the chips "that Father Abraham chopped" for souvenirs.[25] Lincoln once took an axe by its handle, lifted it slowly, and held it out for a minute without a quiver, as in the old days. Yet he was not his old self. He returned to the *River Queen* with an aching arm and went to bed early.

Lincoln visited Grant's telegraph hut several times a day. He tried to appear calm, but the clerks knew he was wound up like a watch spring. The instant a clerk copied a message, the commander in chief grabbed it out of his hand. After reading it carefully, he moved the colored pins stuck into a map he kept in his quarters. The President used the map to follow the army's every movement.

During slow times, Lincoln played with three kittens the telegraphers had adopted. Yet even these harmless animals reminded him of the national tragedy. "There, you poor, little, miserable creatures, what brought you to this camp of warriors? Where is your mother?" he asked as he placed them on his lap. "The mother is dead," a colonel answered. "Then she can't grieve as many a poor mother is grieving for a son lost in battle. . . . Ah, kitties, thank God you are cats, and can't understand the terrible strife that is going on," Lincoln said, stroking their soft coats. He ordered the colonel to give the kittens milk and treat them tenderly. Whenever he visited the hut, he wiped their eyes with his handkerchief, petted them, and listened to their purring.[26]

At night, Lincoln sat by a campfire and swapped stories with Grant and his staff. The general told about an inventor who wished to arm Union soldiers with bayonets a foot longer than those of the Confederates, an easy way to get at the enemy without being hurt themselves. Apparently, the fellow forgot that a bullet has a longer reach than a bayonet.

The President laughed, then offered a story in return. During his circuit-riding days, a thug jumped out of an alley and waved a hunting knife under his nose. Lincoln was so frightened that to him the weapon seemed a yard long. "Stranger," the thug asked, "kin you lend me five dollars?" Why, sure! "I never reached in my pocket and got out money so fast in all my life," Lincoln told the group. "I handed him a bank note and said, 'There's a ten, neighbor; now put up your scythe.' "[27]

Sherman arrived from North Carolina on March 27. That night, he and Grant decided to play a little game. When Julia Grant entered the room, they asked whether they could trust her to keep a military secret. As a test, they questioned her about the geography of Virginia. She had studied her husband's maps and knew Virginia like her hometown. Catching the spirit of the game, she gave answers that were so wrong they became funny. According to her, rivers flowed upstream and cities lay hundreds of miles from their true location. "Well, Grant, I guess we can trust her," said Sherman, smiling. Then, turning to Julia, he grew serious. "Never mind, Mrs. Grant;

perhaps some day women will vote and control affairs, and then they will take us men in hand and subject us to worse cross-examinations than that."[28]

Next morning, Grant, Sherman, and Admiral David Dixon Porter, commander of the North Atlantic Blockading Squadron, joined Lincoln aboard the *River Queen*. They all agreed that the Confederacy was doomed; at most, the war would last another month. In that time, however, more men would be killed and maimed.

As they spoke, the President kept asking: "Must more blood be shed? Cannot this last bloody battle be avoided?"[29] The generals shook their heads. No. There must be another big battle. Robert E. Lee, they explained, was a tenacious fighter. He would give up only when faced with total annihilation, and not a moment sooner. As for the Confederate army in North Carolina, the generals believed its commander, Joseph Johnston, would give up once Lee surrendered.

The meeting turned to the future. Lincoln knew that peace—true peace—is more than the absence of fighting. Peace is also a state of

Friends said that Admiral David Dixon Porter had saltwater for blood. He first went to sea at the age of ten and never left it. As commander of the North Atlantic Blockading Squadron, his chief responsibility was seeing that no ships brought supplies to Confederate seaports.

The conference aboard the River Queen. *On March 28, 1865, President Lincoln met with his top commanders to discuss final plans for bringing the Civil War to a close. Admiral Porter sits on Lincoln's left, Generals Grant and Sherman on his right. The meeting is immortalized in The* Peacemakers, *an 1868 painting by George P. A. Healy, which hangs in the White House today.*

mind, a willingness to forgive and forget. He would make hard war when necessary, but when the fighting ended he would bend over backward to turn former enemies into friends. The kind of peace he wanted must be made in the spirit of his second inaugural address—"with malice toward none and charity for all." Harsh peace terms would only stir up hatred, poisoning the nation for generations to come. There must be no revenge, no treason trials, no fines, and no executions.

Lincoln asked only that the Confederates stop fighting and turn in their heavy weapons. "Let them once surrender and reach their homes, they won't take up arms again. Let them all go, officers and all. . . . Let them have their horses to plow with, and, if you like, their guns to shoot crows with. I want no one punished; treat them liberally all around. We want those people to return to their allegiance to the Union and submit to the laws." As for the Confederate leaders, he wanted them to escape "unbeknownst to me"; that way, no one could accuse him of helping traitors evade justice.[30]

March 29. The Army of the Potomac took battle stations before dawn. Everyone was ready, waiting only for Grant's go-ahead to start the final push. Back at City Point, the general kissed his wife good-bye and walked with the President to the waiting train. The lines in Lincoln's face seemed deeper, Grant recalled, and the rings under his eyes were purple, as if a fist had left its mark.

Lincoln took Grant's hand in both of his and wished him Godspeed. "Well," he said, turning to the general's staff, "your luck is my luck and the country's—the luck of us all . . . except for the poor fellows who are killed. Success won't do them any good."[31]

A whistle tooted, steam hissed, and the train started to move. As it pulled away, Grant and his officers raised their hats out of respect to the commander in chief. Lincoln returned their salute, and in a voice husky with emotion called out, "Good-by, gentlemen. God bless you all!"[32]

Events moved with express-train speed. That afternoon, Sheridan's cavalry cut the Southside Railway, Lee's main supply line. Next morning, April 1, Sheridan defeated a large Confederate force at Five Forks, taking more than five thousand prisoners.

Grant sent Lincoln some captured battle flags. The President fairly glowed with happiness. Seizing the flags, he unfurled them and cried: "Here is something material—something I can see, feel, and understand. This means victory. This *is* victory."[33] Yet it was just the beginning.

At 3:00 A.M. on April 2, the President was nervously pacing the deck of the *River Queen* when explosions rattled windowpanes at City Point and clouds glowed orange in the west. An officer explained that Grant was using hundreds of guns to soften up Confederate positions at Petersburg.

Billy Yanks crouched in their trenches with their fingers in their ears. Johnny Rebs crouched in *their* trenches, fingering their triggers and praying those "damnyankee" shells landed someplace else—someplace far away.

The guns fell silent, and the Union infantry came like a blue tidal wave. Lee organized the retreat, pausing only to send a brief telegram to his president. Jefferson Davis received it during morning services at St. Paul's Church. It contained the worst news possible: Lee's lines were broken and Richmond must be abandoned. The Confederate chief hurried away to arrange for the evacuation. In the panic that followed,

The ruins of Richmond's arsenal, April 1865. Rather than leave behind anything of military value, General Lee's retreating soldiers blew up this and other government buildings. Exploding shells from the arsenal set fire to the rest of the Confederate capital. Notice the piles of solid-iron cannonballs in the foreground.

much of Richmond burned as fires set to destroy its ammunition dumps leaped out of control.

While Richmond burned, Lincoln stayed aboard the *Malvern*, Admiral Porter's flagship, for the two days the *River Queen* was undergoing repairs at Norfolk. His quarters were not exactly "presidential"—just a tiny cabin with a bed six feet long by two feet wide. Yet he thought the *Malvern* a wonderful ship, a ship of miracles.

Lincoln put his boots and socks outside his cabin door the first night. Admirals do not usually examine the commander in chief's footwear, but Porter did. Finding holes in the socks, he had them washed and darned, and the boots polished.

"A miracle happened to me last night," the President announced at breakfast. "When I went to bed I had two large holes in my socks, and this morning there are no holes in them. That never happened before; it must be a miracle!" He added that he was four inches longer than the bed—and you cannot fit a long knife into a short sheath. It had not been a restful night.

That afternoon, as Lincoln visited the troops, carpenters lengthened the bed by two feet and put on new bedding. Porter did not mention the change when the President turned in for the night. Next morning,

Lincoln was all smiles. "A greater miracle than ever happened last night," he said, putting an arm around the admiral's shoulder. "I shrank six inches in length. . . . I got somebody else's big pillow and slept in a better bed than I did on the *River Queen.*"[34]

On April 3, Lincoln was still marveling at the miracle of the socks when he learned that Petersburg had fallen. Immediately he ordered a train to take him to the city. After congratulating Grant and discussing the military situation, he headed back to City Point. As he walked to the train, he met reinforcements moving up to new positions. The soldiers greeted him with shouts of "Three cheers for Uncle Abe!" A private sang out: "We'll get 'em, Abe . . . you go home and sleep sound tonight. We boys will put you through to Richmond."[35]

The President reached City Point at 5:00 P.M. and made a beeline for the telegraph hut. Sure enough, he found a message on the table. It announced that Union forces had occupied Richmond at 8:15 A.M. that very morning. The Confederate government had fled the city only a few hours before. It had left so hurriedly that important documents, not to mention millions of dollars in new banknotes, lay scattered about the capital.

He later learned that a black cavalry unit had arrived first. The troopers galloped up Main Street, driving the Confederate rear guard before them. As the rebels fled, the troopers stood in their stirrups, fired their pistols into the air, and cheered to wake the dead.

Confederate loyalists turned away in disgust and shame. "They certainly were the blackest creatures I ever saw," a lady wrote a friend. "I am almost inclined to the belief that they are a direct importation from Africa."[36] Many other whites, however, saw them as protectors. Soon after the troopers arrived, they organized fire-fighting teams and sent military police to restore order in the streets. They did so respectfully, yet firmly. These were disciplined soldiers, not the bloodthirsty rabble Southerners had imagined.

The cavalry was followed by bands playing "Yankee Doodle," "The Star-Spangled Banner," and, of all things, "Dixie." Fellow blacks shouted: "Thank God! You've come at last, Glory Hallelujah!" The inmates of Lumkin's Jail, part of a slave auction house, sang a new song: "Slavery Chain Done Broke at Last." It was broken—literally. A bullet smashed the lock, and the blacks walked out of Lumkin's as free people.[37]

In Washington, fifteen-year-old Willie Kettles, a junior telegrapher at the War Department, was taking down a message as it came over the wire. Halfway through, he shouted the news at the top of his voice. Fellow clerks threw up the windows and bellowed: "Richmond is fallen!"[38]

Young Kettles burst into Secretary Stanton's office with the telegram. Stanton danced around the room, whooping for joy. Lifting Willie bodily, he stood him in an open window and made him shout the news to the crowd forming below. Already War Department telegraphers were wiring city after city to spread the word.

The entire North exploded with happiness, but no place made more noise than the capital. Secretary Stanton ordered its forts to fire a grand salute of eight hundred guns—three hundred for Petersburg and five hundred for Richmond. Church bells pealed, fire-engine bells clanged, and every locomotive and steamboat whistle went off as if on cue. Offices emptied of workers, and schools dismissed pupils. Banks closed. Courts adjourned. Shopkeepers took the day off. Citizens swarmed into the streets, talking, laughing, and singing. "Babylon has fallen!" people yelled as they strolled arm in arm. Perfect strangers hugged and, yes, kissed. Taverns did a roaring trade—so good that reporters counted five thousand drunks on Pennsylvania Avenue alone.[39]

That night, at City Point, Abraham Lincoln told Admiral Porter before going to bed: "Thank God I have lived to see this. It seems to me that I have been dreaming a horrid dream for four years, and now the nightmare is gone. I want to see Richmond!"[40]

On the morning of April 4, a flotilla of four vessels led by the *River Queen* steamed up the James River. The presidential party consisted of Lincoln, Tad, Admiral Porter, and William H. Crook, the President's personal bodyguard. As the vessel moved upstream, Tad went belowdecks to inspect the engine and make friends with the sailors. His father sat at a table on deck, next to a large bowl of apples. "These must have been put here for us," he said, reaching for one. Before long, every apple had vanished. "I guess I have cleaned that fellow out," said Lincoln, looking at the empty bowl.[41]

They had not gone far before the debris of war closed in around the vessels. Dead horses, broken wagons, and other things floated downstream. The flotilla passed so close to Confederate torpedoes, or floating mines, its passengers could have put out their hands and touched the sheet-metal cylinders. At Drewry's Bluff, wreckage and torpedoes narrowed the channel, making it dangerous for steamboats to pass. The journey had to continue in the admiral's barge, an open boat rowed by twelve sailors armed with rifles.

A pall of smoke hung over Richmond as the barge grounded at Rockett's Landing at the foot of Main Street. Laborers, slaves freed just hours before, were digging a ditch nearby. Looking up, their boss, a white-haired man of about sixty, saw the visitors step ashore. That tall bearded man yonder—he had once admired his picture in a newspaper. "Bress de Lord, dere is de great Messiah!" he shouted, dropping his shovel and racing forward. "I knowed him as soon as I seen him. He's been in my heart four long years and he's come at last to free his chillun from their bondage! Glory, Hallelujah!" With that, the old-timer fell on his knees before the President and kissed his feet.[42] The other workers followed his example.

President Lincoln looks calm and comfortable in this artist's rendition of his tour of Richmond on April 4, 1865. In fact, the visit was a mixture of joy that the war was nearly over and extreme physical discomfort. The picture appeared in the April 22 issue of Frank Leslie's Illustrated Newpaper.

"Don't kneel to me," said Lincoln, embarrassed. "That is not right. You must kneel to God only, and thank Him for the liberty you will hereafter enjoy. I am but God's humble instrument; but you may rest assured that as long as I live no one shall put a shackle on your limbs, and you shall have all the rights which God has given to every other free citizen of this Republic."[43]

Admiral Porter asked the workers to make way; the President had

no time to spare and wanted to see the Confederate capital. "Yes, Massa," the boss said, "but after bein' so many years in the desert without water, it's mighty pleasant to be lookin' at last on our spring of life. 'Scuse us, sir; we mean no disrespect to Mass' Lincoln; we mean all love and gratitude." The workers then formed a circle around the visitors and sang a spiritual. Drawn by the music, every black person in the neighborhood came running.[44]

At Porter's command, the sailors fixed bayonets. Then, with Crook holding Tad's hand, they started up Main Street toward the Confederate White House two miles away.

Hundreds of homes lay in ruins; some were still burning. The heat of the fires combined with the heat of the day to make Lincoln miserable. Dressed in his usual black suit and stovepipe hat, he said he felt as if he was suffocating in a cloud of dust and humidity. Beads of sweat rolled down his face, disappearing under his shirt collar. He fanned himself with his hat, but it did little good.

Wherever Lincoln turned, he saw black people crowding around. They waved to him, yelled into his ear, and reached out to touch him. A mother held up her sick child, telling him to touch the President for a magical cure. "I know I am free, for I have seen Father Abraham and felt him," a man shouted. In a voice choked with emotion, an old woman cried: "God bless Massa Abraham and General Grant; they can't whip me any more, on the order of my old Massa in Richmond."[45]

Blacks were not the only ones to welcome Lincoln. Some whites had hidden their disapproval of secession to avoid trouble. Now that Richmond was again part of the Union, they thanked the man who made it possible. A rough-looking fellow broke through the circle and ran up to the President. "Abraham Lincoln, God bless you! You are the poor man's friend!" he shouted as a sailor drove him away at bayonet point. The sailors allowed a pretty girl of about seventeen to give Lincoln a bouquet of flowers with a card that read: "From Eva to the Liberator of the slaves."[46]

Most whites, however, stood by sullenly. Occasionally, someone yelled, "The old ape is here," or a similar insult. During one such outburst, Lincoln's bodyguard glanced toward an open window and saw a man pointing a rifle. Crook dropped Tad's hand and stood in front of the President, making himself a human shield. The man stepped back into the room, but the danger had been real. At any moment a fanatical Confederate might reach around the sailors to stab the President or fire a bullet into his head. Fortunately, a detachment of cavalry arrived to escort him the rest of the way.[47]

Before fleeing with her husband, Mrs. Jefferson Davis had ordered a servant to tidy up the Confederate White House for the Yankees. Yet Lincoln hardly noticed its condition. Union officers thought he looked like a person drained of every ounce of energy, one who wanted just to rest in a cool place. The President slumped in Davis's chair and asked for a glass of water. After a light lunch, he toured the city in a carriage and paid a social call.

He visited the home of George Pickett, whom he had recommended for West Point as a boy, and who had led the last Confederate charge at Gettysburg as a man.

The general's wife, Sally, answered the knock on the door with her baby in her arms. The tall stranger asked if this was George Pickett's place.

"I am George Pickett's wife," she said.

"And I am Abraham Lincoln."

"The President?"

"No; Abraham Lincoln, George's old friend."

Lincoln smiled when she said her husband was not at home; he already knew that. He had come just to see his friend's home.

Seeing the baby's outstretched arms, Lincoln took him in his arms and got a great big kiss. As he returned him to his mother, the President shook a finger and said, "Tell your father, the rascal, that I forgive him for the sake of your mother's sweet smile and your bright eyes."[48]

The baby's father was retreating from Petersburg with the Army of Northern Virginia. Although Lee still intended to reach North Carolina, his army was falling apart by the minute. Drunk with fatigue, soldiers threw away their weapons and packs. Men marched asleep, awakening with a start when they stumbled into one another or fell into a ditch. Generals' minds wandered; some thought they heard their children's voices, or saw their wives cooking their favorite dishes. "And so the retreat rolls on," an officer scribbled in his diary. "We are passing abandoned cannon and wrecked and overturned wagons and their now useless contents. . . . Horses and mules [lie] dead or dying in the mud. . . . Our march is lighted by the fires of burning wagons. . . . Men who have stood by their flags since the beginning of the war now fall out of ranks . . . simply because it is beyond their power of physical endurance to go any further."[49]

Back at City Point, Lincoln tried to make himself useful. He visited the Confederate prisoners, telling them they would soon be going home. The Johnny Rebs received him politely. Some cheered "Old Abe" when they received Union rations, the best food they had eaten in months.

Lincoln visited the hospitals time and again, because, as a father, he could not stay away. Seeing the wounded drained him emotionally, but he forced himself to make the rounds. In one ward, he halted beside the cot of Captain Charles H. Houghton, age twenty-two, who had lost his left leg up to the hip. "Will he pull through?" he asked a doctor. The doctor averted his eyes. Houghton was feverish and still losing blood, not very good signs. The President put his hand on the captain's forehead, then went down on one knee to kiss him on the cheek. "You must live!" Lincoln said. "Poor boy, you must live!" From the cot came a whisper: "I intend to, sir." And so he did, remembering the President's parting words: "God bless you, my boy."[50]

On April 9, Lincoln returned to Washington aboard the *River Queen*. As he walked down the gangplank, an aide informed him that Secretary Seward had been injured in a carriage accident. Hurrying to Seward's house, he found him in bed, unrecognizable through the bandages that covered his swollen face and broken jaw. Without waiting for an invitation, Lincoln sprawled across the bed on his stomach, his mouth close to Seward's ear. Between grunts of approval from the patient, he described his adventures at the front. Finally, Seward fell asleep, and Lincoln tiptoed out of the room.

Before the President retired for the night, Secretary Stanton arrived with a telegram. Lincoln had never seen "Mars" so excited—or so happy. Frantically waving the paper, he shouted that it came from Grant. The quiet little fellow had done it! That afternoon, as the *River Queen* steamed toward Washington, he had cornered the Confederates

near Appomattox Court House, forcing Lee to surrender. Grant's terms were those outlined by Lincoln aboard the *River Queen*. The rebels were to be paroled on their promise to return home and obey the laws of the United States. Grant also allowed Johnny Reb to keep his pistol and horse "to put in a crop." Except for a few reporters who got the news from War Department clerks, Washington's citizens had to wait until morning.

As U. S. Grant and his staff look on, Robert E. Lee surrenders his army at Appomattox Court House, Virginia, on April 9, 1865.

April 10. Stanton woke the capital with man-made thunder. At dawn, five hundred cannons fired in quick succession. BOOM BOOM BOOM. Not to be outdone, Navy Yard workers dragged six guns through the streets, firing blanks at every corner. The reports echoed across the silent city, sending startled citizens rushing from their beds. Before long, record crowds were surging through the streets. Citizens hung out every flag in town. Fireworks exploded over the Potomac, and the Capitol blazed with colored lights. Miraculously, huge banners and signs appeared on government buildings. They read: "U.S. ARMY, U.S. NAVY, U.S. GRANT," "THIS IS THE LORD'S DOING; IT IS MARVELOUS TO OUR EYES," and "GLORY TO GOD."[51]

Tad Lincoln joined the celebration. Thousands had gathered on the White House lawn to serenade his father with patriotic songs. As they raised their voices, Tad ran around the porch with a Confederate flag, trying to make it snap in the breeze. People laughed when they saw the commander in chief chasing after his son. Lincoln lifted the boy off the ground, tucked him under one arm, and gave him to an aide to take inside.

The crowd called for a victory speech, but Lincoln said he needed time to collect his thoughts. He would speak tomorrow. Meanwhile, he asked the musicians to play "Dixie." "I have always thought 'Dixie' one of the best tunes I had ever heard," he said. "Our adversaries over the way, I know, have attempted to appropriate it, but I insist that on yesterday we fairly captured it."[52] A burst of applause swept the crowd.

The party continued on April 11, noisier than ever. In the afternoon, another crowd gathered before the White House. "Speech! Speech!" people chanted. Lincoln came to a window and began reading from a fistful of handwritten notes. Instead of a rousing victory speech, as expected, it was a detailed lecture on postwar reconstruction. In it he admitted that the future was "fraught with great difficulty." He went on to defend certain actions he had taken in Louisiana, adding that he hoped "the very intelligent" Negro and Negro soldiers would be given the right to vote under Reconstruction.[53] Soon much of the crowd lost interest and drifted away.

Not John Wilkes Booth. When the President finished, Booth turned to a companion. "That's the last speech he will ever make," the actor snarled, his face twisted in rage.[54]

8 O CAPTAIN! MY CAPTAIN!

O Captain! my Captain! our fearful trip is done,
The ship has weather'd every rack, the prize we sought is won,
The port is near, the bells I hear, the people all exulting,
While follow eyes the steady keel, the vessel grim and daring;
But O heart! heart! heart!
O the bleeding drops of red,
Where on the deck my Captain lies,
Fallen cold and dead.

WALT WHITMAN, 1865

Abraham Lincoln's future assassin was born May 10, 1838, the ninth of Mary Ann Holmes's and Junius Brutus Booth's ten children. Named for John Wilkes, an English politician who had supported the patriots during the American Revolution, he belonged to America's first family of the stage. His father, considered the greatest actor of the time, played to full houses on both sides of the Atlantic. The boy's older brothers, Edwin and Junius Brutus, Jr., followed in their father's footsteps. Dubbed the "Prince of Players," Edwin starred in the dramas of William Shakespeare, difficult works that demanded much from a performer. Junius Brutus, Jr., not only acted but became a famous theatrical manager.

"Johnny," as everyone called him, was the family's darling. We know a lot about his early life, thanks to his older sister Asia. In 1874, nine years after his death at the age of twenty-seven, she wrote *The Unlocked Book: A Memoir of John Wilkes Booth*. The person she portrayed did not seem the type to commit murder. A happy, outgoing child, Johnny enjoyed reciting poetry and hiking in the forest behind their home, a farm near Bel Air, Maryland, twenty-five miles from Baltimore. During those hikes, he was "very tender to flowers and . . . insects and butterflies" and would never harm any living being.[1] Yet he also had an adventurous side. Nothing pleased him more than being the hero of imaginary adventures, charging through the woods on horseback after dragons and monsters.

As a teenager, Johnny believed destiny had chosen him to do great deeds. "I must have fame! fame!" he told friends, striking a dramatic pose. Gaining fame—eternal, everlasting fame—became the most important thing of all, more precious than life itself. "I should die," he said, "with the satisfaction of knowing I had done something never before accomplished—something no other man would probably ever do."

John Wilkes Booth, President Lincoln's assassin, belonged to one of the greatest families in the history of the American theater.

Since the Booths were already celebrated actors, it seemed natural for him to seek a career on the stage. So, at the age of seventeen, Johnny took the first steps on the road to fame.[2]

Critics ridiculed his early performances. Audiences threw rotten fruit, stamped their feet, and laughed. Johnny had brought it on himself by refusing to memorize his lines and overacting. Nevertheless, he accepted criticism, learned from his mistakes, and improved steadily.

Johnny's big break came with a series of Shakespeare performances in Richmond during the autumn of 1858. Audiences loved him. Their applause boosted his self-image, encouraging him to work harder. Success in Richmond was followed by tours of the South and sold-out appearances in New York, Boston, and Philadelphia. After Richmond, he never received a bad review. He became a star, a stage idol whose performances rivaled brother Edwin's, who was being hailed as a genius. Fame also brought money—lots of it. Within three years, he was earning seven hundred dollars a week, a fantastic sum in those days.

John Wilkes Booth looked like a star. Five feet eight inches tall, weighing 160 pounds, he had olive-colored skin, jet-black hair, and piercing hazel eyes. A splendid horseman and a crack pistol shot, he spent money freely and made friends easily. Women found him irresistible. They screamed when he came onstage and mobbed him for autographs offstage. Actress Kate Reignolds recalled how "the stage door was always blocked with silly women waiting to catch a glimpse, as he passed, of his superb face and figure." His admirers ranged from barmaids to the daughters of United States senators. Men thought him "handsome as a young god."[3]

Booth loved the South and its way of life. A racist to his fingertips, he believed the United States had been created for white people and not for blacks. Slavery, he insisted, was natural and just. Abolitionists and "black Republicans," he insisted with equal force, deserved to burn in hell. He gladly joined the Richmond Grays for John Brown's execution, but when the Civil War began, he refused to join the Confederate army. Yet he continued to support the South and its Peculiar Institution. More than once, he threatened to kill fellow actors for speaking against Jefferson Davis and the South's "sacred cause."

Sister Asia, who had married a popular comedian, resented such talk. Like her other brothers, she backed the Union and had friends serving in its armies.

During a visit to her home in Philadelphia, Johnny kept harping on the sins of the North. "If the North conquer us, it will be by numbers only," he said, pounding his fist on a table.

"*If the North conquer us*—we are of the North," Asia shot back.

"Not I, not I," he roared. "So help me holy God! My soul, life, and possessions are for the South!"[4]

Oh, really! If that was so, Asia asked, why was he not fighting for the South?

Booth sat silently for a few minutes, his face set in a scowl. Then he admitted that he had promised their mother not to join up. He had kept his word, but not in a way Mother would approve. Although he was not a combat soldier, he served as a secret agent—a more dangerous job, for it meant a firing squad if captured.

The Confederate Secret Service had two branches: sabotage and espionage. Its sabotage branch burnt warehouses, cut telegraph lines, planted bombs on steamships, and did anything else to disrupt the Yankee war effort. Its espionage branch ran spy rings in every Northern city. Agents gathered information and sent it southward by messenger by way of "safe houses," homes belonging to rebel sympathizers. The details of Booth's involvement are still unknown. What is certain is that the actor was also a spy.

Being an actor, he told Asia, was the ideal cover for a spy. Normally, traveling widely in wartime would raise suspicions. Everyone, however, expected actors to be on the road most of the year. "My profession, my name, is my passport," he explained. Indeed, he had a travel permit from none other than Ulysses S. Grant. That permit allowed him to go anywhere, anytime, without having to give an explanation. One week he might be in Tennessee, another in Washington, and still another in New York City. Wherever he went, fans mobbed him and the police left him alone. In return for this privilege, he arranged to smuggle medicines to the Confederate army and carried information collected by agents in the cities where he acted.[5]

Only later did Asia realize that Johnny was using her home as a safe house. He often slept in his clothes on the downstairs sofa, without taking off his riding boots, and kept a pistol by his side. Men rang the doorbell late at night. Asia recognized some of their voices, but they refused to answer to their names. Others were total strangers; they never came in, but stood in the shadows and spoke to her brother in whispers. One night, he offered to show her the code he used to stay in touch with his contacts. She refused to look, saying she did not want to know such things. She would not report him to the police, because he was her brother, but she made it clear that she disapproved of his actions.[6]

Handsome Johnny, gentle Johnny, charming Johnny changed whenever he heard Abraham Lincoln's name. It was a physical change, as if some inner demon had taken possession of his body. His face darkened, his eyes flashed, and the veins swelled in his neck. Few people hated the

President more than John Wilkes Booth. The hatred was both personal and political. Personally, Lincoln's "ugliness" and coarse manners disgusted him beyond words. Politically, he considered Lincoln an enemy of the human race, blaming him for an unjust war to free blacks and slaughter whites.

There was nothing unusual about Booth's views, only the intensity with which he held them. Lincoln was the most hated man in America, North or South. During his years in the White House, he enjoyed little of the love given to his memory after his death. The President became the focus of all the bitterness stirred up by the Civil War. As we have seen, political enemies, including fellow Republicans, thought him the biggest fool in creation. Northern Democrats were forever accusing him of mishandling the war and behaving like a tyrant. "If hell were boiled down to a consistence of a pint of liquid fire," said an Illinois Democrat, "and the whole contents poured down the throat of Abraham Lincoln, the whole dose would be altogether too good for him." A Democratic newspaper once called for a true-blue patriot to "pierce his heart with a dagger for the public good."[7]

Confederate propaganda focused on Lincoln as a magnifying glass focuses the sun's rays on dry twigs. Lincoln haters spread their poison in newspapers, magazines, books, speeches, sermons, and cartoons. No name was too vile to call the President, no charge too disgusting to make against him. Educated people called Lincoln a "savage," "fiend," "beast," and "monster" for invading the South and attacking civilians through the blockade. They accused him of committing every crime imaginable. Lincoln, they said, sent smugglers into Confederate hospitals with poisoned medicines. Why, he even encouraged his soldiers to crucify Confederate officers and insult the Confederate dead by gambling with dice made from their bones.[8] Southern children learned that the Yankee chief planned to enslave white people and put them under black overseers. Ministers described him in Sunday school lessons as a bogeyman with a face like wrinkled bacon and "the snout of a half-starved Illinois pig." Schoolteachers taught poems like this:

> *My name it is Abe Lincoln,*
> *I lead a wretched life.*

Lincoln shows the strain of nearly four years of war in his last formal portrait, Washington, February 5, 1865. After Alexander Gardner snapped the picture, the glass-plate negative cracked. Gardner made only one print and threw the negative away.

I come from Springfield, Illinois,
Me and my dear wife.
We brought with us our dear son Bob,
To let the people know,
That the country I would plunder and rob,
Where ever I would go.

Abraham Lincoln was unfit to lick Jefferson Davis's boots, as we learn from this schoolyard song:

> *Jeff Davis rides a snow-white horse;*
> *Abe Lincoln rides a mule.*
> *Jeff Davis is a gentleman;*
> *Abe Lincoln is a fool.*

Things became so bad that children had tantrums at the mention of Lincoln's name. Seeing his picture in a book, one little boy threw it down and pounded the President's face with his fists.[9]

Words of hate have consequences. In John Wilkes Booth's case, they created a climate that fueled his own resentments and violent feelings. Lincoln's reelection convinced him that the "monster" intended to crown himself king of America. When Asia objected, he sprang to his feet, shouting "No, by God's mercy—never *that*. . . . He is walking in the footprints of old John Brown."[10] Booth would do anything to prevent the coronation of King Abraham the First.

The Booths and the Lincolns had crossed paths several times. Robert Lincoln nearly lost his life during a trip from Harvard University to Washington. Late one night, as passengers were buying their sleeping-car tickets from a conductor in Boston, Robert was leaning against the side of a train. Suddenly the train began to move, tumbling him into the space between the car and the platform. The train would surely have crushed him had not a stranger grabbed his arm and lifted him to the platform. It was Edwin Booth.[11] Thus a Booth saved the life of a Lincoln, a strange irony in view of later events.

Edwin's younger brother, however, left no doubt about his feelings toward Robert's father. Lincoln, we recall, had seen Johnny in *The Marble Heart* a few days before giving the Gettysburg Address. Impressed by the performance, he saw him in several other plays at Ford's Theatre. In the fall of 1864, Booth played a villain in a drama staged in the same theater. Lincoln's box was eye level with the stage, surrounded by a low railing. The President sat at the rail, with the First Lady next to him and guests seated behind. Twice the script called for Booth to threaten other characters. Each time he came up to the railing, he put his finger close to Lincoln's face and hissed the words like a snake spitting venom. The third time, a guest leaned over and said, "Mr. Lincoln, he looks as if he meant that for you." Lincoln replied: "Well, he does look pretty sharp at me, doesn't he?"[12] The play over, Lincoln seemed to have forgotten the incident. Booth did not. Already he was plotting against the man he hated.

Booth began by recruiting a band of loyal followers. His first recruit was John Surratt, age twenty, a Confederate messenger. Surratt quickly dropped out of the picture, but his mother, Mary, who ran a boarding-house at 541 H Street in Washington, let the actor use her place as a safe house. His second recruit was David Herold, age twenty-three, an unemployed drugstore clerk and drifter. Then came George Atzerodt, age thirty-two, a boatman who ferried Confederate agents across the Potomac. Finally, there was Lewis Paine, alias Powell, age twenty, a Confederate soldier who had deserted after being severely wounded. A veteran of Gettysburg and other major battles, Paine liked to show off a drinking cup made from the skull of a Union soldier.[13]

Booth's original plan called for kidnapping Lincoln, not killing him. Historians used to regard him as a lunatic who acted on his own. In 1988, however, William A. Tidwell and two fellow historians, all Southerners, challenged this view in *Come Retribution: The Confederate Secret Service and the Assassination of Lincoln*. After years of studying sources never before utilized, they decided that the kidnapping plan was an undercover operation that turned to murder only after it failed. Their evidence all but proves that the Confederates were involved in the earlier plan.

There is no reason why Confederate leaders should *not* have been involved. By the winter of 1864, the situation had become desperate. Lincoln's reelection guaranteed that Grant and Sherman would renew their offensives in the spring. Unless the Confederacy took drastic steps, defeat was a certainty. Various schemes were discussed in Richmond, including burning New York City and sending the clothes of smallpox victims to Washington to start an epidemic, an early example of germ warfare. There was also talk of sending agents to blow up the White House during a Cabinet meeting.

The Union had already tried some "dirty tricks" of its own. In March 1864, Confederates ambushed a large cavalry force near Richmond. Papers found on the body of the leader, Colonel Ulric Dahlgren, showed that he intended to burn the city and seize or kill Jefferson Davis and his Cabinet. Thus, Confederates felt justified in wanting to kidnap the Yankee chief.

Booth planned to seize Lincoln and take him to Richmond. The Confederacy needed more soldiers. Having already drafted every able-bodied man, and with desertions skyrocketing, only one hope remained: freeing captives held in Union prison camps. If the North released them in a swap for Lincoln, the Confederacy would have a brand-new army. Better yet, the Confederacy could demand peace and independence as the price of his return.

It seemed like a practical scheme—indeed, an easy scheme, thanks to Lincoln himself. The President had plenty of warning that he was in danger, if not from Booth, then from other enemies. The White House mail resembled the outpourings of an insane asylum. Threatening letters arrived daily, signed by "George Washington," "Thomas Jefferson," and "The Angel Gabriel." There were obscene poems and disgusting drawings showing him with a rope around his neck, chains on his feet, and his body covered with tar and feathers. Lincoln filed the threats in an envelope labeled "Assassination." It contained eighty of the choicest items.[14]

Not all threats, however, came by mail. Lincoln knew that an Alabama newspaper had put a price of $1 million on his head. Two people may have tried to collect. A woman spy dressed as a widow boldly came up to him and kissed his cheek. She had smallpox. Lincoln did, in fact, come down with a mild case of the disease on the train back to Washington after the Gettysburg Address. Another time, while driving to the Soldiers' Home in an open carriage, he heard a shot and felt the wind of a bullet passing through the crown of his hat. He joked about the incident.[15]

Yet the President refused to listen to warnings of danger. "I long ago made up my mind that if anybody wants to kill me, he will do it," he told a friend. "If I wore a shirt of mail, and kept myself surrounded by a bodyguard, it would be all the same. There are a thousand ways of getting at a man if it is desired that he should be killed."[16]

Yet nobody made it so easy for an assassin as Lincoln. One reason was the vow he took after the Baltimore Plot never to be called a coward again; this explains his foolish actions at Fort Stevens. Another reason was his quality of fatalism, the belief that events are fixed in advance so that humans are powerless to change them. In short, the President believed that what must be will be, and that one cannot escape destiny.

Lincoln's security arrangements were poor. Guards were posted at the White House, but not always at all entrances. Doors leading into the mansion stayed open day and night. Visitors walked in without anyone checking their identities or searching for weapons. The President did not like to have guards around, saying they made him feel like a European king, not an American President. One wintry night, for example, he told a guard to come in out of the cold. The soldier refused; he had his orders and must make his rounds. "Hold on there!" Lincoln snapped. "It occurs to me that I am commander in chief, and I order you to go inside."[17]

Tad did not help matters, either. He once visited Secretary Stanton at the War Department. Stanton must have been in a jolly mood, because he gave the boy a lieutenant's commission in the United States Army. "Lieutenant" Tad then ordered a supply sergeant to send twenty-five rifles to him at the White House. The sergeant obeyed! Tad promptly dismissed the guards and ordered the gardeners and servants to report to him for duty. He gave them the rifles, drilled them, and put them in place of the soldiers. Seeing this, Robert, who happened to be visiting at the time, reported to "paw." Lincoln thought it a good joke and ordered the servants dismissed. Nobody guarded the White House that night.[18]

Stanton did not repeat his mistake. In November 1864, he assigned plainclothes detectives to guard the President round the clock. In addition, a detail of soldiers was to accompany him during his walks to the telegraph office and when he rode in his carriage. Lincoln complained about the protection, but Stanton insisted. The President *must* be guarded, and that was that. Lincoln gave in.

Nevertheless, he tried to give his protectors the slip. During his carriage rides, Lincoln ordered the driver to speed up suddenly. The cavalry escort was not amused. Lincoln also tried to elude his soldier escort during his nightly visits to the telegraph office, or asked them to stay behind. One rainy night, he told a soldier not to come out in the storm; he had his umbrella and could get back on his own, he said. On second thought, however, he decided to let the man come along, explaining: "If Stanton should learn that you had let me return alone, he would have you court-martialed and shot inside of twenty-four hours."[19]

John Wilkes Booth laid his plans carefully. For six months he followed Lincoln on his carriage rides and hid in the shadows as he walked to and from the telegraph office. Knowing that the President liked to visit Ford's Theatre alone, he staked out the route, hoping to catch him at night without an escort.

On January 16, 1865, Booth and his gang waited for hours, but Lincoln never came. On the night of March 4, he boasted that he could have shot the President from where he stood on the inaugural platform, but hadn't. He tried another kidnapping on March 17, after hearing that Lincoln would be at Ford's Theatre. This time the presidential carriage appeared with a passenger in a black stovepipe hat. It was not Lincoln, but Chief Justice Salmon Chase. Lincoln had intended to go, but changed his mind and asked Chase to go in his place.

Events began to move quickly in the spring. Richmond fell on April 3, and Lincoln visited it the following day. General Lee surrendered the Army of Northern Virginia on April 9. The news stunned Booth. "My God, I have no country now!" he stammered.[20] On April 11, after Lincoln's speech on Reconstruction, he vowed to kill the sixteenth President of the United States. He might die in the attempt, but at least he would take the "tyrant" with him to the grave.

By coincidence, that night Lincoln spoke of a dream he'd had at City Point. In it he was awakened by sobbing coming from somewhere in the White House. Leaving his bed, he went from room to room until he reached the East Room. There he found a crowd of mourners dressed in black. They surrounded a platform on which lay a body wrapped in a black shroud. An honor guard of soldiers stood at attention around the platform.

"Who is dead in the White House?" Lincoln asked a soldier. "The President," the man replied. "He was killed by an assassin!" At that moment, the crowd wailed, and Lincoln awoke with a start. When he described the dream to his wife, she became terrified. "Well, it is only a dream, Mary," he said. "Let us say no more about it, and try to forget it."[21]

Ward Hill Lamon did not allow him to forget. Lamon told his friend that the dream was an omen. Enemies *were* out to kill him, and would succeed if he was not more careful. Lincoln smiled. "For a long time you have been trying to keep somebody—the Lord knows who—from killing me," he said. "Don't you see how it will turn out? In this dream it was not me, but some other fellow, that was killed?"[22]

The President had history, if not good sense, on his side. Assassination was not unusual in Europe, where unpopular rulers had been killed since the days of Julius Caesar. Europe was the Old World, a world of ancient injustices and lingering hatreds. Americans, however, had always prided themselves on being different from other nations. Assassination had never been part of their tradition. It was natural, they said, for the oppressed to kill their oppressors. But the Founding Fathers had created a "people's government." Americans had no reason to kill bad leaders, because they could vote them out of office.

There had only been two attempts on the lives of American leaders. In 1776, a soldier paid with his life for trying to kill General George Washington. In 1835, as President Andrew Jackson was leaving the Capitol, a house painter named Richard Lawrence ran up to him with a pistol. Pointing it at the President's chest, he pulled the trigger. The weapon misfired. Drawing another pistol, he tried again. Another misfire. "Old Hickory" did not give him a chance to reload. He had a cane with a heavy iron knob at the end, and he moved like a cat. Lawrence awoke with a large lump on his head. A court sent him to an insane asylum for the rest of his life.

John Wilkes Booth was no lunatic. Those who knew him best noted that he might be hotheaded and bad-tempered on the subject of Lincoln, but nobody called him insane *before* he killed the President. What he wanted to do was wrong and wicked, but not crazy. The facts were clear enough to Booth. Fact number one: He worshiped the Confederacy and loathed the man who had brought it to ruin. Fact number two: The Confederacy still had a chance of surviving—a slim chance, but a chance nevertheless. Fact number three: Despite Lee's surrender in Virginia, Joseph Johnston still had not surrendered his 30,000 troops in North Carolina. Fact number four: Booth trusted his followers to do anything he asked.

The actor planned to kill President Lincoln, Vice President Andrew Johnson, Secretary of State Seward, and General Grant within minutes of one another. Hatred and revenge were surely factors in Booth's decision. His main reason, however, was more practical. The sudden elimination of the Union's top leadership was likely to produce chaos in Washington and disrupt control of the army in the field. This in turn might allow Jefferson Davis, backed by Johnston's troops, to negotiate a peace treaty rather than surrender unconditionally. The plan was worth a try. With the Confederacy gone, Booth saw no reason to go on living.

April 14. Good Friday, the Friday before Easter and the fourth anniversary of the surrender of Fort Sumter. The defenders' flag would be returned to its rightful place that afternoon.

Lincoln began the day by having breakfast with his eldest son. Robert had seen General Lee surrender, and he described the scene in minute detail. The Southerner had looked magnificent, "with his white head and spotless uniform, his jeweled sword and gold spurs." What a contrast he made with Grant! Robert described "the small, stooping, shabby, shy man in the muddy blue uniform, with no sword and no spurs—only the frayed and dingy shoulder straps of a Lieutenant General on the rumpled blouse of a private soldier." The scene had burnt itself into Robert's memory. "Oh, it was great," he concluded. His father, equally enthusiastic, replied: "Well, my son . . . the war is now closed, and we soon will live in peace with the brave men that have been fighting against us."[23]

After breakfast, the President attended a Cabinet meeting on the military situation. It was excellent, Grant reported; he expected Sherman to report Johnston's surrender any day now. Lincoln reminded the Cabinet there must be "no bloody work." Johnny Reb must be allowed to go home and relearn the ways of peace.[24]

At the close of the meeting, Lincoln took Grant aside. He and the

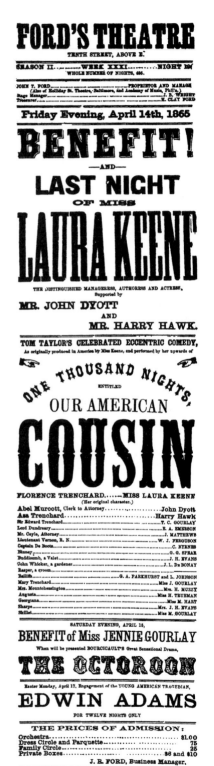

First Lady were going to Ford's Theatre in the evening to see an English comedy called *Our American Cousin*. Would Grant and his wife care to join them?

Nowadays, people pay thousands of dollars to attend banquets with the President; it is even considered an honor to be seen jogging with him in a sweaty running suit. Grant, however, remembered the First Lady's outburst at City Point. Knowing his wife's feelings about Mrs. Lincoln, he turned down the invitation as politely as he could. In place of the Grants, the First Lady asked Major Henry R. Rathbone and his fiancée, Miss Clara Harris, to be their guests.

Meanwhile, Booth learned that his intended victim would be at Ford's Theatre that evening. Perfect! The place had been like a second home for years; even his mail was addressed to its office, where he picked it up each morning during his stays in town. As a famous actor, everyone at the theater knew him, and he could come and go as he pleased.

Booth prepared for the performance of a lifetime. While Lincoln attended to the nation's business, he slipped into the theater through a side entrance. Unnoticed, he made his way across the back of the empty auditorium. To the right of the first balcony he saw the state box, a double box that workers had set up for the presidential party. Then, as now, the box had the flag of the Treasury Guards draped in front of the railing. A portrait of George Washington hung at the center of the flag.

Booth went up a short flight of stairs and opened a door into a narrow hallway. He had rehearsed every action in his mind, and he acted with sure, swift motions. Drawing his knife, he chipped plaster from the wall so that a wooden bar could be wedged in to lock the door from the inside; he found a piece of wood nearby and hid it in a dark corner next to the door. Moving down the hallway, he opened the door to the state box; the lock had been broken for weeks and nobody had remembered to fix it. The walls were covered in dark red cloth, and a Turkish carpet lay on the floor. A rocking chair, the President's favorite, stood near the rail. Booth closed the door, took a small drill from his pocket, and bored a peephole in the door so he could see from the hallway into the box.

Later that afternoon, the Lincolns took their usual carriage ride. The weather had turned raw and windy, and they sat close together as the carriage rolled toward the Navy Yard. The President did not mind the weather. He was happy—truly happy—because a terrible burden had been lifted from his mind. Mary knew Lincoln's moods without his speaking a word. "Dear Husband," she said, "you almost startle me with your great cheerfulness. I have not seen you so happy since before Willie's death."

"And well I may feel so," he replied. "Mother, I consider, *this day,* the war has come to a close. We must *both* be more cheerful in the future. Between the war and the loss of our darling Willie, we have both been very miserable."[25]

Lincoln spoke of the future. After his presidential term, they must take the boys to Europe, perhaps visit the Holy Land, a place he had always wanted to see. When they returned to America, he meant to open a law office in Springfield or Chicago, where they would spend the rest of their lives in peace and quiet. As for Ford's Theatre, neither wanted to go anymore; he was overtired and she had a splitting headache. Nevertheless, they decided they could not disappoint the public. Everyone expected them, so they must attend.

The presidential party arrived at the theater at 8:30 P.M.. Although the play had already begun, Laura Keene, the female lead, saw them from the stage. She stopped in mid-sentence, came to the footlights, and applauded. The audience stood up, cheering and waving handkerchiefs. The orchestra played "Hail to the Chief." Lincoln bowed slightly and kept walking toward the state box.

Lincoln settled into his rocking chair and scanned the audience through gold-rimmed spectacles. He saw another latecomer take his seat. It was General Ambrose Burnside, who had lost so badly at Fredericksburg back in '62. "Old Burn" was a gentleman; he never blamed Lincoln for the disaster.

The President enjoyed the play. During the third act, Mary nestled against her husband. Catching herself, she whispered: "What will Miss

OPPOSITE: *Poster announcing the gala performance of the English comedy* Our American Cousin *at Ford's Theatre on the evening of Friday, April 14, 1865.*

John Wilkes Booth pulls the trigger of a single-shot derringer pistol only inches from President Lincoln's head.

Harris think of my hanging on to you so?" Lincoln smiled. "She won't think anything about it," he said, taking her hand.[26]

At that moment, John Wilkes Booth again entered the auditorium from a side entrance and walked up the aisle toward the rear. Members of the audience who saw him in the half-light noticed that he seemed tense. Still, everyone knew the star, and the play was so much fun that they turned back to the stage. In his belt Booth carried a long hunting knife to silence the guard at the hallway door. In his pocket he had a derringer, a small, single-shot pistol. This was for Abraham Lincoln.

Booth went up a short flight of stairs and found nobody at the door to the hallway leading to the state box. Detective John F. Parker was the only officer assigned to the President that night. Parker had a reputation as a lazy brute who beat up women. Everyone in the Police Department knew his record, but somehow he had drawn the most important assignment in the capital. Bored at sitting outside a closed door, he had left his post. At first he watched the play from a seat in the orchestra. Quickly losing interest, he went to the tavern next door and got drunk. The detective was never brought up on charges, but lost his job three years later for sleeping on duty. It is unclear whether he escaped justice through a police cover-up or police stupidity.

Booth put his eye to the peephole. He could see little more than the back of Lincoln's head, but that was enough. Wait! Wait! Not yet! Take your time!

The actor knew the play by heart and was listening for his cue, a certain line in the third act. At 10:30 P.M., the male lead spoke that line. A gale of laughter swept the audience.

Now!

Booth quietly opened the door, aimed, and fired his pistol six inches from the President's head. In an instant he dropped the gun, raised the knife, and shouted the Latin phrase *Sic semper tyrannis!*—"Thus always to tyrants!"—the motto of the state of Virginia.

Lincoln's only action was to throw up his right arm at the impact of the bullet, while his wife instinctively caught him around the neck and tried to keep him from toppling over.

Startled by the noise, Major Rathbone looked up to see a puff of smoke and a man with a hunting knife poised on the railing of the box. Rathbone reached toward the stranger, who yelled, "Revenge for the South!" and slashed Rathbone's arm from the elbow to the shoulder blade.

The First Lady screamed. Booth jumped. The distance was only nine feet, and Booth had often made twelve-foot leaps from scenery during certain performances. This time, however, the spur on his right boot caught in the folds of the Treasury Guards' flag, throwing him off balance. He crashed to the stage, breaking his left leg above the ankle.

The audience thought the shot and screams had been added to the show, something to liven up the performance. But when Major Rathbone cried, "Stop that man! The President is shot!" they knew it was no act.[27]

Booth limped across the stage, waving his knife and again shouting *"Sic semper tyrannis!"* Reaching the stage door, he mounted a horse waiting in the alley and sped into the darkness. He must have been in agony, for the broken bone had torn through the flesh of his leg.

The audience recognized him at once. "That man was John Wilkes

After shooting the President, the assassin leaped to the stage of Ford's Theatre before making his escape.

Booth," someone yelled. Others took up the cry, chanting "Booth! Booth! Booth!" Shouts of "Kill him!" "Shoot him!" "Lynch him!" filled the auditorium.[28]

People jumped onto seats to get a better view. In the confusion, men's hats were trampled and women lost their shoes. Some women fainted and had to be revived with smelling salts.

Major Rathbone removed the bar and opened the hallway door. At the same moment, Dr. Charles A. Leale, an army surgeon who had been watching the play, burst through and ran to the state box. The major had to give himself first aid, because Dr. Leale was attending to the President. Two more doctors arrived moments later.

Dr. Leale gave Lincoln mouth-to-mouth resuscitation. Laying him flat on the floor, "I leaned forcibly forward directly over his body, thorax to thorax, face to face, and several times drew in a long breath, then forcibly breathed directly into his mouth and nostrils, which expanded his lungs and improved his respiration. After waiting a moment I placed my ear over his thorax and found the action of the heart improving. I rose to the erect kneeling posture, then watched for a short time and saw that the President would continue independent breathing and that instant death would not occur. I then pronounced my diagnosis and prognosis: 'His wound is mortal; it is impossible for him to recover.' "[29]

Six soldiers appeared. Dr. Leale had them lift the dying man and carry him downstairs.

"Oh, God, it can't be true!" cried members of the crowd gathering on the street. "For God's sake, is there no chance for him?"[30]

Cavalrymen ranged along the fringes of the crowd, trying to keep order. Yet their emotions ran high, too, and some could barely control themselves. Sergeant Smith Stimmel, an old campaigner, met such a man. The trooper's face was twisted with grief, and Stimmel could see that he was fighting back tears. They had just brought Lincoln out of the theater, a trail of blood leading down the stairs and across the pavement. "He means more to me than he does to you," the trooper cried. "He signed an order that saved me from being shot." Then the tears came, and he galloped away.[31]

Dr. Leale ordered Lincoln taken across the street to the house of William Petersen. A tailor by profession, Petersen rented rooms to actors from Ford's Theatre. One of those actors favored a room on the second floor, and his friend John Wilkes Booth had spent many hours lying on the bed, talking and smoking his pipe. Now they put Booth's victim in that same bed. Since it was not long enough, he had to be laid diagonally across the mattress.[32]

Even today's medical science is helpless against the kind of wound Lincoln suffered. An ounce of lead had shattered the bone below his left ear, tunneled seven and a half inches across his brain, and come to rest behind his right eye.

The doctors undressed Lincoln and covered him with mustard plasters, a mustard-seed paste used to produce heat. Then they probed for the bullet, not to save the patient, but out of curiosity. Two doctors poked unwashed fingers into the wound; two others inserted unsterilized metal probes. The probes went in three or four inches before being stopped by bone fragments. The only "medicine" given was a mixture of whiskey and water. It nearly choked the patient.

The room grew crowded as more doctors arrived, along with congressmen, government officials, and Cabinet members. The First Lady sat in an adjoining room. "Live! You must live!" she wailed. "Bring Tad—he will speak to Tad—he loves him so."[33] Robert came, but not Tad. He had been in Grover's Theatre a few blocks away, watching a gala production of *Aladdin! or His Wonderful Lamp,* when the manager stepped to the footlights and announced the assassination. An attendant took the boy back to the White House and put him to bed, though not to sleep.

Amid the noise and confusion, one man stood firm. It was as if the secretary of war had been born for this moment in American history.

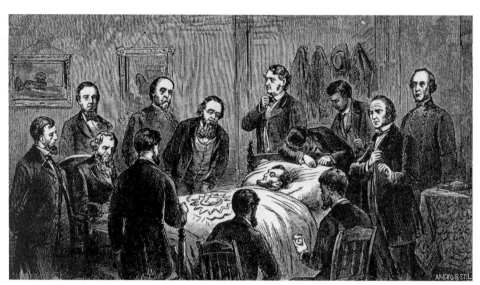

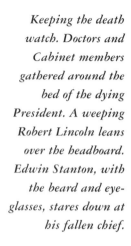

Keeping the death watch. Doctors and Cabinet members gathered around the bed of the dying President. A weeping Robert Lincoln leans over the headboard. Edwin Stanton, with the beard and eyeglasses, stares down at his fallen chief.

Edwin Stanton had said many harsh things about his chief, even called him a "damned fool" and a "baboon."[34] Yet he had been harsh for the President's own good and the good of the country. Lincoln understood. The two men came to admire each other—no, *love* each other.

"Oh, no, no—no!" cried Stanton when he saw Lincoln lying helpless. He sat at the edge of the bed and burst into tears. The tears soon stopped, however. Stanton regained his composure and took charge. Again he was Mars, the man of iron, the human dynamo. He immediately put the capital under martial law and organized the search for Booth. At his orders, troops patrolled the streets and the roads leading out of the city. A telegraph message to the New York City Police Department asked for several detectives. These were not ordinary detectives, but the best of the best, clever fellows who knew the underworld and how to get information in ways not exactly legal. So be it. Stanton wanted results—*fast*.

The vigil continued throughout the night. Lincoln grew weaker, his breathing shallow and his heartbeat irregular. Dr. Leale sat at the bedside holding his hand to "let him know that he was in touch with humanity and had a friend."[35]

The sixteenth President of the United States died at 7:22 A.M. on April 15, 1865. Dr. Leale folded the dead man's arms across his chest, smoothed his tightened facial muscles, and drew a white sheet over his head. Stanton looked at his friend, the tears streaming down his face. Those around the bed had never seen such a hurt expression on a human face as Stanton sobbed, "Now he belongs to the ages."[36]

A cold rain fell as Dr. Leale left the Petersen house. It had been a long night. His uniform was stained with blood and he had lost his hat. Groggy with fatigue, he gradually realized that he was getting soaked to the skin. No matter. The doctor wanted to walk—walk anywhere, so long as he got away from that dreadful place. As he walked, he heard the tolling of a bell. The metallic sound echoed in his aching head. Soon he heard another bell, and another, until the air filled with booming and bonging and changing. All the church bells of Washington were ringing at once. Thus the capital awoke to the death of a President.[37]

Word traveled like wildfire. "Mr. Lincoln is assassinated," people cried, spreading the dreadful news from mouth to mouth. Who? Why? How? What does it mean? What shall we do? Everybody had questions, but nobody had answers.

Yet one thing was certain: the assassination was part of a conspiracy. By late morning, newspapers told how a knife-wielding man had attacked Secretary Seward in bed at the same time as Booth pulled the trigger in the state box. Fortunately, the victim's son and daughter had driven off the attacker at great risk to their own lives. He had run from the house, screaming "I'm mad! I'm mad!"[38] What people did not know (then) was his name: Lewis Paine. Across town, George Atzerodt had been preparing to shoot Vice President Johnson, but changed his mind. Johnson, a Tennessean, carried a pistol and knew how to use it. Atzerodt did not want to meet a man who could shoot back.

The day Lincoln died is unlike any other in American history. A victorious North awoke to continue its week of celebrating. But when the telegraph keys began their clatter, the mood changed. To the end of their days, anyone old enough to understand what had happened remembered where they were when they heard the news.

A little boy heard it from his father, who burst into tears. The boy had never seen a grown man cry. Church bells tolled throughout the day, and when the stars came out at night, he thought it strange that

The cartoon titled "Britannia Lays a Wreath on Lincoln's Bier" appeared in Punch *magazine on May 6, 1865. After mercilessly, and unfairly, criticizing the President for four troubled years, the British magazine tried to make amends.*

they should—for the President was dead.[39]

In Boston, a hotel clerk woke Edwin Booth to tell him his brother was a murderer. "It was just as if I was struck on the forehead with a hammer," Edwin told a fellow actor.[40]

In Charleston, South Carolina, an elderly black woman walked the streets, wringing her hands and wailing "O Lawd! O Lawd! Marse Sam's dead! O Lawd! Uncle Sam's dead!"[41]

In Raleigh, North Carolina, General Sherman's men read the afternoon papers around their cooking fires. Most sat dazed, unable to eat or speak. Veterans who had never flinched in battle covered their faces with their hands and sobbed. During those awful moments, they learned something about themselves and their commander in chief. How thoughtless they had been! How they had taken him for granted! How they missed him now! "I don't think we knew how much we did think of him until then," an officer wrote in his diary.[42]

In Coles County, Illinois, Dennis Hanks was at his chores when a neighbor appeared. "Dennis," the neighbor stuttered, "honest Abe's dead; shot dead!"

Struggling to keep hold of himself, Dennis saddled his horse and rode over to Sarah Lincoln's place. "Aunt Sairy," he told Lincoln's stepmother, "Abe's dead." No hemming and hawing for this simple man; just the plain truth. "Abe's dead."

She heard the words without changing her expression. "Yes, I know, Denny," she replied calmly. "I knowed they'd kill him. I ben awaitin' fur it."[43] She had shared her fears with Abraham before he went to Washington in 1861. He had told her not to worry and that everything would be fine.

The news did not sadden everyone. Many Northerners still hated the

President and said so. They paid the price. Hundreds were fined and thrown into jail for up to six months. Still others came up against "fist justice"—*hard.*

A crowd saw Patrick Travis, of Wrentham, Massachusetts, whipping a scarecrow with a sign around its neck: "Abraham Lincoln, the nigger worshipper." Crowd members beat Travis bloody and tossed him head-first into a manure pile. Elsewhere, people tarred and feathered, even horsewhipped, anyone who spoke badly of Lincoln. Mobs wrecked the offices of anti-Lincoln newspapers and clubbed their editors. Joseph Shaw, editor of the Westminster, Maryland, *Democrat,* died under the blows of an enraged mob. Beatings often took place with policemen looking on. "Served him right," an officer snarled as a man had his head split open with a bottle.[44]

Many Southerners were overjoyed. In their eyes, Lincoln was still the "beast" who had started the war, waged it with brutality, and freed the slaves. At the news of his death, they gave the rebel yell, threw their hats in the air, and burst into song. "All honor to John Wilkes Booth, who has rid the world of a tyrant," a sedate Louisiana lady exclaimed.[45] The Marshall, Texas, *Republican* applauded Booth's action: "It is certainly a matter of congratulation that Lincoln is dead, because the world is happily rid of a monster that disgraced the form of humanity." The newspaper's only regret was that Lincoln had not been killed four years earlier. It called his killer a patriot.[46]

Other Southerners reacted with shock and shame that the crime had been committed in their name. This was particularly true of some former Johnny Rebs. Whatever the merits of their cause, most had fought for it honorably. It angered them that an unarmed man should be shot from behind with his wife sitting beside him. Brave men, real soldiers, did not do such cowardly things. When the news reached the camp at Point Lookout, Maryland, 22,000 prisoners sent a letter to the War Department expressing their horror at the assassination.

Their generals agreed. George Pickett was heartbroken. Joseph Johnston thought the South had lost its best friend. Yet the most eloquent expression of sorrow came from the Confederacy's greatest hero. Upon returning to his home in Richmond after Appomattox, Robert E. Lee learned of the President's death. Calling the assassination a "crime"

A heartbreaking scene on Pennsylvania Avenue: the funeral procession bearing Abraham Lincoln's body from the White House to the U.S. Capitol.

unworthy of Americans, he said he had surrendered as much to Lincoln's "goodness as to Grant's artillery."[47]

Lincoln's funeral took place in the East Room of the White House on April 19. As in the dream, his body lay in a coffin set on a platform surrounded by sobbing mourners. The First Lady was too upset to attend. She allowed no one into her room except Elizabeth Keckley and her sons. Only Tad seemed able to comfort her. He stood beside her bed, cringing at her outbursts. At times he would throw his arms around her neck and plead, "Don't cry so, Mamma! don't cry, or you will make me cry, too! You will break my heart." She could not bear to see her darling boy in misery and would calm herself with great effort—at least for a short time.[48]

Downstairs, Robert Lincoln stood at the foot of his father's coffin, his red, swollen eyes staring blankly into space. Ulysses S. Grant stood at the coffin's head, silently weeping for "the greatest man I have ever known."[49]

After the service, the funeral procession moved slowly down Pennsylvania Avenue. Thousands lined the sidewalks, with more thousands crowding rooftops and windows. A regiment of black troops, just back from the front, became caught in a traffic jam ahead of the procession. Unable to go any farther, the regiment did an about-face and thus led the procession. Although that annoyed some whites, most said the President would have wanted blacks to lead the way.

The troops marched with tears rolling down their cheeks. A black woman told an interviewer years later that they were so sad they got out of step with the band, which was playing the saddest music she had ever heard. "Many even broke out of line and had to sit down on the side of the street. They just could not stand that music and march a single step farther."[50]

Poster offering a reward for the capture of John Wilkes Booth and his accomplices.

Lincoln's body lay in state under the soaring dome of the Capitol. Next day, April 20, thousands stood patiently in the rain, waiting their turn to say good-bye. Most waited two or three hours, some even five or six hours. Silently, sadly, they filed past the open coffin at a rate of three thousand an hour. The President's body lay there, its face gray as the gray sky, dressed in the familiar black suit.

April 21. A nine-car funeral train set out with the bodies of Abraham and Willie Lincoln. Except for bypassing Cincinnati and Pittsburgh, the 1,600-mile journey followed the same route Lincoln had taken as President-elect in 1861, only in reverse.

By day, country folks gathered beside the tracks, waving handkerchiefs and tiny American flags. By night, farm families sat in wagons with flaming torches or stood around roaring bonfires visible for miles. Approaching a city, the train ran between solid walls of humanity. Wherever it stopped, mourners streamed past the open coffin. Many touched the coffin as they

War Department, Washington, April 20. 1865.

$100,000 REWARD!

THE MURDERER

Of our late beloved President, ABRAHAM LINCOLN,

IS STILL AT LARGE.

$50,000 REWARD!

will be paid by this Department for his apprehension, in addition to any reward offered by Municipal Authorities or State Executives.

$25,000 REWARD!

will be paid for the apprehension of JOHN H. SURRATT, one of Booth's accomplices.

$25,000 REWARD!

will be paid for the apprehension of DANIEL C. HARROLD, another of Booth's accomplices.

LIBERAL REWARDS will be paid for any information that shall conduce to the arrest of either of the above-named criminals, or their accomplices.

All persons harboring or secreting the said persons, or either of them, or aiding or assisting their concealment or escape, will be treated as accomplices in the murder of the President and the attempted assassination of the Secretary of State, and shall be subject to trial before a Military Commission and the punishment of DEATH.

Let the stain of innocent blood be removed from the land by the arrest and punishment of the murderers.

All good citizens are exhorted to aid public justice on this occasion. Every man should consider his own conscience charged with this solemn duty, and rest neither night nor day until it be accomplished.

EDWIN M. STANTON, *Secretary of War.*

DESCRIPTIONS.—BOOTH is 5 feet 7 or 8 inches high, slender build, high forehead, black hair, black eyes, and wears a heavy black moustache.
JOHN H. SURRATT is about 5 feet 9 inches. Hair rather thin and dark, eyes rather light, no beard. Would weigh 145 or 150 pounds. Complexion rather pale and clear, with color in his cheeks. Wore light clothes of fine quality. Shoulders square; check bones rather prominent; chin narrow; ears projecting at the top, face rather long and square, fore broad. Parts his hair on the right side; neck rather long. His lips are firmly set. A slim man.
DANIEL C. HARROLD is 22 years of age, 5 feet 6 or 7 inches high rather hard shouldered, otherwise light built, dark hair, little (if any) moustache, dark eyes, weight about 140 pounds.

GEO. F. NESBITT & CO., Printers and Stationers, cor. Pearl and Pine Streets, N. Y.

Shot in the neck and dying, Lincoln's assassin is dragged from the burning Virginia barn in which he had been cornered by Union soldiers.

passed; some kissed it. Occasionally a woman, overcome by grief, bent down to kiss the dead man's face, but she was usually headed off by an alert guard.[51]

Others viewed the body calmly, reflecting the calm they saw in its face. Lincoln appeared contented, as if he had passed through an ordeal and found peace at last. "I saw him . . . in his coffin," wrote David R. Locke, an Ohio newspaper editor. "The face was the same as in life. Death had not changed the kindly countenance in any line. There was upon it the same sad look that it had worn always, though not so intensely sad as it had been in life. It was as if the spirit had come back to the poor clay, reshaped the wonderfully sweet face, and given it an expression of gladness. . . . It was the look of a worn man suddenly relieved."[52]

Meanwhile, the hunt for Lincoln's killer continued. The first clue came from Susan Mahoney, a black housekeeper employed by Mrs. Surratt. The night after the assassination, she had overheard things that made her suspicious. She told her aunt, who told her employer, who told one of Stanton's detectives. Within three days, Booth's accomplices were under arrest. After a speedy trial before nine army officers, Mary Surratt, Lewis Paine, George Atzerodt, and David Herold died on the gallows together. Booth eluded capture until the morning of April 26, when soldiers shot him in a barn near Port Royal, Virginia. He had no regrets about his deed. "Tell mother," he whispered, "tell mother I die for my country." His country, the Confederacy, died only hours later. That afternoon, General Johnston surrendered to General Sherman in North Carolina.[53]

On May 3, at 8:00 A.M., the funeral train pulled into Springfield. Next morning, friends and neighbors escorted the bodies of Lincoln and his son to Oak Ridge Cemetery, two miles north of the city. Workers placed the coffins in a tomb. After mourners said the last prayers and

Soldiers look on as executioners prepare to hang four of John Wilkes Booth's accomplices. Mrs. Mary Surratt, the first woman ever executed by the U.S. government, is seated on the left. The umbrellas were used to shield the condemned from the sun's glare.

sang the last hymns, they sealed the tomb and everyone left. Life went on.

Billy Yank received new marching orders. This time, however, they would not send him into battle. The Union armies were to assemble in Washington for a final ritual before disbanding. There was to be a Grand Review, a parade to beat all parades.

In the days leading up to the review, the hills around the capital blossomed with tents. Troops camped around Robert E. Lee's former home on Arlington Heights had a magnificent view from across the Potomac. Although the Washington Monument remained unfinished, the statue of Freedom crowned the Capitol, where she stands today. Those lucky enough to get passes saw the sights: the Capitol, Supreme Court, Treasury, Smithsonian Institution. Pennsylvania Avenue, filthy as ever, was decorated with flags and flowers. A reviewing stand had been built opposite the White House.

The Grand Review lasted two days, May 23–24. Bugles blared. Drums rolled. Bands played. The blue columns swept around the Capi-

tol and down the long slope to Pennsylvania Avenue. The infantry marched twenty abreast, followed by cavalry and horse-drawn artillery. Names already immortal were stitched on their battle flags: Bull Run, Shiloh, Antietam, Fredericksburg, Chancellorsville, Vicksburg, Gettysburg, Wilderness, Spotsylvania, Cold Harbor, Petersburg, Five Forks, Kennesaw Mountain, Atlanta, Savannah.

Nearing the reviewing stand, the columns passed a flag that had never seen battle. It was the flag of the Treasury Guards, and it had a long tear in one corner. Everyone knew exactly where to look for the tear, and how it came to be there.

As they strode past the flag, more than one veteran swore that a ghostly figure had stepped into line and walked beside him for a few paces before vanishing. The figure was tall and lanky, and he wore a black suit and a stovepipe hat. Although his face was hidden in shadow, there was no mistaking his identity.

OPPOSITE: *The Grand Review along Pennsylvania Avenue, May 23 and 24, 1865. For two days, the victorious Union armies marched from Capitol Hill to the end of the Avenue, where most were discharged and began the journey back to civilian life.*

Notes

PROLOGUE: AN AFFECTIONATE FAREWELL

1. Allen Thorndike Rice, ed., *Reminiscences of Abraham Lincoln by Distinguished Men of His Time* (New York: Haskell House, 1971), 479–80.
2. Saul Sigelschiffer, *The American Conscience: The Drama of the Lincoln-Douglas Debates* (New York: Horizon Press, 1973), 143.
3. Carl Sandburg, *Abraham Lincoln: The War Years,* 4 vols. (New York: Harcourt, Brace and Co., 1939), II: 278.
4. Roy P. Basler, ed., *The Collected Works of Abraham Lincoln,* 9 vols. (New Brunswick, N.J.: Rutgers University Press, 1953–55), I: 190.
5. Webb Garrison, *The Lincoln Nobody Knows* (Nashville: Rutledge Hill Press, 1993), 162; Michael Burlingame, *The Inner World of Abraham Lincoln* (Chicago: University of Illinois Press, 1995), 105.
6. Ibid.
7. Don E. Fehrenbacher and Virginia Fehrenbacher, eds., *Recollected Words of Abraham Lincoln* (Stanford: Stanford University Press, 1996).

CHAPTER 1: BEGINNINGS

1. Eleanor Atkinson, *The Boyhood of Lincoln* (New York: McClure Co., 1908), 6.
2. Ibid., 8.
3. Ibid., 7–8.
4. Benjamin Thomas, *Abraham Lincoln* (New York: Alfred A. Knopf, 1952), 9.
5. Basler, *The Collected Works of Abraham Lincoln*, IV: 62.
6. Benjamin Thomas, *Lincoln's New Salem* (Springfield, Ill.: The Abraham Lincoln Association, 1934), 27.
7. Louis A. Warren, *Lincoln's Youth: Indiana Years Seven to Twenty-One, 1816–1830* (New York: Appleton-Century-Crofts, 1959), 54.
8. Atkinson, *The Boyhood of Lincoln,* 19.
9. Ralph G. Newman, ed., *Lincoln for the Ages* (Garden City, N.Y.: Doubleday, 1960), 51.
10. Stephen B. Oates, *With Malice Toward None: The Life of Abraham Lincoln* (New York: Harper & Row, 1977), 9; Thomas, *Abraham Lincoln,* 12.
11. Atkinson, *The Boyhood of Lincoln,* 40.
12. Warren, *Lincoln's Youth,* 133; Basler, *The Collected Works of Abraham Lincoln,* I: 1.
13. Burlingame, *The Inner World of Abraham Lincoln,* 37.
14. Warren, *Lincoln's Youth,* 107.
15. Basler, *The Collected Works of Abraham Lincoln,* IV: 240.
16. Stephen B. Oates, *Abraham Lincoln: The Man Behind the Myths* (New York: New American Library, 1984), 59; Basler, *The Collected Works of Abraham Lincoln,* IV: 240.
17. James Ford Rhodes, *History of the United States from the Compromise of 1850,* 7 vols. (New York: Macmillan, 1913–1916), I: 323; Warren, *Lincoln's Youth,* 182.
18. Burlingame, *The Inner World of Abraham Lincoln,* 38.
19. Paul Horgan, *Citizen of New Salem* (New York: Farrar, Straus & Cudahy, 1961), 65.
20. Thomas, *Lincoln's New Salem,* 47.
21. Horgan, *Citizen of New Salem,* 25.
22. Thomas, *Lincoln's New Salem,* 57.
23. Horgan, *Citizen of New Salem,* 71.
24. Thomas, *Lincoln's New Salem,* 76–77.
25. Joshua F. Speed, *Reminiscences of Abraham Lincoln and Notes of a Visit to California: Two Lectures* (Louisville: John P. Morton, 1884), 22.
26. Jean H. Baker, *Mary Todd Lincoln: A Biography* (New York: W. W. Norton, 1987), 85.
27. There is a question as to whether or not Mary Todd was Abraham's first love. According to one story, his true love was Ann Rutledge, the daughter of a tavern owner in New Salem, whose death at the age of twenty-two left him devastated. Ann was a good friend, but there is no proof that she

was anything more. He did, however, carry on a brief courtship with Mary Owens, the daughter of a wealthy Kentucky landowner visiting relatives in New Salem. But Miss Owens decided he was, as she put it, "lacking in those links that make up a woman's chain of happiness." While out riding with some other couples, they came to a swift-running stream. Whereas the other men helped their partners across, Abraham rode ahead without looking back to see how she was doing. She decided to look elsewhere for a mate. See Newman, *Lincoln for the Ages,* 67.

28. Oates, *With Malice Toward None,* 57; Paul M. Angle, ed., *Herndon's Life of Lincoln: The History and Personal Recollections of Abraham Lincoln As Originally Written by William H. Herndon and Jesse W. Weik* (Cleveland: World Publishing Co., 1965), 170; Basler, *The Collected Works of Abraham Lincoln,* I: 228–29.

29. Angle, *Herndon's Life of Lincoln,* 179.

30. Ruth Painter Randall, *Lincoln's Sons* (Boston: Little, Brown, 1955), 364.

31. Emanuel Hertz, *The Hidden Lincoln: From the Letters and Papers of William H. Herndon* (New York: Viking, 1930), 176.

32. Ibid., 105, 129, 176–77.

33. Angle, *Herndon's Life of Lincoln,* 385; Baker, *Mary Todd Lincoln,* 89.

34. Thomas, *Abraham Lincoln,* 76.

35. Hertz, *The Hidden Lincoln,* 400–401.

36. Ruth Painter Randall, *Mary Lincoln: Biography of a Marriage* (Boston: Little, Brown, 1953), 104.

37. Oates, *Abraham Lincoln: The Man Behind the Myths,* 45; Randall, *Mary Lincoln,* 68.

38. Oates, *Abraham Lincoln: The Man Behind the Myths,* 49.

39. Burlingame, *The Inner World of Abraham Lincoln,* 155, 156.

40. Basler, *The Collected Works of Abraham Lincoln,* II: 81–82.

41. William E. Barton, *The Women Lincoln Loved* (Indianapolis: Bobbs-Merrill, 1927), 299–300.

42. Randall, *Mary Lincoln,* 105–106.

43. Ward Hill Lamon, *Recollections of Abraham Lincoln, 1847–1865* (Washington, D.C.:

Dorothy Hill Lamon, 1911), 19.

44. Basler, *The Collected Works of Abraham Lincoln,* I, 439.

45. Lloyd Lewis, *Captain Sam Grant* (Boston: Little, Brown, 1950), 164.

CHAPTER 2: THE PECULIAR INSTITUTION

1. Herbert Aptheker, *American Negro Slave Revolts* (Millwood, N.Y.: Kraus Reprint Co., 1977), 201.

2. John Hope Franklin, *From Slavery to Freedom: A History of Negro Americans* (New York: Alfred A. Knopf, 1967), 217.

3. Richard Wheeler, ed., *Lee's Terrible Swift Sword: From Antietam to Chancellorsville* (New York: HarperCollins, 1992), 327.

4. Kenneth M. Stampp, *The Peculiar Institution: Slavery in the Ante-Bellum South* (New York: Alfred A. Knopf, 1956), 202.

5. Avery O. Craven, *The Coming of the Civil War* (Chicago: University of Chicago Press, 1942), 78.

6. Julius Lester, ed., *To Be a Slave* (New York: Scholastic, 1968), 64.

7. James M. McPherson, *Ordeal by Fire: The Civil War and Reconstruction* (New York: Alfred A. Knopf, 1982), 36.

8. Stampp, *The Peculiar Institution,* 145.

9. Belinda Hurmance, ed., *Before Freedom: 48 Oral Histories of Former North and South Carolina Slaves* (New York: Mentor Books, 1990), 145; James Mellon, ed., *Bullwhip Days: The Slaves Remember* (New York: Weidenfeld & Nicholson, 1988), 197–98.

10. Mellon, *Bullwhip Days,* 240.

11. Deborah Gray White, *Ar'n't I a Woman? Female Slaves in the Plantation South* (New York: W. W. Norton, 1985), 33; Stampp, *The Peculiar Institution,* 349.

12. Mellon, *Bullwhip Days,* 147.

13. Ibid., 39.

14. Frederick Douglass, *My Bondage and My Freedom* (New York: Miller, Orton, and Mulligan), 1855, 253–54.

15. Lester, *To Be a Slave,* 47.

16. John W. Blassingame, *The Slave Community: Plantation Life in the Antebellum South* (New

York: Oxford University Press, 1972), 91.

17. John E. Washington, *They Knew Lincoln* (New York: E. P. Dutton, 1942), 128.

18. Lester, *To Be a Slave,* 85, 101.

19. Ibid., 83.

20. Stampp, *The Peculiar Institution,* 128; Lester, *To Be a Slave,* 40.

21. Stephen B. Oates, *The Fires of Jubilee: Nat Turner's Fierce Rebellion* (New York: Harper Perennial, 1990), 125.

22. Aptheker, *American Negro Slave Revolts,* 307.

23. James M. McPherson, *The Struggle for Equality: Abolitionists and the Negro in the Civil War and Reconstruction* (Princeton: Princeton University Press, 1964), 153.

24. Martin Duberman, ed., *The Antislavery Vanguard: New Essays on the Abolitionists* (Princeton: Princeton University Press, 1965), 169–70.

25. Franklin, *From Slavery to Freedom: A History of Negro Americans,* 264.

26. Leon F. Litwack, *North of Slavery: The Negro in the United States, 1790–1860* (Chicago: University of Chicago Press, 1961), 98.

27. Henrietta Buckmaster's *Let My People Go: The Story of the Underground Railroad and the Growth of the Abolitionist Movement* (Columbia, S.C.: University of South Carolina Press, 1995) is an excellent account of these daring rescuers.

28. Rhodes, *History of the United States from the Compromise of 1850,* I: 369.

29. Philip S. Foner, ed., *The Life and Writings of Frederick Douglass,* 4 vols. (New York: International Publishers, 1950), II: 207.

30. Louis A. Warren, *The Slavery Atmosphere of Lincoln's Youth* (Fort Wayne, Ind.: Lincolonia Publishers, 1933), no page numbers given.

31. William H. Townsend, *Lincoln and His Wife's Home Town* (Indianapolis: Bobbs-Merrill, 1929), 81, 147–48; Baker, *Mary Todd Lincoln,* 68.

32. Basler, *The Collected Works of Abraham Lincoln,* III: 315.

33. Ibid., II: 130.

34. Burlingame, *The Inner World of Abraham Lincoln,* 27.

35. Ibid., 78; Benjamin Quarles, *Lincoln and the*

Negro (New York: Oxford University Press, 1962), 36, 40; Eugene A. Berwanger, *The Frontier Against Slavery: Western Anti-Negro Prejudice and the Slavery Extension Controversy* (Chicago: University of Illinois Press, 1967), 4.

36. Basler, *The Collected Works of Abraham Lincoln,* II: 461–62.

37. P. M. Zall, ed., *Abe Lincoln Laughing: Humorous Anecdotes from Original Sources by and About Abraham Lincoln* (Berkeley: University of California Press, 1982), 5.

38. Charles Hamilton and Lloyd Ostendorf, *Lincoln in Photographs: An Album of Every Known Pose* (Norman: University of Oklahoma Press, 1963), 217.

39. Don E. Fehrenbacher, *Prelude to Greatness: Lincoln in the 1850s* (Stanford: Stanford University Press, 1962), 103.

40. Sigelschiffer, *The American Conscience,* 148.

41. Oates, *With Malice Toward None,* 19; Randall, *Mary Lincoln,* 152.

42. Robert W. Johannsen, ed., *The Lincoln-Douglas Debates* (New York: Oxford University Press, 1965), 46.

43. Ibid., 162.

44. Ibid., 53.

45. Oates, *With Malice Toward None,* 160.

CHAPTER 3: AND THE WAR CAME

1. J. C. Furnas, *The Road to Harpers Ferry* (New York: Wiliam Sloane Associates, 1955), 19.

2. Stephen B. Oates, *To Purge This Land with Blood: A Biography of John Brown* (New York: Harper & Row, 1970), 230.

3. Furnas, *The Road to Harpers Ferry,* 44.

4. Paul Finkelman, ed., *His Soul Goes Marching On: Responses to John Brown and the Harpers Ferry Raid* (Charlottesville: University of Virginia Press, 1995), 42; David M. Potter, *The Impending Crisis, 1848–1861* (New York: Harper Torchbooks, 1976), 381; Oswald Garrison Villard, *John Brown* (New York: Alfred A. Knopf, 1943), 565.

5. After Brown's failure at Harpers Ferry, the Secret Six refused to take responsibility for their actions. Some lied about their

involvement or fled to Canada, and one suffered a nervous breakdown. See Edward J. Renehan, Jr., *The Secret Six* (New York: Crown, 1995).

6. Richard Wheeler, ed., *A Rising Thunder: From Lincoln's Election to the Battle of Bull Run* (New York: HarperCollins, 1994), 10–11.

7. Garrison, *The Lincoln Nobody Knows*, 74–75.

8. Philip B. Kunhardt, Jr., *A New Birth of Freedom: Lincoln at Gettysburg* (Boston: Little, Brown, 1983), 150.

9. Oates, *With Malice Toward None*, 179.

10. Quarles, *Lincoln and the Negro*, 56.

11. McPherson, *The Struggle for Equality*, 17, 25.

12. Paul M. Angle, *"Here I Have Lived": A History of Lincoln's Springfield, 1821–1865* (Springfield, Ill.: The Abraham Lincoln Association, 1935), 245.

13. Randall, *Lincoln's Sons*, 75.

14. Villard, *John Brown*, 565.

15. Randall, *Mary Lincoln*, 167; Katherine Helm, *The True Story of Mary, Wife of Lincoln, Containing Recollections of Mary Lincoln's Sister (Mrs. Ben Hardin Helm), Extracts from Her War-Time Diary, Numerous Letters and Other Documents Now First Published* (New York: Harper & Brothers, 1928), 153.

16. Henry Villard, *Lincoln on the Eve of '61* (New York: Alfred A. Knopf, 1941), 19.

17. Belle Irvin Wiley, *The Road to Appomattox* (Memphis: Memphis State University Press, 1956), 44.

18. Wheeler, *A Rising Thunder*, 73–74.

19. Merton E. Coulter, *The Confederate States of America* (Baton Rouge: Louisiana State University Press, 1959), 14–15.

20. Wheeler, *A Rising Thunder*, 33.

21. Victor Searcher, *Lincoln's Journey to Greatness* (Philadelphia: John C. Winston Co., 1960), 11.

22. Lamon, *Recollections of Abraham Lincoln*, 33.

23. Searcher, *Lincoln's Journey to Greatness*, 11.

24. A. K. McClure, *Abraham Lincoln and the Men of War Times: Some Personal Recollections of War and Politics During the Lincoln Administration* (Philadelphia: The Times Publishing Co., 1892), 45.

25. Basler, *The Collected Works of Abraham Lincoln*, II: 253.

26. Noah Brooks, *Washington in Lincoln's Time* (New York: Rinehart & Co., 1958), 46.

27. William E. Baringer, *A House Dividing: Lincoln as President Elect* (Springfield, Ill.: The Abraham Lincoln Association, 1945), 303; Kunhardt, *A New Birth of Freedom: Lincoln at Gettysburg*, 63.

28. Villard, *Lincoln on the Eve of '61*, 70–71; Burlingame, *The Inner World of Abraham Lincoln*, 281.

29. Julia Taft Bayne, *Tad Lincoln's Father* (Boston: Little, Brown, 1931), 20.

30. Wheeler, *A Rising Thunder*, 68. When the Civil War began, Douglas gave Lincoln his full support. The Little Giant died in June 1861.

31. Ibid.

32. C. Vann Woodward, ed., *Mary Chesnut's Civil War* (New Haven: Yale University Press, 1981), 48.

33. Margaret Sanborn, *Robert E. Lee: A Portrait*, 2 vols. (Philadelphia: J. B. Lippincott, 1966, 1967), I: 302.

34. David S. Reynolds, *Walt Whitman's America: A Cultural Biography* (New York: Alfred A. Knopf, 1995), 417–18.

35. Courtlandt Canby, ed., *Lincoln and the Civil War: A Portrait and a History* (New York: George Braziller, 1960), 62.

36. Oates, *With Malice Toward None*, 233.

37. Canby, *Lincoln and the Civil War*, 61.

38. Oates, *With Malice Toward None*, 235.

39. Randall, *Mary Lincoln*, 206.

40. Wheeler, *A Rising Thunder*, 344.

41. Ibid., 346.

42. Bayne, *Tad Lincoln's Father*, 121.

43. Wheeler, *A Rising Thunder*, 366.

44. Ibid., 359.

45. Zall, *Abe Lincoln Laughing*, 212.

46. Civil War battles often had two names. This was because Yankees named them after the nearest body of water; rebels after a landmark, such as a town.

47. Wheeler, *A Rising Thunder*, 381.

48. Ibid., 372.

49. Stefan Lorant, *Lincoln: A Picture History of His Life* (New York: Harper & Brothers, 1952), 127.

50. Basler, *The Collected Works of Abraham Lincoln*, IV: 439.

CHAPTER 4: THE FIERY TRIAL

1. The area later seceded from Virginia to form the state of West Virginia.
2. T. Harry Williams, *Lincoln and His Generals* (New York: Alfred A. Knopf, 1952), 44.
3. Richard Wheeler, ed., *Sword over Richmond: An Eyewitness History of McClellan's Peninsula Campaign* (New York: Harper & Row, 1986), 36.
4. James B. Murfin, *The Gleam of Bayonets: The Battle of Antietam and the Maryland Campaign of 1862* (New York: Thomas Youseloff, 1965), 45; Stephen W. Sears, *George B. McClellan: The Young Napoleon* (New York: Ticknor & Fields, 1988), 22.
5. Wheeler, *Sword over Richmond,* 49.
6. Helen Nicolay, *Lincoln's Secretary* (New York: Longman, Green, 1949), 227; Justin G. Turner and Linda Levitt Turner, *Mary Todd Lincoln: Her Life and Letters* (New York: Alfred A. Knopf, 1972), 89.
7. Canby, *Lincoln and the Civil War,* 246–47.
8. Sandburg, *Abraham Lincoln: The War Years,* III: 433.
9. John Hay, "Life in the White House in the Time of Lincoln," *Century Magazine* (November 1890): 33–34.
10. Philip B. Kunhardt, Jr., et al., *Lincoln: An Illustrated Biography* (New York: Alfred A. Knopf, 1992), 330.
11. Oates, *With Malice Toward None,* 248.
12. Helen Nicolay, *Personal Traits of Abraham Lincoln* (New York: D. Appleton Century Co., 1939), 210; Sandburg, *Abraham Lincoln: The War Years,* I: 278.
13. Ibid., II: 319.
14. Nicolay, *Personal Traits of Abraham Lincoln,* 281; Sandburg, *Abraham Lincoln: The War Years,* III: 477.
15. Richard N. Current, *The Lincoln Nobody Knows* (New York: Hill & Wang, 1990), 166.
16. Nicolay, *Personal Traits of Abraham Lincoln,* 204.
17. Sandburg, *Abraham Lincoln: The War Years,* II: 241.
18. Bayne, *Tad Lincoln's Father,* 165.
19. Ibid., 108–10.
20. Ibid., 136.
21. Elizabeth Keckley, *Behind the Scenes; or, Thirty Years a Slave and Four Years in the White House* (New York: Oxford University Press, 1988), 104–105. This story has been questioned because the asylum was not visible from the White House. It could, however, be seen from the Soldiers' Home. Mrs. Keckley may simply have gotten the places mixed up in the retelling of the story.
22. Quarles, *Lincoln and the Negro,* 201–203.
23. Sandburg, *Abraham Lincoln: The War Years,* I: 496.
24. Francis B. Carpenter, *Six Months in the White House with Abraham Lincoln: The Story of a Picture* (New York: Hurd & Houghton, 1866), 46.
25. Sears, *George B. McClellan,* 25.
26. Sanborn, *Robert E. Lee,* II: 177.
27. David Herbert Donald, *Lincoln* (New York: Simon & Schuster, 1995), 359.
28. Sandburg, *Abraham Lincoln: The War Years,* I: 495.
29. Gerald F. Linderman, *Embattled Courage: The Experience of Combat in the American Civil War* (New York: Free Press, 1987), 125.
30. Basler, *The Collected Works of Abraham Lincoln,* V: 474.
31. Keckley, *Behind the Scenes,* 137; Sanborn, *Robert E. Lee,* II: 87.
32. James M. McPherson, *The Negro's Civil War: How Black Americans Felt and Acted During the War for the Union* (New York: Ballantine Books, 1991), 39.
33. Joseph T. Glatthaar, *Forged in Battle: The Civil War Alliance of Black Soldiers and White Officers* (New York: Free Press, 1990), 30.
34. McPherson, *The Struggle for Equality,* 108–109.
35. Oates, *Abraham Lincoln: The Man Behind the Myths,* 94. Moving from west to east, Tennessee's neighbors were Arkansas, Mississippi, Alabama, Georgia, North Carolina, South Carolina, and Virginia.
36. Canby, *Lincoln and the Civil War,* 312.
37. David H. Bates, *Lincoln in the Telegraph Office* (New York: Century Co., 1907), 138–41.
38. Basler, *The Collected Works of Abraham Lincoln,* V: 372.
39. *Douglass' Monthly* (September 1862): 707.
40. Mark E. Neely, *The Last Best Hope of Earth:*

Abraham Lincoln and the Promise of America (Cambridge: Harvard University Press, 1993), 107.

41. Basler, *The Collected Works of Abraham Lincoln,* V: 388.

42. Sears, *George B. McClellan,* 318.

43. Belle Irvin Wiley, *The Life of Johnny Reb: The Common Soldier of the Confederacy* (Baton Rouge: Louisiana State University Press, 1978), 75.

44. McPherson, *Ordeal by Fire,* 306.

45. Washington, *They Knew Lincoln,* 90–91.

46. Oates, *With Malice Toward None,* 333.

47. Washington, *They Knew Lincoln,* 91; James B. McPherson, *Marching Toward Freedom: The Negro in the Civil War, 1861–1865* (New York: Alfred A. Knopf, 1967), 40; Oates, *With Malice Toward None,* 333.

48. Robert Penn Warren, *Who Speaks for the Negro?* (New York: Random House, 1966), 262. In a famous article, the black historian Lerone Bennett, Jr., accused Lincoln of being a racist. See "Was Abe Lincoln a White Supremacist?" *Ebony* 23 (February 1968): 35–42.

49. *Douglass' Monthly* (October 1862): 721.

50. Frederick Douglass, *Life and Times of Frederick Douglass Written by Himself* (reprint of 1892 rev. ed., London: Collier, 1962), 489.

51. Mellon, *Bullwhip Days,* 344.

52. Belle Irvin Wiley, *The Plain People of the Confederacy* (Baton Rouge: Louisiana State University Press, 1943), 73.

53. Washington, *They Knew Lincoln,* 85–87.

CHAPTER 5: NEW BIRTH OF FREEDOM

1. James McPherson, *Abraham Lincoln and the Second American Revolution* (New York: Oxford University Press, 1991), 57.

2. Basler, *The Collected Works of Abraham Lincoln,* VI: 266–67.

3. Current, *The Lincoln Nobody Knows,* 179, 180.

4. Office of the Deputy Assistant Secretary of Defense, *Black Americans in Defense of Our Nation* (Washington: Department of Defense, 1985), no pages given.

5. Ibid.

6. *Douglass' Monthly* (August 1863).

7. Basler, *The Collected Works of Abraham Lincoln,* V: 423.

8. Reid Mitchell, *Civil War Soldiers* (New York: Viking, 1988), 141; Belle Irvin Wiley, "Billy Yank and Abraham Lincoln," *The Abraham Lincoln Quarterly* VI (June 1950): 112; Belle Irvin Wiley, *The Life of Billy Yank: The Common Soldier of the Union* (Baton Rouge: Louisiana State University Press, 1978), 120, 283.

9. McPherson, *Ordeal by Fire,* 355; Forrest G. Wood, *Black Scare: The Racist Response to Emancipation and Reconstruction* (Berkeley and Los Angeles: University of California Press, 1968), 46.

10. Glatthaar, *Forged in Battle,* 79.

11. James M. McPherson, *Battle Cry of Freedom: The Civil War Era* (New York: Oxford University Press, 1988), 566.

12. Glatthaar, *Forged in Battle,* 156–58.

13. Quarles, *Lincoln and the Negro,* 173.

14. Glatthaar, *Forged in Battle,* 80.

15. Basler, *The Collected Works of Abraham Lincoln,* VI: 409–10; Burlingame, *The Inner World of Abraham Lincoln,* 83.

16. Quarles, *Lincoln and the Negro,* 173; McPherson, *The Negro's Civil War,* 158.

17. Oates, *With Malice Toward None,* 338.

18. Basler, *The Collected Works of Abraham Lincoln,* VI: 78–79.

19. Wheeler, *Lee's Terrible Swift Sword,* 341.

20. Randall, *Lincoln's Sons,* 140.

21. Ibid., 181.

22. Wheeler, *Lee's Terrible Swift Sword,* 351.

23. Brooks, *Washington in Lincoln's Time,* 56.

24. Wheeler, *Lee's Terrible Swift Sword,* 351.

25. Brooks, *Washington in Lincoln's Time,* 60–61.

26. Noah Brooks, *Abraham Lincoln and the Downfall of American Slavery* (New York: G. P. Putnam's Sons, 1894), 358; Sandburg, *Abraham Lincoln: The War Years,* II: 97.

27. Wheeler, *Voices of the Civil War,* 1.

28. Earl Schenck Miers, *The Web of Victory: Grant at Vicksburg* (New York: Alfred A. Knopf, 1955), 86.

29. Sandburg, *Abraham Lincoln: The War Years,* III: 63.

30. Gabor S. Boritt, ed., *Lincoln's Generals* (New York: Oxford University Press, 1994), 85.

31. Sandburg, *Abraham Lincoln: The War Years,* III: 63.

32. Ibid., II: 342.

33. Clifford Dowdy, *Death of a Nation: The Story of Lee and His Men at Gettysburg* (New York: Alfred A. Knopf, 1963), 266.

34. Wiley, *The Life of Johnny Reb,* 75.

35. Paul M. Angle and Earl Schenck Miers, eds., *Tragic Years, 1860–1865: A Documentary History of the Civil War* (New York: Simon & Schuster, 1960), 665.

36. Earl Schenck Miers and Richard A. Brown, eds., *Gettysburg* (New Brunswick, N.J.: Rutgers University Press, 1948), 277.

37. Basler, *The Collected Works of Abraham Lincoln,* VI: 409.

38. Boritt, *Lincoln's Generals,* 96.

39. Glenn Tucker, *High Tide at Gettysburg: The Campaign in Pennsylvania* (New York: Morningside Bookshop, 1973), 387.

40. Sandburg, *Abraham Lincoln: The War Years,* II: 354.

41. Kunhardt, *A New Birth of Freedom,* 122.

42. Mrs. General Pickett, "President Lincoln: Intimate Personal Recollections," *Lippincott's Magazine* (May 1906): 559.

43. Basler, *The Collected Works of Abraham Lincoln,* VII: 23.

44. Sandburg, *Abraham Lincoln: The War Years,* II: 470.

CHAPTER 6: A QUIET LITTLE FELLOW

1. William O. Stoddard, *Inside the White House in War Times* (New York: Charles L. Webster, 1890), 158–59.

2. Margarita Spalding Gerry, ed., *Reminiscences of Colonel William H. Crook* (New York: Harper & Brothers, 1910), 13; Brooks, *Washington in Lincoln's Time,* 15; George S. Bryan, *The Great American Myth* (Chicago: Americana House, 1990), 127.

3. J. C. Fuller, *Grant & Lee: A Study in Personality and Generalship* (Bloomington: University of Indiana Press, 1982), 83.

4. McClure, *Abraham Lincoln and the Men of War Times,* 180. Some historians have questioned the authenticity of this famous statement. See Fehrenbacher and Fehrenbacher, *Recollected Words of Abraham Lincoln,* 315.

5. Lamon, *Recollections of Abraham Lincoln,* 185. Although Lamon may not have heard this anecdote from Lincoln himself, it had appeared in print as early as 1864. See Fehrenbacher and Fehrenbacher, *Recollected Words of Abraham Lincoln,* 288.

6. David Dixon Porter, *Incidents and Anecdotes of the Civil War* (New York: D. Appleton & Co., 1885), 19.

7. Brooks, *Washington in Lincoln's Time,* 135.

8. Ulysses S. Grant, *Personal Memoirs of Ulysses S. Grant and Selected Letters, 1839–1865,* 2 vols. in 1 (New York: The Library of America, 1990), II: 473.

9. Burke Davis, *Gray Fox: Robert E. Lee and the Civil War* (New York: Fairfax Press, 1981), 276.

10. William E. Barton, *Lincoln at Gettysburg* (Indianapolis: Bobbs-Merrill, 1933), 109.

11. Gene Smith, *Lee and Grant: A Dual Biography* (New York: McGraw-Hill, 1984), 185.

12. Bruce Catton, *A Stillness at Appomattox* (Garden City, N.Y.: Doubleday, 1953), 46.

13. Sandburg, *Abraham Lincoln: The War Years,* II: 551.

14. Richard Wheeler, ed., *On Fields of Fury: From the Wilderness to the Crater: An Eyewitness History* (New York: HarperCollins, 1991), 83.

15. Sandburg, *Abraham Lincoln: The War Years,* III: 43.

16. Henry Wing, *When Lincoln Kissed Me: A Story of the Wilderness Campaign* (New York: Eaton and Mains, 1913), 38.

17. Wheeler, *On Fields of Fury,* 243.

18. Davis, *Gray Fox,* 261.

19. Sandburg, *Abraham Lincoln: The War Years,* III: 409.

20. Thomas, *Abraham Lincoln,* 423; Carpenter, *Six Months in the White House with Abraham Lincoln,* 19.

21. Keckley, *Behind the Scenes,* 133–34.

22. Ibid.

23. Oates, *With Malice Toward None*, 390.

24. John Henry Cramer, *Lincoln Under Enemy Fire* (Baton Rouge: Louisiana State University Press, 1948), 32.

25. Nicolay, *Personal Traits of Abraham Lincoln*, 222–23.

26. Alexander Woollcott, "Get Down, You Fool!" *The Atlantic Monthly* (February 1938): 170. Although at least two historians doubt the authenticity of this incident, Justice Holmes described it to several people, including Justice Felix Frankfurter. See Fehrenbacher and Fehrenbacher, *Recollected Words of Abraham Lincoln*, 259.

27. Lloyd Lewis, *Sherman: Fighting Prophet* (New York: Harcourt, Brace and Co., 1958), 233.

28. Sandburg, *Abraham Lincoln: The War Years*, III: 154.

29. Ibid.

30. Henry Steele Commager, ed., *The Blue and the Gray: The Story of the Civil War As Told by Participants* (Indianapolis: Bobbs-Merrill, 1950), 578–79.

31. Randall, *Mary Lincoln*, 146–47; William A. Evans, *Mrs. Abraham Lincoln* (New York: Alfred A. Knopf, 1932), 183.

32. Thomas, *Abraham Lincoln*, 297–98.

33. Randall, *Mary Lincoln*, 264.

34. Emanuel Hertz, *Abraham Lincoln: A New Portrait*, 2 vols. (New York: Horace Liveright, 1931), I: 239.

35. Randall, *Mary Lincoln*, 274; Sandburg, *Abraham Lincoln: The War Years*, II: 141; Newman, *Lincoln for the Ages*, 315.

36. Basler, *The Collected Works of Abraham Lincoln*, VII: 507.

37. Ibid., 514.

38. Sandburg, *Abraham Lincoln: The War Years*, III: 193; McPherson, *Ordeal by Fire*, 449; McPherson, *Battle Cry of Freedom*, 790. The President was no dictator. Dictators were no different in Lincoln's day than in our own; that is, they acted as a law unto themselves. Lincoln never did that. Despite his restrictions on individual liberties, he was still accountable to Congress, the courts, and the voters. No dictator would have tolerated the kind of criticism he received every day.

39. Ida Tarbell, *The Life of Abraham Lincoln*, 4 vols. (New York: Lincoln History Society, 1895–1900), III: 199.

40. Wiley, "Billy Yank and Abraham Lincoln," 117. The "Hood" in the song refers to General John Bell Hood, the Confederate commander at Atlanta.

41. McPherson, *Ordeal by Fire*, 458.

CHAPTER 7: RICHMOND AT LAST

1. Sandburg, *Abraham Lincoln: The War Years*, III: 621.

2. Bruce Catton, *Never Call Retreat* (Garden City, N.Y.: Doubleday, 1965), 415.

3. Sandburg, *Abraham Lincoln: The War Years*, III: 625; Burke Davis, *Sherman's March* (New York: Random House, 1980), 44.

4. Ibid., 45.

5. Ibid., 45–46.

6. McPherson, *Marching Toward Freedom*, 60.

7. Sandburg, *Abraham Lincoln: The War Years*, III: 625.

8. Davis, *Sherman's March*, 180.

9. Coulter, *The Confederate States of America*, 549–50.

10. Bruce Levine, *Half Slave and Half Free: The Roots of the Civil War* (New York: Hill and Wang, 1992), 103.

11. Oates, *Abraham Lincoln: The Man Behind the Myths*, 117.

12. Brooks, *Washington in Lincoln's Time*, 187. Though passed by Congress, the amendment could take effect only after being ratified by three-fourths of the states. Ironically, Tennessee, a former Confederate state, cast the deciding vote in December 1865. By then, however, the Civil War was over and Lincoln in his grave for eight months.

13. Oates, *With Malice Toward None*, 405.

14. Hamilton and Ostendorf, *Lincoln in Photographs*, 210.

15. Basler, *The Collected Works of Abraham Lincoln*, VIII: 333.

16. Ibid.

17. Rice, *Reminiscences of Abraham Lincoln by Distinguished Men of His Time*, 191–92.

18. Rudolph Marx, *The Health of the Presidents* (New York: G. P. Putnam's Sons, 1960), 173.

19. John S. Barnes, "With Lincoln from Washington to Richmond in 1865," *Appleton's Magazine* (May 1907): 522.

20. Sandburg, *Abraham Lincoln: The War Years,* IV: 147.

21. Smith, *Lee and Grant,* 241–42.

22. W. E. Woodward, *Meet General Grant* (New York: Horace Liveright, 1928), 346.

23. Ibid.

24. Ibid.

25. Lamon, *Recollections of Abraham Lincoln,* 99.

26. Porter, *Incidents and Anecdotes of the Civil War,* 286–87.

27. Clarence E. Macartney, *Grant and His Generals* (New York: McBride, 1953), 336.

28. Richard Wheeler, ed., *We Knew William Tecumseh Sherman* (New York: Thomas Y. Crowell, 1977), 105–106.

29. Earl Schenck Miers, *The Last Campaign: Grant Saves the Union* (Philadelphia: J. B. Lippincott, 1972), 168.

30. Porter, *Incidents and Anecdotes of the Civil War,* 213–14; Thomas, *Abraham Lincoln,* 509.

31. Sandburg, *Abraham Lincoln: The War Years,* IV: 163.

32. Ibid.

33. Thomas, *Abraham Lincoln,* 510.

34. Porter, *Incidents and Anecdotes of the Civil War,* 384–85.

35. Ibid., 191.

36. A. A. Hoehling and Mary Hoehling, *The Last Days of the Confederacy* (New York: Fairfax Press, 1981), 206.

37. Rembert W. Patrick, *The Fall of Richmond* (Baton Rouge: Louisiana State University Press, 1960), 68; Quarles, *Lincoln and the Negro,* 236.

38. Jim Bishop, *The Day Lincoln Was Shot* (New York: Harper & Brothers, 1955), 43.

39. Brooks, *Washington in Lincoln's Time,* 221; Bryan, *The Great American Myth,* 9.

40. McPherson, *Battle Cry of Freedom,* 846.

41. Gerry, *Reminiscences of Colonel William H. Crook,* 51.

42. Ibid., 295.

43. Ibid., 296. Fehrenbacher and Fehrenbacher (*Recollected Words of Abraham Lincoln,* 366)

doubt that these were the President's exact words. If not, they certainly expressed his deepest beliefs.

44. Ibid.

45. McPherson, *Ordeal by Fire,* 481; Porter, *Incidents and Anecdotes of the Civil War,* 302; Patrick, *The Fall of Richmond,* 80.

46. Ibid., 300, 301.

47. Ibid., 130; William T. Crook, "Lincoln's Last Day," *Harper's Monthly* (September 1907): 521.

48. Pickett, "President Lincoln," 560.

49. Richard Wheeler, ed., *Witness to Appomattox* (New York: Harper & Row, 1989), 202.

50. Sandburg, *Abraham Lincoln: The War Years,* IV: 186.

51. Smith, *Lee and Grant,* 280. Margaret Leech, *Reveille in Washington, 1860–1865* (New York: Harper & Brothers, 1941), 417.

52. Thomas Reed Turner, *Beware the People Weeping: Public Opinion and the Assassination of Abraham Lincoln* (Baton Rouge: Louisiana State University Press, 1982), 19.

53. Basler, *The Collected Works of Abraham Lincoln,* VIII: 399–404.

54. Sandburg, *Abraham Lincoln: The War Years,* IV: 330.

CHAPTER 8: O CAPTAIN! MY CAPTAIN!

1. Asia Booth Clarke, *The Unlocked Book: A Memoir of John Wilkes Booth* (New York: G. P. Putnam's Sons, 1938), 73.

2. Stanley Kimmel, *The Mad Booths of Maryland* (Indianapolis: Bobbs-Merrill, 1940), 150; Bryan, *The Great American Myth,* 81.

3. Ibid., 94; Francis Wilson, *John Wilkes Booth: Fact and Fiction of Lincoln's Assassination* (New York: Benjamin Bloom, 1972), 82.

4. Clarke, *The Unlocked Book,* 115.

5. Ibid.

6. Ibid., 123, 125.

7. Kenneth A. Bernard, "Glimpses of Lincoln in the White House," *The Abraham Lincoln Quarterly* (December 1952): 183; the La Crosse, Wisconsin, *Democrat* (August 29, 1864), quoted in Bryan, *The Great American Myth,* 391.

8. Richard Bardolph, "Malice Toward One: Lincoln in the North Carolina Press," *Lincoln Herald* 53 (Winter 1951): 41; Sandburg, *Abraham Lincoln: The War Years,* II: 148.

9. Newman, *Lincoln for the Ages,* 205; Michael Davis, *The Image of Lincoln in the South* (Knoxville: University of Tennessee Press, 1971), 63; Woodward, *Mary Chesnut's Civil War,* 412–13.

10. Clarke, *The Unlocked Book,* 124.

11. Helm, *The True Story of Mary, Wife of Lincoln,* 251–52.

12. Ibid., 243.

13. Wilson, *John Wilkes Booth,* 96.

14. Villard, *Lincoln on the Eve of '61,* 52–53; Stoddard, *Inside the White House in War Times,* 32.

15. Sandburg, *Abraham Lincoln: The War Years,* IV: 241; Theodore Roscol, *The Web of Conspiracy: The Complete Story of the Men Who Murdered Abraham Lincoln* (Englewood Cliffs, N.J.: Prentice-Hall, 1959), 13; Lamon, *Recollections of Abraham Lincoln,* 265–66.

16. Brooks, *Washington in Lincoln's Time,* 43–44.

17. Sandburg, *Abraham Lincoln: The War Years,* II: 211.

18. Carpenter, *Six Months in the White House with Abraham Lincoln: The Story of a Picture,* 42.

19. Sandburg, *Abraham Lincoln: The War Years,* III: 346.

20. Wilson, *John Wilkes Booth,* 76.

21. Lamon, *Recollections of Abraham Lincoln,* 117. Fehrenbacher and Fehrenbacher (*Recollected Words of Abraham Lincoln,* 293) dismiss this as a "fantastic" story. However, other authorities (Sandburg, *Abraham Lincoln,* IV: 243–45; Oates, *With Malice Toward None,* 425–26; Bishop, *The Day Lincoln Was Shot,* 54–56) follow Lamon's version—and I follow them.

22. Ibid., 117–18.

23. Ibid., 16–17.

24. W. Emerson Reck, *A. Lincoln: His Last 24 Hours* (Jefferson, N.C.: McFarland & Co., 1987), 37.

25. Ibid., 47; Randall, *Mary Lincoln,* 342.

26. Ralph Borreson, *When Lincoln Died* (New York: Appleton-Century, 1965), 55.

27. Ibid., 22, 24.

28. Reck, *A. Lincoln: His Last 24 Hours,* 114.

29. Charles A. Leale, *Lincoln's Last Hours: An Address Delivered Before the Commandry of the State of New York Military Order of the Loyal Legion,* 1909, 24–25.

30. Sandburg, *Abraham Lincoln: The War Years,* IV: 285.

31. Victor Searcher, *The Farewell to Lincoln* (New York: Abingdon Press, 1965), 33.

32. Reck, *A. Lincoln: His Last 24 Hours,* 131.

33. Sandburg, *Abraham Lincoln: The War Years,* IV: 288.

34. Nicolay, *Personal Traits of Abraham Lincoln,* 245; Hamilton and Ostendorf, *Lincoln in Photographs,* 217.

35. Leale, *Lincoln's Last Hours,* 29.

36. Sandburg, *Abraham Lincoln: The War Years,* IV: 297.

37. Leale, *Lincoln's Last Hours,* 30.

38. Lloyd Lewis, *The Assassination of Lincoln: History and Myth* (Lincoln: University of Nebraska Press, 1994), 178.

39. Wilson, *John Wilkes Booth,* 138.

40. Sandburg, *Abraham Lincoln: The War Years,* IV: 300.

41. Ibid., 353.

42. Glatthaar, *Forged in Battle,* 51.

43. Atkinson, *The Boyhood of Lincoln,* 54–55.

44. Lewis, *The Assassination of Lincoln,* 59, 61; Turner, *Beware the People Weeping,* 50.

45. Oates, *Abraham Lincoln: The Man Behind the Myths,* 18.

46. Martin Abbott, "Southern Reaction to Lincoln's Assassination," *The Abraham Lincoln Quarterly* (September 1942): 126.

47. Philip Van Doren Stern, *An End to Valor: The Last Days of the Civil War* (Boston: Houghton Mifflin, 1858), 330.

48. Keckley, *Behind the Scenes,* 192.

49. Bruce Catton, *Grant Takes Command* (Boston: Little, Brown, 1969), 479.

50. Washington, *They Knew Lincoln,* 148.

51. Reck, *A. Lincoln: His Last 24 Hours,* 80, 82.

52. Rice, *Reminiscences of Abraham Lincoln by Distinguished Men of His Time,* 452–53.

53. Bryan, *The Great American Myth,* 265. Mrs. Surratt was the first woman ever hanged by the United States government. Dr. Samuel A. Mudd, a physician who had set Booth's broken leg, and two other men were sentenced to life in prison.

More Books About Abraham Lincoln

Abraham Lincoln is the most written-about person in American history. Here are some of the books I have found most helpful in preparing my own study.

Anderson, Nancy Scott, and Dwight Anderson. *The Generals: Ulysses S. Grant and Robert E. Lee.* New York: Alfred A. Knopf, 1988.

Angle, Paul M., ed. *Herndon's Life of Lincoln: The History and Personal Recollections of Abraham Lincoln As Originally Written by William H. Herndon and Jesse W. Weik.* Cleveland: World Publishing Co., 1965.

———, and Earl Schenck Miers, eds. *Tragic Years, 1860–1865: A Documentary History of the Civil War.* New York: Simon & Schuster, 1960.

Atkinson, Eleanor. *The Boyhood of Lincoln.* New York: McClure Co., 1908.

Baker, Jean H. *Mary Todd Lincoln: A Biography.* New York: W. W. Norton, 1987.

Barton, William E. *Lincoln at Gettysburg.* Indianapolis: Bobbs-Merrill, 1933.

Basler, Roy P., ed. *The Collected Works of Abraham Lincoln.* 9 vols. New Brunswick, N.J.: Rutgers University Press, 1953–1955.

Bates, David H. *Lincoln in the Telegraph Office.* New York: Century Co., 1907.

Bayne, Julia Taft. *Tad Lincoln's Father.* Boston: Little, Brown, 1931.

Bennett, Lerone, Jr. *Before the Mayflower: A History of Black America.* New York: Penguin Books, 1982.

Berwanger, Eugene A. *The Frontier Against Slavery: Western Anti-Negro Prejudice and the Slavery Extension Controversy.* Chicago: University of Illinois Press, 1967.

Bishop, Jim. *The Day Lincoln Was Shot.* New York: Harper & Brothers, 1955.

Blassingame, John W. *The Slave Community: Plantation Life in the Antebellum South.* New York: Oxford University Press, 1972.

Boritt, Gabor S., ed. *Lincoln's Generals.* New York: Oxford University Press, 1994.

———, ed. *Lincoln, the War President.* New York: Oxford University Press, 1992.

Brooks, Noah. *Washington in Lincoln's Time.* New York: Rinehart & Co., 1958. Reprint of an 1896 book.

Bryan, George S. *The Great American Myth.* Chicago: Americana House, 1990. The best book on Lincoln's assassination.

Buckmaster, Henrietta. *Let My People Go: The Story of the Underground Railroad and the Growth of the Abolitionist Movement.* Columbia, S.C.: University of South Carolina Press, 1995.

Burlingame, Michael, *The Inner World of Abraham Lincoln.* Chicago: University of Illinois Press, 1995.

Cain, William E., ed. *William Lloyd Garrison and the Fight Against Slavery: Selections from* The Liberator. New York: St. Martin's Press, 1995.

Canby, Courtlandt, ed. *Lincoln and the Civil War: A Profile and a History.* New York: George Braziller, 1960.

Carpenter, Francis B. *Six Months in the White House with Abraham Lincoln: The Story of a Picture.* New York: Hurd & Houghton, 1866.

Clarke, Asia Booth. *The Unlocked Book: A Memoir of John Wilkes Booth.* New York: G. P. Putnam's Sons, 1938. Written in 1874.

Commager, Henry Steele, ed. *The Blue and the Gray: The Story of the Civil War As Told by Participants.* Indianapolis: Bobbs-Merrill, 1950.

Coulter, Merton E. *The Confederate States of America.* Baton Rouge: Louisiana State University Press, 1959.

Cramer, John Henry. *Lincoln Under Enemy Fire.* Baton Rouge: Louisiana State University Press, 1948.

Craven, Avery O. *The Coming of the Civil War.* Chicago: University of Chicago Press, 1942.

Current, Richard N. *The Lincoln Nobody Knows.* New York: Hill & Wang, 1990.

Davis, Burke. *Gray Fox: Robert E. Lee and the Civil War.* New York: Fairfax Press, 1981.

————. *Sherman's March.* New York: Random House, 1980.

Davis, Michael. *The Image of Lincoln in the South.* Knoxville: University of Tennessee Press, 1971.

Donald, David Herbert. *Lincoln.* New York: Simon & Schuster, 1995.

Donovan, Frank. *Mr. Lincoln's Proclamation: The Story of the Emancipation Proclamation.* New York: Dodd, Mead, 1964.

Douglass, Frederick. *The Life and Writings of Frederick Douglass.* 4 vols. Edited by Philip S. Foner. New York: International Publishers, 1950.

————. *My Bondage and My Freedom.* New York: Arno Press, 1968. Reprint of a book first published in 1855.

Fehrenbacher, Don E. *Prelude to Greatness: Lincoln in the 1850s.* Stanford: Stanford University Press, 1962.

————, and Virginia Fehrenbacher, eds. *Recollected Words of Abraham Lincoln.* Stanford: Stanford University Press, 1996.

Franklin, John Hope. *The Emancipation Proclamation.* Garden City, N.Y.: Doubleday, 1963.

————. *From Slavery to Freedom: A History of Negro Americans.* New York: Alfred A. Knopf, 1967.

Furnas, J. C. *Goodbye to Uncle Tom.* New York: William Sloane Associates, 1956.

————. *The Road to Harpers Ferry.* New York: William Sloane Associates, 1955.

Garrison, Webb. *The Lincoln Nobody Knows.* Nashville: Rutledge Hill Press, 1993.

Genovese, Eugene D. *Roll, Jordan, Roll: The World the Slaves Made.* New York: Pantheon Books, 1974.

Glatthaar, Joseph T. *Forged in Battle: The Civil War Alliance of Black Soldiers and White Officers.* New York: Free Press, 1990.

Hamilton, Charles, and Lloyd Ostendorf. *Lincoln in Photographs: An Album of Every Known Pose.* Norman: University of Oklahoma Press, 1963.

Helm, Katherine. *The True Story of Mary, Wife of Lincoln, Containing Recollections of Mary Lincoln's Sister (Mrs. Ben Hardin Helm), Extracts from Her War-Time Diary, Numerous Letters and Other Documents Now First Published.* New York: Harper & Brothers, 1928.

Hertz, Emanuel. *The Hidden Lincoln: From the Letters and Papers of William H. Herndon.* New York: Viking, 1930.

Horgan, Paul. *Citizen of New Salem.* New York: Farrar, Straus & Cudahy, 1961.

Hurmance, Belinda, ed. *Before Freedom: 48 Oral Histories of Former North and South Carolina Slaves.* New York: Mentor Books, 1990.

Johannsen, Robert W., ed. *The Lincoln-Douglas Debates.* New York: Oxford University Press, 1965.

Keckley, Elizabeth. *Behind the Scenes; or, Thirty Years a Slave and Four Years in the White House.* New York: Oxford University Press, 1988. Reprint of an 1868 book.

Kimmel, Stanley. *The Mad Booths of Maryland.* Indianapolis: Bobbs-Merrill, 1940.

Kunhardt, Philip B., Jr. *A New Birth of Freedom: Lincoln at Gettysburg.* Boston: Little, Brown, 1983.

————, et al. *Lincoln: An Illustrated Biography.* New York: Alfred A. Knopf, 1992.

Lamon, Ward Hill. *Recollections of Abraham Lincoln, 1847–1865.* Washington, D.C.: Dorothy Hill Lamon, 1911.

Leale, Charles A. *Lincoln's Last Hours: An Address Delivered Before the Commandry of the State of New York Military Order of the Loyal Legion.* 1909.

Leech, Margaret. *Reveille in Washington, 1860–1865.* New York: Harper & Brothers, 1941.

Lester, Julius, ed. *To Be a Slave.* New York: Scholastic, 1968.

Lewis, Lloyd. *The Assassination of Lincoln: History and Myth.* Lincoln: University of Nebraska Press, 1994. Reprint of a book first published in 1929.

Litwack, Leon F. *North of Slavery: The Negro in the United States, 1790–1860.* Chicago: University of Chicago Press, 1961.

McKitrick, Eric L., ed. *Slavery Defended: The View of the Old South.* Englewood Cliffs, N.J.: Prentice-Hall, 1963.

McPherson, James M. *Abraham Lincoln and the Second American Revolution.* New York: Oxford University Press, 1991.

———. *Battle Cry of Freedom: The Civil War Era.* New York: Oxford University Press, 1988.

———. *Marching Toward Freedom: The Negro in the Civil War, 1861–1865.* New York: Alfred A. Knopf, 1967.

———. *The Negro's Civil War: How Black Americans Felt and Acted During the War for the Union.* New York: Ballantine Books, 1991.

———. *Ordeal by Fire: The Civil War and Reconstruction.* New York: Alfred A. Knopf, 1982.

———. *The Struggle for Equality: Abolitionists and the Negro in the Civil War and Reconstruction.* Princeton: Princeton University Press, 1964.

Mellon, James, ed. *Bullwhip Days: The Slaves Remember.* New York: Weidenfeld & Nicholson, 1988.

Merrill, Walter M. *Against Wind and Tide: A Biography of William Lloyd Garrison.* Cambridge: Harvard University Press, 1963.

Miers, Earl Schenck. *Lincoln Day by Day.* 3 vols. Washington, D.C.: Lincoln Sesquicentennial Commission, 1960.

Neely, Mark E. *The Abraham Lincoln Encyclopedia.* New York: McGraw-Hill, 1982.

———. *The Last Best Hope of Earth: Abraham Lincoln and the Promise of America.* Cambridge: Harvard University Press, 1993.

Nevins, Alan. *The Emergence of Lincoln.* 2 vols. New York: Charles Scribner's Sons, 1950.

Newman, Ralph G., ed. *Lincoln for the Ages.* Garden City, N.Y.: Doubleday, 1960.

Nicolay, Helen. *Personal Traits of Abraham Lincoln.* New York: D. Appleton Century Co., 1939.

Oates, Stephen B. *Abraham Lincoln: The Man Behind the Myths.* New York: New American Library, 1984.

———. *The Fires of Jubilee: Nat Turner's Fierce Rebellion.* New York: Harper Perennial, 1990.

———. *Our Fiery Trial: Abraham Lincoln, John Brown, and the Civil War Era.* Amherst: University of Massachusetts Press, 1979.

———. *To Purge This Land with Blood: A Biography of John Brown.* New York: Harper & Row, 1970.

———. *With Malice Toward None: The Life of Abraham Lincoln.* New York: Harper & Row, 1977.

Porter, David Dixon. *Incidents and Anecdotes of the Civil War.* New York: D. Appleton & Co., 1885.

Potter, David M. *The Impending Crisis, 1848–1861.* New York: Harper Torchbooks, 1976.

Quarles, Benjamin. *Lincoln and the Negro.* New York: Oxford University Press, 1962.

Randall, Ruth Painter. *Lincoln's Sons.* Boston: Little, Brown, 1955.

———. *Mary Lincoln: Biography of a Marriage.* Boston: Little, Brown, 1953.

Reck, W. Emerson. *A. Lincoln: His Last 24 Hours.* Jefferson, N.C.: McFarland & Co., 1987.

———. "When the Nation Said Farewell to Lincoln." *Bulletin of the Forty-Eighth Annual Meeting of the Lincoln Fellowship of Wisconsin,* 16 April 1989.

Rice, Allen Thorndike, ed. *Reminiscences of Abraham Lincoln by Distinguished Men of His Time.* New York: Haskell House, 1971. Reprint of a book first published in 1888.

Roscol, Theodore. *The Web of Conspiracy: The Complete Story of the Men Who Murdered Abraham Lincoln.* Englewood Cliffs, N.J.: Prentice-Hall, 1959.

Sandburg, Carl. *Abraham Lincoln: The War Years.* 2 vols. New York: Harcourt, Brace and Co., 1926.

———. *Abraham Lincoln: The War Years.* 4 vols. New York: Harcourt, Brace and Co., 1939.

Searcher, Victor. *The Farewell to Lincoln.* New York: Abingdon Press, 1965.

———. *Lincoln's Journey to Greatness.* Philadelphia: John C. Winston Co., 1960.

Sears, Stephen W. *George B. McClellan: The Young Napoleon.* New York: Ticknor & Fields, 1988.

Shutes, Milton H. *Lincoln and the Doctors.* New York: Pioneer Press, 1933.

Sigelschiffer, Saul. *The American Conscience: The Drama of the Lincoln-Douglas Debates.* New York: Horizon Press, 1973.

Smith, Gene. *Lee and Grant: A Dual Biography.* New York: McGraw-Hill, 1984.

Stampp, Kenneth M. *The Peculiar Institution: Slavery in the Ante-Bellum South.* New York: Alfred A. Knopf, 1956.

Thomas, Benjamin P. *Abraham Lincoln.* New York: Alfred A. Knopf, 1952.

———. *Lincoln's New Salem.* Springfield, Ill.: The Abraham Lincoln Association, 1934.

———, and Harold M. Hyman. *Stanton: The Life and Times of Lincoln's Secretary of War.* New York: Alfred A. Knopf, 1962.

Tidwell, William A., James O. Hall, and David Winfred Gaddy. *Come Retribution: The Confederate Secret Service and the Assassination of Abraham Lincoln.* Jackson: University Press of Mississippi, 1988.

Turner, Justin G., and Linda Levitt Turner. *Mary Todd Lincoln: Her Life and Letters.* New York: Alfred A. Knopf, 1972.

Villard, Henry. *Lincoln on the Eve of '61.* New York: Alfred A. Knopf, 1941.

Villard, Oswald Garrison. *John Brown.* New York: Alfred A. Knopf, 1943.

Warren, Louis A. *Lincoln's Youth: Indiana Years Seven to Twenty-one, 1816–1830.* New York: Appleton-Century-Crofts, 1959.

———. *The Slavery Atmosphere of Lincoln's Youth.* Fort Wayne, Ind.: Lincolonia Publishers, 1933.

Wheeler, Richard, ed. *Lee's Terrible Swift Sword: From Antietam to Chancellorsville: An Eyewitness History.* New York: HarperCollins, 1992.

———. *On Fields of Fury: From the Wilderness to the Crater: An Eyewitness History.* New York: HarperCollins, 1991.

———. *A Rising Thunder: From Lincoln's Election to the Battle of Bull Run: An Eyewitness History.* New York: HarperCollins, 1994.

———. *Sword over Richmond: An Eyewitness History of McClellan's Peninsula Campaign.* New York: Harper & Row, 1986.

———. *Voices of the Civil War.* New York: Thomas Y. Crowell, 1976.

White, Deborah Gray. *Ar'n't I a Woman? Female Slaves in the Plantation South.* New York: W. W. Norton, 1985.

Wiley, Belle Irvin. "Billy Yank and Abraham Lincoln." *The Abraham Lincoln Quarterly* VI (June 1950): 103–120.

———. *The Life of Billy Yank: The Common Soldier of the Union.* Baton Rouge: Louisiana State University Press, 1978.

———. *The Life of Johnny Reb: The Common Soldier of the Confederacy.* Baton Rouge: Louisiana State University Press, 1978.

———. *The Plain People of the Confederacy.* Baton Rouge: Louisiana State University Press, 1943.

Wills, Garry. *Lincoln at Gettysburg: The Words That Remade America.* New York: Simon & Schuster, 1992.

Wilson, Francis. *John Wilkes Booth: Fact and Fiction of Lincoln's Assassination.* New York: Benjamin Bloom, 1972. Reprint of a book first published in 1929.

Woodward, C. Vann, ed. *Mary Chesnut's Civil War.* New Haven: Yale University Press, 1981.

Zall, P. M., ed. *Abe Lincoln Laughing: Humorous Anecdotes from Original Sources by and About Abraham Lincoln.* Berkeley: University of California Press, 1982.

Index